1890 – 1941

EL LISSITZKY

architect
painter
photographer
typographer

EL LISSITZKY

1890–1941

architect

painter

photographer

typographer

Municipal Van Abbemuseum, Eindhoven

Fundaçion Caja de Pensiones, Madrid

Musée d'Art Moderne de la Ville de Paris/ARC

ISBN 90-70149-28-1

CIP – DATA KONINKLIJKE BIBLIOTHEEK, DEN HAAG

El

El Lissitzky 1890-1941: architect, painter,
photographer, typographer / [final ed.: Jan Debbaut
... et al.; ed.: Mariëlle Soons... et al.; transl.:
by Kathie Somerwil-Ayrthon... et al.]. – Eindhoven:
Stedelijk Van Abbemuseum. – Ill., foto's
Catalogus van de tentoonstelling in het Stedelijk
Van Abbemuseum, Eindhoven, 15-12-1990/03-
03-1991, de Fundación Caja de Pensiones, Madrid,
01-04/26-09-1991 en het Musée d'Art Moderne
de la Ville de Paris / ARC, Parijs,
18-06/30-09-1991. - Met bibliogr., index.
ISBN 90-70149-28-1
SISO eu-rusl 707.8 UDC [72+75/77](47)"19"
Trefw.: Lissitzky, El; tentoonstellingscatalogi.

Contents

Acknowledgements

We would like to express our deep gratitude to all who have made very valuable works available for this exhibition and whose interest, efforts and advice have helped to make the exhibition possible.
We would especially like to thank:

Yen Lissitzky, Bad Karlshafen
Yuri K. Korolev, Moscow
Lidija Iovleva, Moscow
Mirra Nemirovskaya, Moscow
Nathalia Sekolova, Moscow
Ludmila Smirnova, Moscow
Ekatarina Selezneva, Moscow
Catherina Semenova, Moscow
Tatiana Goubanova, Moscow
Valentin Rivkind, Moscow
Jean Leering, Amsterdam
Henk Puts, Groningen
Kai-Uwe Hemken, Marburg
Peter Nisbet, Cambridge
Willem G. Weststeijn, Department of Slavonic Languages and
    Literature, University of Amsterdam
Annely and David Juda, London
Nicolas Ilyine, Frankfurt/Main
Anthony Wouters, Eindhoven
Eef Kamerbeek, Eindhoven
Hannie van Houtum, Best
Fré Ilgen, Pro-Pro Art and Architecture Foundation, Eindhoven
Axel Bruchhäuser, Lauenförde

and the staff of the Prints Department of the Tretiakov Gallery
the Dutch Ambassador and staff members of the Dutch embassy in Moscow
the students of the Department of Slavonic Languages and Literature at the University of Amsterdam

Lenders to the exhibition:

GERMANY
Berlinische Galerie,Berlin
Galerie Berinson, Berlin
Deutsches Hygiene-Museum, Dresden
Stadtmuseum, Dresden
Kunstsammlung Nordrhein-Westfalen, Düsseldorf
Staatliche Galerie Moritzburg, Halle
Sprengel Museum, Hanover
Museum Ludwig, Cologne
Stuhlmuseum Burg Beverungen + TECTA,
    Lauenförde
Deutsches Buch- und Schriftmuseum der
    Deutschen Bücherei, Leipzig
Gg.G. Weisbrod

GREAT BRITAIN
Eric Estorick, London
Annely Juda Fine Art, London

ISRAEL
The Israel Museum, Jerusalem

THE NETHERLANDS
Stedelijk Museum, Amsterdam
Hans Biezen, Eindhoven
Coll. A.J. v. D.H.

SOVIET UNION
State Tretiakov Gallery, Moscow

UNITED STATES
Busch-Reisinger Museum, Harvard University,
    Cambridge, Massachusetts
Los Angeles County Museum of Art, Los Angeles
Robert Shapazian, Los Angeles
Getty Center for the History of Art and the
Humanities, Malibu
The Museum of Modern Art, New York
Thomas Walther, New York
Philadelphia Museum of Art, Philadelphia

SWEDEN
Private collection courtesy of Annely Juda Fine Art,
    London

SWITZERLAND
Museum für Gestaltung, Basel
Galerie Dr. I. Schlégl, Zürich

and those who wish to remain anonymous

Foreword

El Lissitzky was born in 1890. He played an important role in the development of the Russian avant-garde, not only as an artist working in widely different fields but as a mediator between the rival movements and views of art of the time. He was for ever in search of the all-embracing synthesis which would contribute towards creating a new and better world.

The years 1890 and 1990 are more than arbitrary points in time marking the passing of a century. This period has seen both turbulent times in art and enormous political and social changes in the world. The utopian model, whose beginnings Lissitzky experienced, seems now to have developed in a completely perverted way and has recently been abandoned as a derelict system.

These dramatic developments have reawakened interest in both the position of the Russian avant-garde as a whole and in Lissitzky's work, in which the paradox of a utopian artist is evident, an artist who – at a point when belief in utopia was still possible – put himself at the service of the pursuit of a reality that could never exist.

He did this with all available means and in many fields; this makes his work coherent in its conception but eclectic in its execution. Historically, this makes him a remarkable artist, for he had the strength of a fundamental vision but was sometimes unsuccessful in having his projects realized. He was fully occupied with his many international contacts, with the constant exchange of ideas, seeking for the synthesis . . . his 'Proun' project, his project 'for the affirmation of a new art' which would change the world.

With the bringing together of the major Lissitzky collections from Moscow and Eindhoven, his quest can be reconstructed for the first time. We are very grateful to our Russian colleagues at the State Tretiakov Gallery for making this possible.

Jan Debbaut
director Municipal Van Abbemuseum, Eindhoven

Maria Corral
director Fine Arts Program, Fundacion Caja de Pensiones, Madrid

Suzanne Pagé
director Musée d'Art Moderne de la Ville de Paris /ARC, Paris

Autobiography

El Lissitzky

1890 Born 23 November in Pochinok, district Smolensk.

1909 Graduation at Smolensk Grammar School.

1909 Matriculation at the Polytechnic in Darmstadt. Education for graduated engineer (architect). Wandering through Europe, including Paris, I teach myself about the fine arts. I cover more than 1200 km in Italy on foot - making sketches and studying.

1912 My works are included for the first time in an exhibition of the St. Petersburg Artists Union.

1914 Outbreak of World War I, return to Russia.

1915 Diploma in architecture in Moscow; I work with various architects as assistant.

1916-1917 Represented at art shows *Mir Iskusstva* and *Bubowi Valet* (Knave of Diamonds).

1917 Since the beginning of the Revolution member of the art commission. Creation of the first Soviet flag.

1917-1920 Jewish books.

1919 Invited by Marc Chagall to join the Vitebsk Art Labour Cooperative as a professor of Architecture and the Graphic Arts. Album *Unovis* appeared in 7 hand-printed copies. First *Proun*. Collaboration with Malevich. The poster *Red Wedge*.

1920 Plan of a tribune of the students' collective (1924 revised as *Lenin Tribune*).

1921 Called to Moscow as head of the faculty of Architecture of the school *Vkhutemas*, the Russian Bauhaus. First constructivist exhibition *Obmokhu*.

1922 During a temporary stay in Berlin I publish together with the writer Ilia Erenburg the journal *Veshch* (object).

1922-1923 I participate in the organization and creation of the *Erste Russische Kunstausstellung* in Berlin and Amsterdam.

1923 During Mayakovsky's stay in Berlin I was asked to design his book *Dlia Golosa* (For the Voice). It was recognized as the starting point of a new kind of typography. I was appointed member of the Gutenberg society. Temporary stay in Hanover. Here the 1º *Kestnermappe Proun* and the *Figurinenmappe Sieg über die Sonne* came into being.

Late autumn serious illness, wich requires immediate treatment in Switzerland, tuberculosis.

1924 In Brione near Locarno. Pneumothorax. In Brione was created: 1. *ABC, Beiträge zum Bauen* together with Mart Stam, Hans Schmidt, Emil Roth et al. 2. Issue of the *Merz*-journal called *Nasci* together with Kurt Schwitters. 3. Layouts for Pelikan publicity, which are regarded as guarantee for the granting of the cure. 4. The *Kunstismen* together with Hans Arp. 5. The essay *K. und Pangeometrie*. 6. The photograhic self-portrait.

1925 With the technical help of Emil Roth the *Wolkenbügel* project is executed, a skyscraper on three posts planned for Moscow (illustrated for the first time on the front cover of Adolf Behne's book *Der moderne Zweckbau*. Order to leave Switzerland. In June back to Russia via Leningrad. Moscow: Professor for interior decoration and furniture, wood- and metalwork at the school *Vkhutemas*.

1926 My most important work as artist begins: the creation of exhibitions. In this year I was asked by the committee of the *Internationale Kunstausstellung* in Dresden to create the room of non-objective art and was sent there by *Voks* (the intermediary with countries abroad). After an educational trip with the new architecture in Holland as subject, I returned to Moscow in autumn.

1927 Typographical exhibition in Moscow. Layout for *Raum der Abstrakten* in the Landes-Museum in Hanover on request of Dr. Dorner.

1928 Through a state decision I was appointed chief artist for the Soviet pavilion at the *International Press exhibition* in Cologne. The foreign press praised the creation as a big success of the Soviet culture. For this pavilion I had designed a photomontage frieze which was 24 meters long and 3,5 meters wide. It became the model for all those gigantic montages, which became the symbol for future exhibitions. For this work I received much appreciation from the state. Another part of my work at that time was the artistic and polygraphic creation of albums, journals etc.

El Lissitzky in his Vitebsk studio,
1919/20
Photo: private archives

El Lissitzky climbing the Eiffel
Tower, Paris 1928
Photo: private archives

El Lissitzky and Ossip Zadkine, Paris
1912
Photo: private archives

Group Unovis, Vitebsk 1920
On the right El Lissitzky
Photo: private archives

Group photograph of participants
in the International congress of
progressive artists, Düsseldorf 1922
El Lissitzky (with cap) standing
fourth from the right
Photo: private archives

Party in the Gallery Sturm, Berlin
1923
In front (with cap) El Lissitzky,
beside him Ilia Erenburg
Photo: private archives

**El Lissitzky and his wife Sophie
Lissitzky-Küppers,** 1938
Photo: private archives

**Ruben Lissitzky, El Lissitzky, Sophie
Lissitzky and Dziga Wertov,**
Schodnia 1932
Photo: private archives

El Lissitzky, Bauhaus, 1928
Photo: private archives

**Mart Stam, Gerrit Rietveld and
El Lissitzky,** Utrecht 1926
Photo: private archives

Lissitzky's address book
Photo: Municipal Van
Abbemuseum, Eindhoven

12

El Lissitzky working on the album:
15 Years of the Red Army, Moscow
1934
Photo: private archives

1929 Construction of the Soviet stand at the *Film und Foto* exhibition in Stuttgart. Theatre project. Reconstruction of the stage for Tretjakov's play *I want a child*, stage-manager was Meyerhold.

1930 I was appointed chief artist for the Soviet pavilion by the Ministry of Health at the *Internationale Hygiene-Ausstellung* in Dresden. At the same time I set up the Soviet section at the *internationale Pelz-Fachausstellung IPA* in Leipzig on request of Narkom-Meschtorg (Ministry of the fur-trade). Thus I became pioneer of the artistic construction of our exhibitions abroad with their new political responsibility. In the following years I was asked continually to participate in our important exhibitions.

As from 1931 I was chief artist-architect at the permanent building exhibition in the park of culture *Gorki*. But with the years, with my failing health, less and less strength is left for the realization of big exhibitions and similar works.

1932 Album for the 15th anniversary of the Soviet Union (Isogis Publishers). Russian section at the *International Avia Exhibition* in Paris.

1934 I was appointed chief artist for the *Agricultural Exhibition of the Soviet Union*. I fought against the mistakes of my predecessors and resigned. Then, while I was still in the sanatorium, I undertook the creation of the main pavilion. The construction of the main hall still bears my imprint until today. I succeeded in working out a project for the museum exhibition of the Narkomat for social security. *Soviet subtropics*, editor M. Kolzov (Ogonjok Publishers).

1935 Album for the 15th Anniversary of the Red Army (Isogis Publishers).

1936 Album and large portfolio for the Food industry (Za Industralisazia Publishers).

1940 Design for the restaurant at the Soviet exhibition in New York. USSR-Album Isostat (Institut for artistic statistics) for the American exhibition *Soviet Georgia* (Publishers: Gosplanizdat).

1941 The last piece of exhibition work for Vnesh-torga (Foreign Trade): the Soviet pavilion at Beograd. Although ready to be shipped the exhibition had to be left in Moscow: war. The Germans were in Beograd. Together with my work on exhibitions I have worked a lot as book-artist and with photomontage. As such work I can do when illness forces me to stay in bed.

As from 1932 I was permanent collaborator as book-artist for the journal *USSR im Bau*. Layout for particulary complicated issues such as *Dneprostroj, Tcheluskin, Red Army*. A special volume consisted of four issues, which were dedicated to the Constitution. The editorial office received approving letters from among others: Lion Feuchtwanger, Heinrich Mann, Martin Andersen-Nexö.
I designed posters some of which are illustrated in journals at home and abroad. I wrote about questions on art and architecture and also some books.
Many newspapers all over the world reported on my books. Presently, while I am ignoring my serious illness, I still hope to be able to create something for the 25th Anniversary of the October revolution.

June 1941

Postscript: During the months before the 30th December 1941, the day Lissitzky died, a large poster *For Peace* (the original is lost) was being designed and also the poster *Give us more tanks!* (which was printed). Even the night before his death, Lissitzky had left a plan on his little notepad, but I couldn't decipher that anymore.

Sophie Lissitzky-Küppers

El Lissitzky (1890-1941) his life and work

Henk Puts

Lissitzky lived from 1890 to 1941; he grew up in a Jewish family in czarist Russia, studied in the German empire, experienced the Russian Revolution, the years of the blockade of Russia and of the inflation in Germany and, in his later years, the terror of Stalin's rule. He was an important leader of the Jewish cultural renaissance in Eastern Europe and became famous as an artist with his *Prounen*. He played a significant role in the transfer of two-dimensional Suprematism to three-dimensional Suprematism and architecture. He was recognized as a prominent architect, an innovator in typography and a pioneer in the field of exhibition design. He moreover acted as an intermediary for artists from Eastern and Western Europe. In the 1930s he designed exhibitions, books and magazines which contained propaganda for Stalin's communism.

Many of Lissitzky's ideas were far ahead of their time: his *Prounen* were projections about utopian architecture; his plans for a horizontal skyscraper on pilings, for a fundamental restructuring of the Meyerhold Theater, and for an electromechanical puppet theater remained on paper, never to be carried out. This text gives an idea as to the course of Lissitzky's life and the diverse areas in which he worked.

Vitebsk and Smolensk 1890-1909

El Lissitzky was born on November 23, 1890[1] as Lazar

Morduchovitch Lissitzky in the Russian town Pochinok, fifty kilometers southeast of Smolensk, along the eastern border of the vast region in Eastern Europe where many Jewish people then lived. He spent his childhood in Vitebsk; during his secondary school years, he lived with his grandparents in Smolensk. Early on he became interested in drawing: around his thirteenth year he received instruction from the Jewish artist Jehuda Pen, and by the age of fifteen he was already giving lessons himself. After finishing secondary school, he took the admissions examination for the art academy in Petersburg but was not accepted, despite the fact that he passed it; at that time in czarist Russia, the law prevented more than a limited number of Jews from being admitted to schools and universities. In 1909 he went to Germany, like many other Russian Jews, and registered himself at the Technical Institute of Darmstadt.

Darmstadt 1909-1914

We don't know why Lissitzky chose to study architecture; the program of study did, in any case, include free drawing as well. In the works that he produced at that time, we see, aside from a single portrait and a tree study, buildings from places that Lissitzky knew: from Vitebsk and Smolensk, where he had lived and from cities that he had visited in the summer of 1912 while hiking through northern Italy. He drew these buildings in heavy outlines within a rounded-off frame and filled in the areas with bright colors, by which the works assume a somewhat illustrative character. These early drawings show the relationship to work of artists from the *Mir Iskusstva* (World of Art), a group which can be regarded as the Russian counterpart of Jugendstil.

Several of these drawings from Darmstadt had been done by Lissitzky as part of his examination at the Technical Institute, which he did in 1914. When the World War broke out shortly thereafter, Lissitzky was forced to return to Russia, along with many of his countrymen (e.g. Kandinsky and Chagall).

Moscow 1915-1919

In 1915 Lissitzky took up residence in Moscow and entered the Polytechnic Institute of Riga, which had been evacuated to Moscow because of the war. Three years later he received the 'engineer / architect' diploma from the school. During this period he worked for architectural firms and, as an artist, took part in exhibitions by such groups as the *Mir Iskusstva*. But the most outstanding of his work from this time is his achievement as a designer and illustrator of Jewish books.

1. Modern calendar date; according to the old Russian calendar, November 10.

Revolution (1917)
Jewish Renaissance (1916-1919)

Lissitzky's transition to specifically Jewish art was not an extraordinary move at that time: Jewish culture was flourishing in those years. The regime of the czar had always been openly anti-semitic in its politics, which had seriously hindered the cultural and political potential of Jews. The fall of the czar's empire and the arrival of the new government, which removed restrictions for Jews, strengthened the will and the potential of Jewish people, particularly those of Eastern Europe, to shape their own identity. It was not so much a form of religion as a form of nationalism. Artists looked for Jewish subject matter; writers began to publish plays and stories in Yiddish; their books were illustrated by El Lissitzky and other well-known leaders of this Jewish Renaissance such as Nathan Altman, Lissitzky's former teacher Jehuda Pen and Marc Chagall, who remained true to Jewish art throughout his entire life.

Between 1916 and 1919 Lissitzky devoted himself almost totally to the cause of Jewish national art. He took part in the organization of exhibitions by Jewish artists and was represented with work; moreover, he himself studied the Jewish culture, undertaking a journey to Mogilev to investigate the paintings in the synagogue there; later he published an article about this in Yiddish, with depictions of the copies that he had made of these frescos.[2] But for the most part he occupied himself with the designing of illustrations and covers for Jewish books; many of his drawings from this time are reminiscent of Chagall's work. In 1917 he made the drawings for the Yiddish book *Sikhes Khulin. A Prager Legende* (An everyday conversation. A legend of Prague) by Moshe Broderson, several copies of which were published in the form of a Torah scroll, in a wooden case, in addition to the normal edition [repr.8].

In the year of the revolution, Lissitzky made designs in gouache for *Khad Gadya* (One billy goat) [repr.6], a song that is sung in Jewish families on the first evening of Passover. The song tells of a billy goat which is menaced by a cat, which in turn is attacked by a dog. The billy goat stands for the Jewish people, and the cat, the dog, followed then by a stick, fire, water, ox, butcher and angel of death stand for their oppressors, from the Assyrians to the Turks, who successively defeat each other, until God himself defeats the angel of death and thus liberates the Jewish people. In 1919, in Kiev, Lissitzky published a book containing lithographs of these ten subjects. The style of these works differs greatly from that of the gouaches: he designed the forms of the figures according to a geometric motif. Lissitzky drew, for example, the dog and the cat fighting [repr.7.2], each with their arched backs within a circle. The two circles overlap. The way in which Lissitzky drew their legs seems to set the circles in motion; this brings about a dynamic force. In the other lithographs we see more of such circular and spiral movements. These cubiform lithographs seem to foreshadow the basic turnabout toward geometric / abstract art which would take place in Lissitzky's work during that same year.

Lissitzky did not actively participate in the upheavals of 1917. Shortly after the revolution, he appears to have done work for the cultural department of the new government and to have designed a Soviet flag, which was carried across Red Square by members of the government on May 1, 1918.

Vitebsk 1919-1921

In 1918 Marc Chagall was appointed commissioner for artistic affairs in Vitebsk, his hometown. One of his accomplishments was the founding of an art academy, at the beginning of 1919, where he himself, Jehuda Pen and others started to teach. In July of that same year, he gave his kindred spirit in matters of Jewish art, Lissitzky, a position as instructor in the department of architecture and head of the graphics workshop.

Suprematism

Shortly after Lissitzky's arrival, Kasimir Malevich also joined the faculty at Vitebsk. Malevich had undergone a rapid development from Impressionism, via Primitivism and Cubism, to totally abstract art. Around 1915 he produced his first suprematist paintings, in which squares, triangles and other flat geometric shapes float in a field of white. He built his art on sound theoretical groundwork and thereby achieved great recognition. Malevich had stopped depicting everyday reality, something which he regarded as an illusion. What we see appears to be made up of matter, but physics had demonstrated that the smallest building blocks of this matter, the atoms, could be split into forms of energy, into something immaterial. He believed true reality to be made up of forces and their reciprocal relationships; these forces form energy patterns, which are able to stir our senses and allow us to experience something. Malevich considered it the duty of the artist to visualize this true, but invisible reality, which he called the "world of non-objectivity", in the most succinct manner possible. To achieve this, he made use of simple geometric shapes and bright colours. He called this form

15

2. 'Vegen der Mohilever Schul', *Milgroim* (1923) nr. 3, p. 9-13.

of art, which for him was the only plausible one, Suprematism. Malevich regarded Suprematism as being eminently suitable as the art of the new revolutionary society and engaged in fierce disputes with artists who did traditional paintings. At the art academy in Vitebsk he began to teach according to methods that he had developed on the basis of Suprematism; he united his students in the group *Unovis*, the abbreviation for 'Advocates of the new art'.[3] A somewhat explosive situation arose at the school; Chagall, who remained true to the more traditional Jewish art, became Malevich's opponent. Lissitzky, who was influenced by the powerful personality of Malevich and by his art, chose to take his side in the conflict, much to the disappointment of Chagall, who left Vitebsk not long afterwards. Lissitzky broke away from Jewish art and became a disciple of Suprematism.

Lissitzky's poster *Beat the whites with the red wedge* [repr.76] shows triangles, rectangles, bars and circles as Malevich used them in his suprematist paintings. He gave the elements a much more concrete meaning than Malevich, since the poster was an assignment to make propaganda for the Red Army in their battle against the Whites; the civil war was now in full progress. On the poster, the point of a red triangle penetrates a white circle surrounded by black. Two arched rectangles yield to the onrushing red wedge, and a smaller red wedge chases after a small white circle at the upper right. Shapes like these were used as symbols on military maps [4], and this is what makes the poster comprehensible.

Proun

By about 1920, Malevich had taken Suprematism to a point where it was difficult to go any further. Malevich distinguished between three phases within the development of Suprematism: the black, the coloured and the white. Several years prior to this, he had painted his black square, which he regarded as the end of traditional art and the beginning of the new, suprematist art. He wrote that his brightly coloured geometric shapes came about by dissecting the black square into separate colours and shapes. In 1919 these shapes had meanwhile dissolved into almost entirely white paintings (white shapes on a white background), whereby it looked as though Malevich had reached the end of his new painting. In Vitebsk he nevertheless sought for possibilities to extend Suprematism into space; architecture offered prospects for this. It was his colleague, the architect and artist El Lissitzky, who would carry out this task and arrive at his most famous creation: the *Proun*.

In Vitebsk, at the end of 1919 or beginning of 1920, Lissitzky produced the first paintings in which he expanded the visual language of Suprematism with spatial elements. Most of these early compositions were based on an architectonic idea, such as a bridge or a city, but Lissitzky's concern was not for concrete architectural plans. In a gouache [repr.40], for instance, we see two large vertical blocks with two flat shapes at their sides. At first the gouache resembles a perspective drawing of skyscrapers, but on further observation the perspective proves to be all wrong; the large shapes have a horizontal base but do not stand on the ground; they appear to be flat on the underside, spatial at the top, and they have different vanishing points. All sorts of spatial and flat objects float to the fore from between the vertical blocks. The manner in which Lissitzky has placed all of these large and small shapes along side and on top of each other on the white surface makes for an intricate and fascinating complex of various spatial relationships which contradict each other.

We also see architectonic forms floating about in many other paintings by Lissitzky. The notions of 'floating' and 'weightlessness' had already played a significant role in the theories of Malevich, and Lissitzky became fascinated with them as well: he expected that, in the future, gravity would be conquered and that it would thus become possible to construct buildings that would float in the air. Such paintings are visions of this future. In his first article, Lissitzky wrote, "The artist constructs a new symbol with his brush. This symbol is not a recognizable form of anything which is already finished, already made, already existent in the world – it is a symbol of a new world, which is being built upon and which exists by way of people."[5]

One aspect of Lissitzky's work which greatly differs from the suprematist paintings of Malevich is his use of colour: in his gouaches we see no bright colours, but various shades of gray and ochre, colours that we actually encounter today in the architecture of big cities. Lissitzky hereby wanted to indicate, very concretely, something about the visual effect of the materials which were going to be used in the architecture of the future: "We will turn the ruggedness of concrete, the smoothness of metal and the reflection of glass into the skin of the new life,"[6] he wrote in 1920. In order to convey this all the more clearly, he combined a range of materials in various paintings, such as tempera paint with pencil and metal foil; occasionally he mixed sand into the paint in order to convey coarseness; some surfaces

16

3. Russian: Utverditeli NOVogo ISkusstva.
4. Alan C. Birnholz, *El Lissitzky* (Ph. D. Diss. Yale University, New Haven), Ann Arbor, Mich. and London 1973, p. 131.

5. Quoted from the German translation of 'Suprematizm tvortsjestva' (The Suprematism of the creative work) from 1920, Sophie Lissitzky-Küppers and Yen Lissitzky, ed., *El Lissitzky. Proun und Wolkenbügel. Schriften, Briefe, Dokumente*, Dresden 1977, p.15-20.
6. Sophie Lisstizky-Küppers, *El Lissitzky. Life, Letters, Texts*, London 1980 (second edition), p. 332.

were painted with pure varnish in order to achieve a glass-like transparency.

Wanting to emphasize the fact that he was not creating ordinary works of art, Lissitzky called his suprematist compositions *Prounen*. He only began to do this, however, after about a year. The provenance of his two-syllable trademark *'pro-oon'* was never revealed by Lissitzky, but the word has been explained in different ways by others. It could very well be a contraction of the Russian 'proekt unovisa', which means 'architectonic design of Unovis', but no one can be kept from reading it as the Latin 'pro' unovis, or as an abbreviation of 'proekt utverzhdenya novogo' (design for the confirmation of the new). This very ambiguity is well suited to the art for which it stands.

In Lissitzky's *Prounen* we often see a movement which emerges from the picture plane: in *Proun 1D* [repr.52] a series of bars hovers like a complex of buildings in front of a black circle. Two broad strips run through the picture plane, from the inside of the circle to the edge of the painting; because the circle cuts across these strips and the group of bars, in turn, do this to the circle, the floating complex of spatial forms clearly seems to come forward.

Many of Lissitzky's compositions are known to have different versions. *Proun 1D* was done by Lissitzky in at least three versions, all of which reveal various small differences. One of these can be seen in a photograph of Lissitzky in his studio in Vitebsk. It is probably this earliest version that he wished to publish as a lithograph, in a portfolio together with ten other lithographs. Lissitzky made several designs for the cover of this *Proun portfolio*, but its actual publication appears to have never taken place.

Architecture

Lissitzky gave shape to a rather concrete architectonic idea in *Proun 1E*, a composition of which only a lithograph now remains [repr. 21]. The painting of this which he had made earlier was not yet titled *Proun 1E* but *Suprematism – Town*. In this composition we see strips which come out of a black square and continue to the edge of the painting. Lissitzky placed, alongside that square, a number of blocks which suggest buildings. The different colours and materials were replaced by various cross-hatchings in the lithograph. On one of the prints,[7] he wrote the following: 'system for a town square'. With *Proun 1E* Lissitzky gives us a bird's eye view of a suprematist town square. Lissitzky used the composition of *Proun 1E* in a propaganda sign [repr.74] from his time in Vitebsk. A large segment of the popu-

lation had fled to the country during the years of the civil war. The government wanted to start up industrial production again and therefore needed to bring people back to the cities. Lissitzky designated this direction with a couple of arrowheads that point to the city; these look very much like those in his poster *Beat the whites with the red wedge*. He later applied his town *Proun* once again on the cover of his book *Russland. Die Rekonstruktion der Architektur in der Sowjetunion* (Russia. The reconstruction of the Architecture in the Soviet Union) [repr.103]. Lissitzky also made attempts to actually apply Suprematism to architecturè. He gave his *Unovis* students the assignment of designing a podium on which leaders of the revolution could speak to the people. Lissitzky himself made various sketches for this, basing his ideas on the curved and straight, flat and spatial forms that appear in his *Prounen*. In some of these drawings, it is almost impossible to see that they involve plans for a podium. Not until 1924, in Switzerland, would Lissitzky create the design that became known as the *Lenin Tribune*, using these studies done by him and his students [repr.152].

Moscow 1921

At the beginning of 1921 Lissitzky left Vitebsk for Moscow, in order to give instruction in monumental painting and architecture at *Vkhutemas* (Higher State Art and Technical Workshops). This year was a turning point for many artists. The contention between supporters of a spiritual, utopically oriented art on the one hand and proponents of a utilitarian art on the other seemed to have been sorted out in favour of the latter. One of the instructors at *Vkhutemas* was Vladimir Tatlin, a fervent advocate of utilitarian art.

Tatlin had made a model for a *Monument for the third international*, a 400-meter-high spiralled tower. Three large, geometrically formed areas, intended for scientific and government use, were to be built inside this tower. With this design Tatlin wanted to place his art at the service of society, as it was his conviction that the individual artist was subordinate to the community. This conviction also led him to design industrial mass products in new forms and with new materials. Lissitzky, who was by no means insensitive to these ideas, also carried out assignments in the field of typographic design in Moscow and would even begin to concentrate totally on applied arts in the future. But the atmosphere of his own utopic and very personal, almost romantic creations – the *Prounen* – clashed with the constructivist belief in its subjection to the immediate needs of society.

7. In the Costakis collection, nr. 151.78

Germany 1922-1923
Cultural exchange

At the end of 1921, Lissitzky was given the opportunity to go to Berlin. This was not an escape from government politics; with the activities which he developed in Germany, he seemed, on the contrary, to have taken on the job of cultural representative for the Soviet government.[8] In doing so he fulfilled a significant role as intermediary for artists from Eastern and Western Europe. Shortly after his arrival, he set up a periodical, *Veshch-Gegenstand-Objet* [repr.92], together with the Russian writer Ilia Erenburg; it was intended as a means to provide Western Europe with information about Russian art and literature and, in turn, to provide Russians with information about Western European art. Consequently they published articles in German, French and Russian, sometimes in three languages at once, as was done with the opening article 'The blockade of Russia is coming to an end'.

Lissitzky designed the magazine. No more than two issues of the periodical were published, but the two had managed to gather contributions from prominent artists, writers, filmmakers and architects throughout the whole of Europe.

Lissitzky also took part in the organization and development of the *Erste Russische Kunstausstellung* (First Russian Art Exhibition), held in the autumn of 1922 at Galerie Van Diemen in Berlin. This was the first opportunity, since the world war and the subsequent blockade of the Soviet Union by Western powers, for the Western public to become acquainted with the newest art movements which had emerged in Russia, such as Suprematism and Constructivism, in addition to traditional art and movements that preceded Social Realism. It also became evident that Russian and Western art had been developing in a surprisingly similar way.

Lissitzky designed the cover of the catalogue [repr.78] and was also represented with work, which included a series of *Proun* lithographs and the paintings *Town (Proun 1E)* and *Proun 19D.* The latter work was purchased by Katherine Dreier for the Museum of Modern Art in New York.

A year later, the exhibition went to the Stedelijk Museum in Amsterdam. Lissitzky travelled to The Netherlands and held lectures there on the new art in Russia. During his visit to The Netherlands, he established contacts with artists and architects, among them Huszar and Oud. The architect J.J.P. Oud was a member of the *Algemeen Comité voor Economische Opbouw van Rusland* (General Committee for the Economic Develop-

ment of Russia), the association which was partly responsible for the organization of the exhibition in The Netherlands. An interesting exchange of correspondence came about between Oud and Lissitzky; this lasted until 1928.

Lissitzky established numerous contacts in Germany as well. He took part in the important artists congresses that were being held at that time, such as the *International Congress of Progressive Artists* in Düsseldorf in 1922. Afterwards, along with such others as Theo van Doesburg, he passed out statements which were published in *De Stijl.* Art was seen as a universal expression of creative energy, which could be used for the betterment of mankind. The idea was to fight for a universally intelligible and applicable art and to become organized in order to bridge the considerable gap which was felt to exist between theory and practice.

Typgraphic designs

In addition to all of these organizational duties, Lissitzky continued to paint *Prounen* in Germany. He moreover began to concentrate increasingly on the designing of covers and illustrations for books, primarily for the Russian publishing houses in Berlin. A book that Lissitzky designed and wrote entirely himself was *Suprematicheskii skaz pro dva kvadrata v 6ti postroikakh*; Suprematist story about two squares in six constructions) [repr.86]. The drawings for this had already been done in Vitebsk, two years before the book was published in Berlin in 1922. In *Pro dva kvadrata* Lissitzky made use of suprematist forms. The work resembles a film script with six illustrations, six constructions, as the title reads. The text is made up of letters in various sizes, most of them placed diagonally to the illustrations. The story deals with two squares, one red and one black, that fly to earth: 'They see black, turmoil. One blow, and everything bursts apart. Bright red is placed on top of the black.' The suprematist shapes hereby depict the advent of a new society, where socialism (the red square) and Suprematism (the black square) work together. Lissitzky made this book especially for children: on the first page, he encouraged them to act out the event with paper, sticks and the like. Theo van Doesburg was quite impressed by Lissitzky's book and published a Dutch adaptation of *Pro dva kvadrata* as a special issue of *De Stijl.*[9] He also included an article by Lissitzky, which dealt with the *Prounen*, in his magazine.[10]

At the end of 1922, Mayakovsky asked Lissitzky to design a book with thirteen of his best known poems intended for reading aloud, *Dlia Golosa* (For the voice) [repr.80]. In order to make

8. It is not known as to whether he actually did leave for the West on government assignment, as is often suggested.

9. *De Stijl* V (1922) nr. 10 / 11.
10. 'Proun. Nicht Weltvisionen, SONDERN – Weltrealität', *De Stijl* V (1922) nr. 6, p.81-85.

it easier for the reciter to find a particular poem, Lissitzky introduced a thumb index, which was a great innovation in the field of typography. The texts were typeset in the traditional manner, but at the beginning of each poem Lissitzky designed a title page. "My pages are more or less to the poem as a piano is to the violin that it accompanies,"[11] wrote Lissitzky. For this, he used only typesetting materials, such as large and small letters, lines, circles and grids, making figures with these which are highly reminiscent of his *Prounen*.

The Proun in Germany
A linoleum print from 1922, which Lissitzky made for the cover of the Hungarian periodical *MA* [repr.83], was literally taken from one of his *Prounen*, albeit in reverse: in *Proun 43* [repr.41] we see two intersecting white strips inside a rectangle and a circle; the corners are rounded off. On and across these corners, Lissitzky painted a circle, several elongated forms and a transparent triangle. The composition has the look of a map, but this association is not as obvious as in *Proun 1E* [repr.21]. *Proun 43* appears to be a much more careful arrangement of forms; the thought of architecture seems to have dissolved into the background. By way of its relative simplicity and clarity, the composition functions more as a sign. With the same elements, though, Lissitzky was able to make an entirely different sign; this is shown by two works that are closely related to this gouache, the painting *Proun G7* [repr.33] and the collage *Proun* [repr.34], both done in a wide range of materials. In these two works, Lissitzky changed the direction, size and colour of the strips and other elements. The glistening triangle of varnish was omitted by him in the collage, although it still does appear in the design for this [repr.35]. The number of different materials, each with its own expression, was perhaps already enough for him: crepe tape, metal powder, pencil, various kinds of paper – matter and glossy in assorted tints – and yellow paint on top of tape and paper.

Lissitzky regarded the elements of his *Prounen* as indicative marks; their construction and scale were to give the space a certain tension. 'When we change the marks, we alter the tension of the space, which is formed from the very same void,'[12] Lissitzky wrote in 1920. These three *Prounen* show how Lissitzky worked out that idea.

Prounenraum
At the *Grosse Berliner Kunstausstellung* (Great Berlin Art Exhibition) in 1923, Lissitzky had the use of a small square space. He decided to not hang any existing *Prounen* there, but to put new *Proun* compositions with reliefs on the wall and to connect these with long slats. [repr.59] "The first form, which 'leads' in those who come from the large room, is diagonally placed and 'leads' him to the large horizontal on the back wall and, from there, to the third wall with the verticals. At the exit – Stop! There below is the square, the basic element of the entire design."[13]
We still know what the *Prounenraum* (Proun Room) looked like, because designs for it have been kept. Moreover, Lissitzky assigned some of its components to a painting and several lithographs. One of these lithographs portrays the space in collapsed form [repr.55.7]. By means of this, it was possible to reconstruct the room [repr.60].

Kestnermappe
The lithographs from this *Prounenraum* were part of Lissitzky's *1° Kestnermappe Proun* (First Kestner portfolio Proun) [repr.55.1-7], a particularly fine portfolio with six lithographs, most of them in colour and some with collage, and a page of text; this was printed in an edition of fifty. Early in 1923, Lissitzky had his first solo exhibition at the Kestner Gesellschaft in Hanover. Encouraged by its success, the directors of the Gesellschaft decided to commission Lissitzky to create this portfolio of lithographs, which was to be presented as an annual gift to its members.
Lissitzky came to Hanover to etch the stones himself. He was given a studio on one of the upper floors at the Kestner Gesellschaft, where he was able to work until the end of that year. During this time he also met Sophie Küppers, widow of Paul Küppers, who had been the artistic director of the Kestner Gesellschaft. Some years later El Lissitzky would marry Sophie Küppers and move with her to Moscow.

Figurinenmappe
Commissioned by the owner of the graphic workshop where the *Kestnermappe* was printed, Lissitzky made another portfolio with lithographs, but one of a completely different nature. Here he used gouaches that he had brought from Russia [repr.61-71], designs for mechanical dolls which he had made for the futuristic opera *Victory over the Sun* by painter / poet Aleksei Kruchenykh and the painter / composer Michail Matyushin. This opera was performed for the first time in 1913 in Moscow; the

19

11. Sophie Lissitzky-Küppers, op. cit.
(note 6), text accompanying ill. 95-108.
12. Ibidem, p.347.

13. Ibidem, p.365.

costumes and sets were designed by Malevich. His stage set with the black/white square was the beginning of Suprematism. The opera tells the story of a battle against the sun, which is banished from the heavens as an old source of energy, then imprisoned and replaced by a new source of energy which modern man has invented himself with his technical capability.[14] In 1920, the opera was re-staged by students from *Unovis*; costumes were done by Vera Ermolaeva. During that time Lissitzky produced his designs for nine of the figures from the opera, but he based these ideas on electromechanical dolls rather than actors and actresses. He described the project in his Page of Text [ill.1]. The dolls were to move about mechanically within a setting. This *Schaumaschinerie* was to become an open network of scaffolding, situated on a plaza which was accessible from all sides and controlled by one person, the *Schaugestalter*. His voice would be electromechanically altered, according to the noise to be spoken or sung by the figure. Lissitzky deliberately wanted to leave this plan in the form of colour lithographs; at the conclusion of his text, he wrote that he was leaving the execution of these ideas and forms to others.

On the first page of the portfolio, Lissitzky depicted part of the *Schaumaschinerie* [ill.2]; in and on a number of circles, strips and plateaus, we can see four of the nine figures from the portfolio. *Totengräber* (Gravediggers) [repr.69] shows coffins with crosses on them that serve as bodies; their high hats are depicted clearly, even somewhat sculpturally, but only disjointed details of their faces can be seen, such as the eye of the right-hand figure. *Ansager* (Announcer) [repr. 62] has a body in the shape of a red piano, connected to a megaphone; his head is an egg. The figures of *Ängstliche* (The Terrified) [repr.64] also have eggs for heads; due to the diagonal position of their body forms, they seem to be literally stricken with fear. And that of *Neuer* (The New) [repr.70] has a red square on its body, the sign of *Unovis*, and two heads with the Soviet star, sign of the new society.

The development of the *Figurinenmappe Sieg über die Sonne* (Figurine Portfolio Victory over the Sun) is particularly well documented. Aside from the splendid designs which he made in Russia (now owned by the Tretiakov Gallery), there is also a series of sketches, transfer sheets and proofs (in the collection of the Van Abbemuseum) that gives us a fairly good glimpse of Lissitzky's studio. He first traced his design onto a transfer sheet, laid this with the image side on the litho stone and then traced the lines onto the stone by pressing hard. The stone could then be processed further; a stone was needed for each colour, a method common to lithography. Lissitzky also did the initial designs for many of his paintings, collages and gouaches on such a transfer sheet; several of these still exist. On the framework that Lissitzky drew around such a sketch, he marked off numerous measurements which served as a basis for the construction with compass and ruler; in chalk, he scratched these marks onto the backside of the sheet, so that the design could be transferred onto canvas or wood.

Secondary colours were created where colours overlap each other in the lithographs; by mixing speckled ochre on top of black, for instance, Lissitzky obtained a surface resembling sheet metal with a layer of rust. Just as with the *Prounen*, the colours in these figures also had to be seen as being equivalent to materials. A subtle use of grays in various shades and textures, as in *Neuer* [repr.70], is striking as well. The working sketch for this lithograph was used by Lissitzky to designate, in gouache, that which was to be printed in red: the red square and the five-point star.

Switzerland 1924-1925

Shortly before the *Figurinenmappe* was completed at the end of 1923, Lissitzky became seriously ill. Symptoms of tuberculosis became manifest. A stay at a sanatorium in Switzerland only became possible when the office supply firm *Pelikan*, in Hanover, appeared to be prepared to help with a fixed monthly allowance, in exchange for advertisement designs for the company. Lissitzky left for Switzerland early in February 1924. Despite his illness, he was quite active and worked on all sorts of projects there. He no longer painted *Prounen*, but focused his attention on typography and architecture; he wrote articles, translated writings by Malevich into German [15] and occasionally produced advertising material for *Pelikan* [repr.94-95].

While in Switzerland, Lissitzky also became involved in photography and began to experiment with photograms and multiple exposures. This is how his well-known photographic self-portrait *The Constructor* [repr.117] was made from six exposures, for example. He also made use of photography in his advertisement designs for *Pelikan*.

Typographic Designs

In Hanover, Lissitzky became friends with Kurt Schwitters. Schwitters was the best known avant-garde artist of this city; he produced Dadaist poems and Dadaist collages, which he called

14. A German translation of the text with reproductions of the score and of Malevich's costume designs can be found in exib. cat. Berlin (Akademie der Kunst) 1983, *Sieg über die Sonne. Aspekte Russischer Kunst zu Beginn des 20. Jahrhunderts*, Berlin 1983.

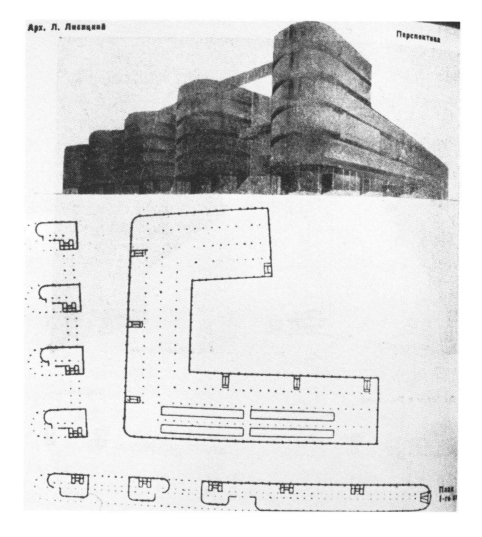

ill. 4
Asnova-bulletin, 1926
Municipal Van Abbemuseum,
Eindhoven

ill. 5
Give more tanks!, propaganda-
poster, 1941
Photo: Sophie Lissitzky-Küppers,
1976, nr. 252

Merz-Bilder, and published the periodical *Merz*; one issue of this, the *Nasci-Heft* [repr.93], was published together with Lissitzky. Lissitzky wrote an article for this issue and was responsible for its design. In the magazine, the authors compare art and architecture with forms from nature and suggest that both fields are basically interrelated.[16]

On March 30, 1924 Lissitzky wrote, "I have an idea for the last *Merz* of 1924: 'Final parade of all the isms of 1914-1924"[17] [repr.96]. Kurt Schwitters had little regard for the idea. Hans Arp, whom Lissitzky had met in Switzerland, did appear to be interested. During the summer of 1924, they started working on this "mass grave of all the isms in art".[18] Arp wrote the articles for the various isms in collaboration with Lissitzky, and Lissitzky saw to the design.

Architecture

Lissitzky had created his design for a podium, which became known as the *Lenin Tribune* [repr.152], on the basis of sketches done by a student of his, Ilia Tsyasnik; these were published in *Almanakh Unovis*. The *Lenin Tribune* was to be made of iron, eternite and glass and measure approximately twelve meters in height. The bottommost cube, made of transparent material, was to contain the motor which would set the whole contraption in motion: a glass elevator would have the capacity to transport several speakers to the lowest balcony, where they would wait their turn to be brought to the upper level. Once they had arrived at the uppermost balcony, this would then shift forward, so that balcony and speaker would become the center of attention; the diagonal construction was to accentuate the gesture of the speaker. On top of this, there was to be a removable screen on which maxims could be displayed and news reels projected.

A second well-known architectural design from Lissitzky's Swiss period is the *Wolkenbügel* (Cloud ironer) [repr.129], a building that he designed, like the *Lenin Tribune*, specially for the Soviet Union. It is an office building which is meant to be built high above the ground, on pilings; Lissitzky had taken urban planning into consideration here. He believed that as long as free-floating buildings were an impossibility, we tend more toward horizontal than toward vertical movement. Because there was insufficient room on the ground, he raised the horizontal building into the air and placed it on three vertical supports. Traffic, consequently, would be given more space, and the street would remain light and airy. The structure was intended for certain major intersec-

tions of the ring boulevard and radial arteries in Moscow, and was thus to become a fixed point of orientation in the city; one of the three supports was to have access to a metro station. Lissitzky described a number of technical details, such as lightweight insulation and soundproofing material and chemically processed glass which was to let light in, but not heat. By way of the open construction and the abundance of glass, the building was to acquire a non-solid, almost immaterial character. From each angle it was to look completely different; Lissitzky indicated this in his various drawings of the building, which are reminscent of the *Prounen*. The *Wolkenbügel* is much less utopic however; the building was never realized, but its execution is not impossible.

Moscow 1925-1928
Asnova

In May 1925 Lissitzky left Switzerland and returned to Moscow. He spent his first years there focusing primarily on architecture. Two important groups of architects with different ideas were working in Moscow at that time. The constructivists, united in the *Osa* (League of Contemporary Architects), were predominantly concerned with the practical problems of residential building. They approached architecture from a functional standpoint and criticized the architects of the other group, *Asnova*, for what they regarded as their old-fashioned ideas and a lack of feasible plans. *Asnova*, the Association of New Architects, opposed what they saw as extreme utilitarianism on the part of the constructivists. *Asnova* was founded in 1923 by Nikolai Ladovsky, an instructor at *Vkhutemas*, and several of his colleagues. They advocated a synthesis of painting, sculpture and architecture, and they placed value on the appearance of a building, the organization of its space and the effect that its architectonic forms would have on people. Lissitzky understandably felt more allied with the *Asnova* architects; when he was still in Germany he had, at Ladovsky's request, taken charge of all representation for the organization abroad. On returning to Moscow he and Ladovsky set up a magazine, the *Asnova Bulletin* [ill.4], and published his plans for the *Wolkenbügel* in it, showing photographs of his designs and ground plans. Lissitzky designed the magazine himself. Due to a scarcity of paper, only one issue was published, and this did not come out until 1926. Lissitzky made more architectonic plans and took part in competitions, but none of his ideas were realized. This was the fate of most work done by architects from *Asnova*.

15. Its publication in book form was never realized. Part of the translation was published as K. Malewitch: Lenin (Aus dem Buch: 'Über das Ungegenständliche'), *Das Kunstblatt* VIII (1924), p.289-293.
16. For a discussion of 'the organic' with regard to Lissitzky and his interest in the philosopher Oswald Spengler and the biologist Raoul Heinrich Francé, see Peter Nisbet, 'An Introduction to El Lissitzky', Cat. Cambridge MA (Busch Reisinger Museum) 1987, *El Lissitzky (1890-1941)*, Cambridge MA 1987, p.28-30.
17. Sophie Lissitzky-Küppers, op. cit. (note 6), p.48.
18. Letter to Oud, dated 8-9-1924, Van Abbemuseum archives, Eindhoven.

At the end of 1925, Lissitzky was again given a position at *Vkhutemas*, this time as an instructor for interior design and furniture, in the department of wood and metal. He taught there until 1930.

During this period, Lissitzky published various articles on architecture, for the most part in the periodical *Building Industry*. These dealt with much more concrete subject matter than his previous articles on Suprematism and the *Proun*; Lissitzky covered such topics as building in reinforced concrete, the construction of flat roofs, Bauhaus and the new train station in Rotterdam.

Demonstration Spaces
One of Lissitzky's most important activities during the late 1920s and 1930s was the designing of exhibition spaces. In 1926 he created two exceptional spaces for modern art: a temporary space for the *Internationale Kunstausstellung* in Dresden, his *Raum für konstruktive Kunst* (Room for constructivist art) [repr.119-121], and a permanent space for the abstract art at the Provinzialmuseum in Hanover, the *Abstraktes Kabinett* (The abstract cabinet) [repr.122-124]. He applied the same principles to both sites.

Lissitzky regarded the walls as optical background and not as carriers; he decided to resolve this issue by placing, in front of the walls, vertical slats that were painted black on one side and white on the other. The wall itself became gray; as the visitor walked through the space, the walls constantly changed from white to gray to black and vice versa. In addition to this, he wanted to limit the large number of artworks that the viewer was seeing at one time. In order to achieve this and moreover make the viewer active, he installed sliding panels, whereby the visitor could discover a painting at his own discretion and then take out another one.

Since his stay in Switzerland, Lissitzky had not painted any *Prounen*. Specially for the space in Dresden, he produced a new version of *Round Proun* [ill.6] and, in addition to this, a large print of the photograph of his hand with a compass, which he had made in Switzerland.

Pressa
After 1927, the year in which he married Sophie Küppers, Lissitzky concentrated almost totally on exhibitions and publications for the Soviet government. The success that he had with his first big assignment in the Soviet Union, the *Polygraphic exhi-*bition in Moscow in 1927, brought about his appointment as head of a team of artists who were to design the Soviet pavilion for the *Internationale Presse-Ausstellung Pressa* (International Press Exhibition Pressa) in Cologne in 1928 [repr.155-158]. Sophie Lissitzky also assisted in the preparations for this exhibition. With this exhibition, Lissitzky entered the realm of pure Soviet propaganda in the time of Stalin. The pavilion became something entirely different than what people had been accustomed to seeing: the information was not simply set against the walls and attached to partitions, but incorporated into all sorts of installations. There were long conveyor belts which could roll up to the ceiling, making a continuous display of assorted texts and propaganda posters. Near this was a gigantic star, which was to give an idea of the structure of the Soviet Union. According to the catalogue which Lissitzky designed a vast eclipse on the ceiling was to represent the Russian nation, six spheres the six republics. Connective wires and rings with text served to indicate how the republics were related to each other. The center was formed by a three-dimensional hammer and sickle. For the *Pressa* exhibition, Lissitzky also designed an enormous photographic frieze measuring three-and-a-half by twenty-four meters, the theme of which was: 'The duty of the press in the transition period from capitalism to communism is to educate the masses.' Such photographic friezes were to become a routine part of Soviet exhibitions.

The design of the Soviet pavilion greatly impressed its visitors. "Everything in it is exceptionally interesting, and the author of these lines should consider himself lucky if he could say the same of the British pavilion," read an English newspaper.[19] Lissitzky himself was not wholly satisfied with the result. He wrote to Oud: "It was a great success for us, but artistically it remains an unsatisfying achievement, as the haste and lack of time violate the plans and necessary completion of the form, and then it actually ends up being stage scenery."[20]

Die vier Grundrechnungsarten
Lissitzky proved to be a loyal propagandist for the brand of socialism envisioned by Stalin.

In Austria, to which he travelled with Sophie after the exhibition, he produced designs for a book which was meant to introduce children to the principles of arithmetics and Soviet communism at the same time: *Die vier Grundrechnungsarten* (The four arithmetical functions) [repr.97.6]. '1 worker + 1 peasant + 1 soldier of the Red Army = 3 comrades,' he wrote next to the figures

24

19. Sophie Lissitzky-Küppers, op. cit. (note 6), p.85.
20. Letter to Oud, dated 26-12-1928, Van Abbemuseum archives, Eindhoven.

that he had assembled from letters and other typesetting elements, like those of the *Dlia Golosa*. But the drift was quite different now. *Die vier Grundrechnungsarten* was never published.

Contacts

Lissitzky and Sophie subsequently went to Vienna, Stuttgart, Frankfurt and Paris and visited various architects and artists in these places. The contacts established by Lissitzky at this time were the reason for which some people later decided to go and work in the Soviet Union; among these individuals were Ernst May, who had masterminded the expansion of Frankfurt, and Neurath in Vienna, who would later set up an 'Institute for artistic statistics' with his group in Moscow.

In Paris, Sophie and El Lissitzky saw Piet Mondrian; it was the first time they had met. "Despite a lack of fluency in French and German, the two artists understood each other immediately. Their experiments, those of Lissitzky in space and those of Mondrian on the picture plane, complemented each other. In Mondrian's studio, Lissitzky was deeply impressed by the vivid planes of colour; he predicted a great future for him in the application of colour as a component of architecture."[21]

Moscow 1928-1941
Architecture

At the end of 1928 Lissitzky returned to Moscow permanently. He still continued to work on several architecture projects until 1931; as an entry to a competition, he submitted a design for a new Pravda building [ill.3], in which five separate units and several building segments behind them were interlinked by footbridges; like the *Wolkenbügel*, this was to give the building an openness and a different aspect from every angle. Again, this plan was never carried out; this was also to be the fate of his proposal for a complete renovation of the Meyerhold Theater [repr.143-145], which seems to be a continuation of his ideas from the *Figurinenmappe*. Meyerhold wanted to play down the distinction between stage and audience; Lissitzky therefore moved the stage toward the center of the theater and made it an open construction, reminiscent of the *Schaumaschinerie*, with platforms, footbridges and winding staircases. The actors would be able to approach the transparent stage surface from the orchestra pit below as well as from the balconies above and bridges at the side; stage props could be rolled down via block and tackle and then disappear into the depths after each scene.

Exhibitions

During the 1930s politics began to leave a heavier mark on Lissitzky's work; exhibitions and books increasingly took on the look of propaganda for Stalin; the pavilions that he designed for locations abroad were to show off the achievements of the Soviet Union.

Yet an interesting model apartment by Lissitzky was shown at the *Internationale Hygiene-Ausstellung* in Dresden in 1930 [repr.149-150]. A movable wall, with built-in shelves and writing surfaces in standard sizes, made it possible to divide the space in different ways. Lissitzky thus left it to the inhabitant to determine where he would eat, sleep or spend time during the day. Lissitzky placed a chair designed by himself in this apartment.

In his later years, the exhibitions changed dramatically in character. We see, for instance, a design for a pavilion at the agriculture show in Moscow in 1938 that incorporates figures holding the emblems of the Soviet republics into a kind of classical architecture, which Lissitzky himself would have fulminated against fifteen years earlier. For a restaurant in the Soviet pavilion of the 1939 World's Fair in New York, he designed a frieze in bright folkloristic colours, depicting dancing peasants in national costumes.

Typographic Designs

From 1932 onward Lissitzky did the design and lay-out for various issues of the Soviet propaganda magazine *USSR im Bau* (USSR in construction) [repr.106-107]. It had been set up by Maxim Gorky and was published from 1931 to 1941 in four languages, its aim being to give foreign publicity to the achievements of the Soviet Union under Stalin. Sometimes Lissitzky only saw to the lay-out, other times he also sketched in the photographs that were to be included. Frequently we see a glimpse of his earlier work: he cropped photographs diagonally or placed them in round frames; he sometimes used wide strips to divide parts of the page and allowed photographs of varying scales to contrast with each other. He made use of fold-out pages, and as a last echo of his fascination with a diversity of materials, he frequently used different varieties of paper and materials. Each issue was dedicated to one subject, such as the new dam in the Dniepr, the Red Army, the constitution drawn up by Stalin or the new territories in Eastern Europe, acquired since the Hitler-Molotov Pact of 1939.

Lissitzky moreover did the design for various other publications by the Soviet government, which dealt with such topics as the

25

21. Sophie Lissitzky-Küppers, op. cit. (note 6), p.87.

Red Army, heavy industry and the foodstuffs sector. The tuberculosis from which he was suffering, however, made it very difficult for him to work during those years. In 1935 he stayed for some months in the Caucasus Mountains for a cure; there he worked on an issue of *USSR im Bau* about Georgia.

Conclusion

One can only guess how Lissitzky must have felt in his later years as a supporter and propagandist of Soviet communism, when more and more people began to disappear, some of them having been his colleagues from the editorial staff of *USSR im Bau*. Lissitzky continued to work within a system that he had regarded as an ideal, a system in which he believed. His feeling probably began to change gradually, but he could no longer turn back. One may wonder about the extent to which fear may have played a role in this. Perhaps Lissitzky ignored his inner aversion. His illness, too, must have had a great influence on him and his work; during the last years of his life, his health declined steadily. When the Soviet Union became involved in World War II, he was still able to design one more poster (a photomontage) with an appeal to produce more war supplies [ill.5]. On December 21, 1941 Lissitzky died at his home in Schodnia, near Moscow.

From – ∞ to 0 to + ∞

Axonometry,
or Lissitzky's mathematical paradigm

Yve-Alain Bois

In *K. und Pangeometrie* (A. and Pangeometry), a formidable essay published in 1925, El Lissitzky writes:

"Suprematism has advanced the ultimate tip of the visual pyramid of perspective to infinity. It has broken through the 'blue lampshade of the firmament'. For the colour of space, it has taken not the single *blue* ray of the spectrum, but the whole unity – the *white*. Suprematist space may be formed not only forward from the plane but also backward in depth. If we indicate the flat surface of the picture as 0, we can describe the direction in depth by – (negative) and the forward direction by + (positive) or the other way around. We see that Suprematism has swept away from the plane the illusions of three dimensional perspective space, and has created the ultimate illusion of *irrational* space, with its infinite extensibility into the background and foreground."[1]

This section is illustrated by a diagram without a caption, and the particular purpose of the following pages will be to comment on both these few lines and this diagram, while drawing from other sections of the text as well as a few others of Lissitzky's writings.

At first, his very use of the term *Suprematism* might lead us to conclude that he is simply describing the work of his mentor, Kasimir Malevich. A simple reading of this passage would argue that for Lissitzky, Suprematism has replaced the perspectival representation of space, invented in the Renaissance, by another mode of spatial projection. However, but for a few specific exceptions, Malevich does not resort to any kind of projection for depicting the third dimension of space. His paintings are entirely planimetric, using geometrical planes of a single colour, either overlapping or not, and seem to be requiring the kind of description Lissitzky devotes, earlier in his text, to Egyptian art. Indeed, Lissitzky's characterization of Suprematism is biased by his own pictorial interpretation of this style, as from the outset his *Proun* paintings appeared as combinations of geometric volumes floating in space.

In fact, what Lissitzky is describing in this passage is a mode of geometric projection which was called *cavalière perspective* by the military engineers who first used it in the 16th century (etymologically, the term means *perspective of a horse rider*, that is: seen from above). In this type of projection, one of the planes of the represented solids is projected without any foreshortening – one face of a cube is represented as a perfect square. More important is the fact that in this mode of projection receding parallel lines do not converge in a vanishing point but remain parallel. As such, *cavalière perspective* can be characterized as a particular case of axonometric projection, or axonometry (which Lissitzky indeed uses very often in his *Proun*), and whose main difference with it is that no face of a represented solid would appear in its true figure. As the theoretical issues pertaining to both types of projection are the same, from our point of view, and as axonometry covers a broader territory, I will subsume here both types of projection under this latter term. Axonometry was invented many times in the history of mankind, and *rejected* as often until it finally appeared, during the 19th century, as an ideal tool of representation in fields as various as crystallography, mechanics, descriptive geometry or architectural archeology. But although this positivist use of axonometry can be traced back to the 1820's, it is only after abstract painters like Lissitzky or Theo van Doesburg had magnified axonometry in their works, one century later, that architects of the modern movement choose this mode of representation as a stylistic landmark of their drawings. Thus Lissitzky, among others, can be credited for opening the eyes of modern archi-

1. This essay, which appeared in German in *Europa Almanach*, Carl Einstein and Paul Westheim (Potsdam: Kiepenheuer) is poorly translated into English in Sophie Lissitzky-Küppers, *El Lissitzky: Life. Letters. Texts.*, London 1968 (Thames and Hudson), p. 348-354 (in most of the quotations made here the translation has been modified). Throughout the essay, Lissitzky abbreviated the word Art (Kunst became K., thus Art becomes A.)

Diagram

tects of the esthetic potentialities of axonometry, a graphic device they knew well at least since Auguste Choisy's magnificent plates of his archeological books at the end of the 19th century.[2]

In a very elliptical manner, the long quote I made at the beginning of this essay evokes: perspective; the notion of infinity; the blue versus white colours; a plus/minus, or protention/retention reversibility of the figures in suprematist space; the zero of the picture plane; irrationality; and the history of art as a Hegelian series of sublations or replacements of one type of illusion by another.

I shall start with the last issue. Although he begins his article by stressing the stratified character of the history of art ("A. is a graduated glass. Every era pours in a certain quantity"), Lissitzky conceives here of the various modes of representation of space in art as related by a kind of negative engendering, each one evolving from and superseding the precedent, in the manner of the Hegelian dialectics. To articulate his narrative, Lissitzky uses a metaphor which, as Peter Nisbet has shown recently, he borrows from Oswald Spengler's famous book, *Der Untergang des Abendlandes* (The Decline of the West).[3] This metaphor is that of mathematics, or rather, of the *numeration systems* of various epochs and civilizations, as analogous in some ways to the artistic achievements of those specific eras.

Just as the Russian formalist literary critics will do shortly thereafter, Lissitzky begins his metaphorical account of the relationships between art and science with a proviso of caution; to apply directly and uniformly facts drawn from the history of science to those drawn from the history of art would be as harmful as the more common vulgarity of the *Widerspiegelung* theory, according to which art simply 'reflects' society: "the parallels between A. and mathematics must be drawn very carefully, for everytime they overlap it is fatal for A." Nevertheless, he does not seem to be so cautious later in his text. Like Spengler, Lissitzky seems to envision the relationship of art and mathematics as an exemplification of the *Zeitgeist* of a given time (Spengler speaks of the 'soul'), and to hold to the concept of the cultural totality of an epoch or a civilization.

To measure Lissitzky's debt to Spengler, I will mention a few points of the opening chapter of his magnum opus, a chapter devoted to the 'meaning of numbers'. First of all, Spengler states that "one should not speak of the evolution of high arts without looking at the same time at the mathematics which is contemporary to it"; second, he considers that the systems of numeration can be understood as cultural symptoms; third, he insists on the fact that there are two kind of mathematics: the theoretical mathematics, which is formalized by numbers and symbolic notations, and the empirical mathematics, which presides over many productions of mankind – art, for example can be interpreted as embodying this 'unconscious' type of mathematics which can in fact anticipate the corresponding discovery in the field of mathematics proper (and Spengler gives here a perfectly accurate example when he states that the elaboration of Renaissance monocular perspective antedates Descartes' work for two centuries); fourth, Spengler shows that there is a gap between Greek geometry, grounded in arithmetics and the visible world, and modern geometry, whose emphasis on function and continuity by way of its dependence on algebra requires an altogether different language and envisions a space totally remote from our actual experience of the phenomenal world; fifth, Spengler claims that the problem of infinity is at the core of modern western thought, and that the invention of the zero played a major role in the elaboration of infinitesimal calculus; finally, he states that the euclidian space, which Kant thought of as *a priori*, as independent of experience, is only but one possibility for conceiving of spatial relationships. All that, and more, constitutes the lesson which Lissitzky would retain from Spengler. In a few words, it could be characterized as that of a mathematical relativism grounded on a cultural relativism: "a number as such does not and cannot exist", writes Spengler, "there are many universes of numbers", he adds, "because there are many cultures."

Let us look at the way this relativism and the mathematical metaphor works in Lissitzky's account of the 'evolution' of art. The first iconic representations produced by men were purely planimetric, thus, Lissitzky: "Plastic F. begins, like elementary arithmetic, with counting. Its space is the physical two-dimensional flat plane. Its rhythm is the elementary harmony of the natural numerical progression 1,2,3,4...", which he illustrates by a diagram of three segments of a horizontal line, each surmounted by an Egyptianlike cow, standing for the artistic production of Antiquity in the East and in Greece prior to the appearance of foreshortening. Then the first illusion of space was created, with the overlapping of planes as a symbol for depth: "the plane begins to presume upon space and there arises the numerical progression 1, 1½, 2, 2½..." The numerical suite is still arithmetic, although it already departs from integers and starts dealing with fractions, which indeed were discovered by the Egyptians:

28

2. See for examples the plates of Choisy's first book, *L'Art de bâtir chez les Romains*, Paris 1873. His *Histoire de l'architecture* (1899) was Le Corbusier's bed-table book.

3. Cf. Nisbet, *El Lissitzky*, Busch-Reisinger Museum, Cambridge 1987, p. 29. Nisbet states this interest for Spengler in relation to an earlier text by Lissitzky, but 'A. and Pangeometry' is a reshaping of this earlier essay and retains strong Spenglerian overtones.

the virtual line relating the different numbers is still discontinuous and it is still a planimetric entity, but it is already slightly oblique. (In the second diagram corresponding to this transitional stage, this lesser discontinuity is represented by the overlapping of the three cows and by the three lines stacked one upon another as a series of steps). Avoiding speaking of the Middle Ages (not because of a lack of interest in the period, but I suspect, because his mathematical metaphor would not hold true), Lissitzky turns directly to perspective: "Perspective defined space and made it infinite, then enclosed it; but the 'body of numbers' of A. became richer" and in a footnote Lissitzky defines this 'body of numbers' *(Zahlkörper)* as "the totality of all possible numbers, which may be represented geometrically by a straight line consisting of an infinite number of contiguous points, each of whom correspond to a number"). To sum up:

"Planimetric space provided us with the arithmetical progress. There the objects stood in the relation: 1,2,3,4,5... In perspective space we acquired a new geometric progression; here the objects stand in a relation: 1,2,4,8,16,32... Up to the present time the 'body of numbers' of A. has acquired no new enrichment."

Although the difference between those two last sets of numbers is clear enough as expressing the visual acceleration one encounters in the representation of depth by the kind of foreshortening produced by monocular perspective, where things become smaller as they recede, one wonders what prevented Lissitzky from using a continuous series of numbers as a formula for the step which would logically follow his characterization of the transitional stage. The answer is quite simple, and can be deduced from the first and the last sentence of the paragraph I just quoted as well as from the footnote attached to it: on the one hand, Lissitzky denies (contra Spengler, for once) that perspective deals with an infinite space (which is the corollary of the idea of a continuum), on the other hand, he asserts that what he calls the 'body of numbers' of art, that is, the representation of space as formulated by his mathematical metaphors, has received no new enrichment up to the present time (that is until Malevich or rather until himself). The next lines of Lissitzky's text are quite explicit: although modern art as a whole can be understood as an attack against this mode of representation of space, neither the impressionists, nor the cubists, nor the futurists drew the final conclusion: "the establishing of the square, by Malevich, was the first manifestation of expansion in

the 'body of numbers' of A", writes Lissitzky (and again, one must read here, under the name of Malevich, Lissitzky's own interpretation of Suprematism, i.e., the *Prounen*). So it is not by chance that he saves the diagram of the absolute expansion of his so-called 'body of numbers' – the continuous line consisting of an infinity of continuous points – for this last development of art: "This is where we first arrive at an A. complex, which we can compare analogically to the unbroken straight line of mathematics, which comprises within itself the series of natural numbers, with integers and fractions, the 0, the negative and positive numbers, and the irrational numbers." We shall come back later to the minus and plus infinity which are framing this continuous line, and which certainly could not have been used for a formula of perspective space.

The text then unfurls in an investigation of what would be the next step, which would supplant the axonometric space just described and correspond in art to the new mathematical discovery of the imaginary numbers, for they cannot lead to any geometrical representation (for example $\sqrt{-1}$). Lissitzky stipulates that the abstract films of Vicking Eggeling are a first attempt in the direction leading towards this imaginary space which would be best set forth, according to him, by the virtuality of volumes engendered by rotational movement, something he called an *immaterial materiality*. Lissitzky fell short of pursuing these experiments in his own work, perhaps because he realized, as Erwin Panofsky put it in the criticism he wrote of Lissitzky's article, that this supposedly imaginary space was no less euclidian than that of perspective nor even, for that matter, of axonometry, that is, of which it was supposed to replace.[4]

Lissitzky's radical critique of perspectival space posits axonometry as its sublation on the path leading towards the fulfillment of the 'body of numbers' of art, that is toward infinity. We have reached here the point where Lissitzky's loose adaptation of Hegelian dialectics becomes most significant: as a sublation of perspective, axonometry must be born out of the contradictions of the latter system. And indeed, it is Lissitzky's idiosyncratic interpretation of Suprematism, via axonometry, which leads him to point out the major contradiction of perspectival space. Let us recall, to state briefly the problem, that in the system of monocular perspective, based on Euclid's geometry, the vanishing point is the representation of the infinite, of the non-existing point at which parallels meet. But if the infinite is represented, if the meeting of parallels is actually portrayed for our human perception, how could one state that they never meet in the phe-

"Plastic F. beginns, like elementary arithmetic, with counting. Its rhythm is the elementary harmony of the natural numerical progression 1,2,3,4..."

"The plane beginns to presume upon space and there arises the numerical progression 1, 1$^{1/2}$, 2, 2$^{1/2}$, ..."

4. Cf Panofsky, 'Die Perspektive als 'symbolische Form'' (1927), reprinted in Erwin Panofsky, *Aufsätze zu Grundfragen der Kunstwissenschaft*, Berlin 1974 (Bruno Hessling), (H. Oberer and E. Verheyen eds.), p. 166, note 73.

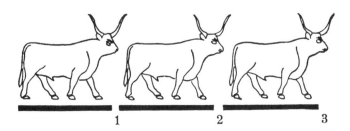

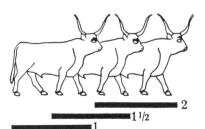

nomenal world axiomatized by Euclid? The fraud of perspective, for Lissitzky, is that while it is constructed as an analogon to human perception, it pretends to give to us an equivalent of the infinite and continuous extension of space through the receding patterns of the foreshortened lines. But this is impossible: the infinite is inaccessible to human perception, and cannot be apprehended via a system grounded on the subjectivity of human vision. Such a system is *structurally* limited: theoretically, there is only one *point of view* which the spectator is supposed to hold, at a specified distance, in front of a perspectival painting, and it corresponds as in a mirror to the vanishing point in the painting.[5] Theoretically, this is Lissitzky's claim, perspective is *Medusa*, it petrifies the spectator and can in no way lead him towards an apprehension of the infinite. Only a fully abstract, conceptual system of the representation of space, a system which would claim its independence from human vision, could lead us to such an apprehension: it would not try to let us *see* the infinite, for that is impossible, but grasp it. This is what axonometry achieves, for Lissitzky, via the virtual extensibility of receding lines forward or backward: from the picture plane, it sets forth the virtual possibility of the negative infinity (in depth) and of positive infinity (towards beyond us).

One begins to understand, now, why blue is discarded at the benefit of white in suprematist space. Lissitzky's emphasis on white is grounded in his knowledge of Malevich's white on white paintings of 1918, and of the numerous texts of the painter dismissing the blue as the color of infinity. Blue is the color of *distance*, which is antithetic to the notion of infinity in so far as it presupposes a *point of view* and an *object*. The pictorial tradition acknowledged this at least since Leonardo's theorization of the so-called 'atmospheric perspective': the more an object is removed from us, the more bluish it will appear (and hence should be pictured so). This phenomenon, which was scientifically explained by Von Helmholtz at the end of the 19th century, is alluded to, by Malevich and Lissitzky, as evidence of the ties of perspective to the phenomenal world: perspective is bound to earth, hence its incapacity to present abstractly, the only possible way, the concept of the infinite. But Lissitzky's metaphor implies something more. As a sublation of perspective, as its *Aufhebung*, to use Hegel's term, axonometry must surpass it while retaining its purpose, it must include it as a limited, somewhat inferior possibility: this is exactly the status of the white in relationship to the blue: as the color of the whole spectrum, it englobes blue as one of its components and destroys it

at the same time.

The contradiction of monocular perspective regarding the infinite is not, however, the only one Lissitzky is able to discern, via his use of axonometry, in this system of representation of space. Thus reads *A. and Pangeometry:*

"It is generally accepted that perspective representation is the clear, objective, obvious way to represent space. [... But in fact:] Perspective has comprehended space according to the concept of Euclidian geometry as a constant three-dimensional state. It has fitted the world into a cube, which it has transformed in such a way that in the plane it appears as a pyramid. The tip of this visual pyramid either lies in our eyes - therefore in front of the object – or we project it onto the horizon -behind the object. The former concept was chosen by the East, the latter by the West."

At this juncture, the text is illustrated by a three part diagram bearing these legends: under the square on the left (a schematic rendering of a still life in the so called 'inverted perspective' one encounters indeed in chinese painting), the word *chinese*; under the square of the right (an as schematic rendering of the *Last Supper*), the name *Leonardo*; and for the square of the middle, empty but for the two diagonals that bisect it, this riddle: "this is the perspective representation of a pyramid. Where does the tip lie? In depth, or in front?" What Lissitzky is trying to say here, besides pointing to cultured differences in the representation of space, is first that perspective consists in a rationalist reduction of space to a cube and of human binocular vision to a monocular one, and second, which only seems paradoxical, that its very rationalism is flawed by its incapacity to solve one of the most famous aporia of human perception. Indeed, it is only because paintings made according to the laws of perspective are peopled by objects and figures that one has a clear sense of the direction of space as receding from one's point of view, that one can claim to know where the tip of the visual pyramid lies. Without this population, without the *istoria*, there is no way to know if a foreshortened line recedes or advances towards us. Being monocular, the system of perspective does not deal with visual accommodation, that is, the capacity of our organism, having two eyes, to eliminate such ambiguities.

Two consequences have to be drawn from Lissitzky's advocacy for a system where the protension/retention dodeling, inherent to perception, would not be repressed. First, the perspective sys-

5. On the issue of the theoretical specularity, cf. Hubert Damisch, *L'origine de la perspective*, Paris 1987 (Flammarion), passim.

tem is as such incapable of depicting the spatial void. It can function only in a world fully inhabited, it is bound to earth. Hence the numerous metaphors of flight one can find in Malevich's texts as well as in Lissitzky's. If perspective is Medusa, the deadly petrification of the spectator, axonometry is Pegasus, the flying horse which was born from the blood of Gorgon. Second, as a rationalist system, perspective wished to ignore every occurrence where human consciousness finds itself at loss: as it structurally avoids dealing with the issue of binocular accommodation, it does not take into consideration those very moments where such a human capacity is faulted. Such occurrences fill the pages of numerous treatises of optical physiology of the 19th century under the name of reversible figures (for example the axonometric diagram of a cube whose main receding side will shift direction in space and, as a consequence, be seen either as its top or its bottom but never as both simultaneously). It is such an aporia regarding the perception of depth that Lissitzky presented rather crudely in his diagram of a pyramid, and that will be magnified in a playful way in Joseph Albers' axonometric *Structural constellations*. Just as Von Helmholtz was convinced, via the loss of power of human consciousness once confronted to optical illusion, of the existence of an 'optical unconscious' – Lissitzky was convinced that a whole section of our perception of visual phenomena escapes human reason and that these ambiguous perceptions, which had been repressed by the rationalism of perspective, were precisely those which a truly abstract conception of space should exemplify. Hence the characterization of Suprematism as *irrational*.

The sentence I quoted at the beginning of this essay, concerning the −, the +, and the 0, is, I hope, becoming clearer. Axonometry is chosen as a means of underlining the protension/retention oscillation which perspective had repressed, the words "or the other way around" stressing the fact that unlike perspective, it does now rely on the choice of a necessarily arbitrary point of view – that there is, indeed, no point of view at all in axonometry. Like Albers, Lissitzky wants to emphasize by all possible means this deep ambiguity of perception. Let us read, for example, his only text on the *Proun* published in the West during his lifetime (it appeared in 1922 in *De Stijl*, the journal directed by Theo van Doesburg):

"We saw that the surface of the *Proun* ceases to be a picture and turns into a structure round which we must circle, looking at it from all sides, peering down from above, investigating from

below. The result is that the one axis of the picture which stood at right angles to the horizontal was destroyed. Circling round it, we screw ourselves into the space. We have set the *Proun* in motion and so we obtain a number of axes of projection."[6]

This passage is important as it reveals how Lissitzky wished to exacerbate the plus/minus effect inherent to axonometry and transform it into a radical reversibility. What he wants to destroy is the certainty of the spectator and his usual position in *front* of the painting, in front of the horizon. This position is clearly anthropomorphic; it is bound to our standing still on the ground, it is bound to our submission to the law of gravitation. In order to "free ourselves away from the horizon of form", as would say Malevich, in order to reach a totally abstract mode of representation of space, we must sever all ties to the phenomenal space, which is a space oriented around and from the pole constituted by our body. "To turn an object upside down", submitted the French philosopher Maurice Merleau-Ponty, "is to deny its signification". In his *Prounen*, Lissitzky wanted to invent a space in which such a fundamental orientation of space and in space would be deliberately abolished. They are made to be hung in various positions (at least one *Proun* painting bears this potential reversibility in its title, the famous *8 position Proun* [repr.14] of 1923, but examples abound of this concern, particularly in his lithographs). Furthermore, although he was fully aware, of course, of the engineers' rationalist use of axonometry (he was trained as an architect), Lissitzky could not resist underlining the potential reversibility of axonometric space in his depiction of the various exhibition rooms he designed in the 1920's: in the graphic interpretation he gave of it in the *1° Kestnermappe Proun* (First Kestner portfolio Proun) [55.7], the surfaces of the 1923 *Prounenraum* (Proun Room), which is a cube, are tilted in such a way that negative and positive space shift constantly, and the same occurs for his gouache and collage rendering of the *Abstraktes Kabinett* (The abstract cabinet) [repr.122] of 1928, which we must turn upside down in order to be able to read the lower half properly. During this operation of reversal, not only positive space becomes negative, and vice-versa, but the ambiguous position of the ground on which the figure stands is clearly demonstrated. This oscillation of a plane in various directions of space, as well as its shifting from two-dimensional to three and back to two is essential to Lissitzky's *Proun* paintings. And one of the ways by which he achieves this amphibology is given in the quote I just made: he is using, for the direction of   31

6. Reprinted in Lissitzky-Küppers, op. cit. (note 1), p. 343.

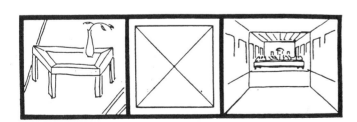

Chinese   This is the perspective   Leonardo
               representation of a pyramid.
               Where does the top lie?
               In depth, or in front?

depth, several axis of projection within a single image. This practice, which contradicts a rationalist use of axonometry, engenders the impression of floating, of non-gravitation one is given by his *Prounen*: we are again dealing with flight, but also with the idea of an isotropic space, a space where no direction is more important than another, and for which the sky is a perfect metaphor.

This search for a radical reversibility went even further. In a letter dating from 1923, he writes:

"You go on to enquire on which wall you should hang my work.... When I made my *Proun*, I did not think of filling one of these surfaces with yet another decorative patch. You should be treating the problem in quite the right manner, as prescribed by common sense, if you wanted to order a cupboard for these documents of my work. Subsequently, labels will be attached to them, indicating to what sphere of human activity these documents belong and in which epoch these documents originated. You say that we are hung on walls in the museums? It is not my fault that the museum directors are convinced of the perpetual infallibility of their own spectacle lenses so that it never occurs to them to devise another method of exhibiting."[7]

What is at stake here is not so much the struggle against the usual mode of visibility available to works of art in a museum, but the change of status Lissitzky envisions for his *Prounen*: they are not paintings any more, but documents, and they should be stored as such, that is horizontally. But horizontality is another inversion of the pictorial mode of relationship (between object and beholder) being criticized by Lissitzky. In fact, he himself directly connected horizontality to the disorientation in space that he wanted to achieve, in the magazine cover he designed for *Broom* [repr.88]: "the fact that magazines frequently lie on the table with their titles upside down gave Lissitzky the idea,"[8] his wife tells us. In this shift of the verticality of the painting to the horizontality of the document, I am inclined to read a fundamental transformation, an antecedent to the shift which Leo Steinberg perceived twenty years ago in the works of Rauschenberg, but which I see as essential to major productions of 20th century art (Cubism, Mondrian, Pollock, Minimalism). For Steinberg, who coined the concept, Rauschenberg's paintings are 'flatbeds,' that is, similar to surfaces like "tabletops, studio floors, charts, bulletin boards – any receptor surface on which objects are scattered, on which data is entered, on which

information may be perceived, printed, impressed". A flatbed does not offer a "conception of the picture as representing a world, some sort of worldspace which reads on the picture plane in correspondence with the erect human posture", it is "no longer the analogue of a visual experience of nature but of operational processes". In short, "the horizontality of the bed relates to making as the vertical of the Renaissance picture plane relates to seeing".[9]

We reach here the last point I want to make, concerning the use of the zero in Lissitzky's text. His interest in this number which has no geometric equivalent, as Spengler puts it, stems in three directions. First, obviously referring to Malevich's numerous allusions, in his writings, to Suprematism as the zero of forms, Lissitzky adopts the typically formalist interpretation of the flatness of the picture as the irreducible essence, the zero degree of the art of painting: this is the function of Malevich's black square. Then Lissitzky dwells on the structural marvel which is constituted by the *positional* numeration system invented by Indian Buddhism, a system for which the zero played a major role, far greater than in the West where it was theorized as such only in the 16th century by Cardano and Tartaglia, both of whom Lissitzky refers to. It is there that his discussion of Malevich's work seems the most appropriate, for he introduces one of the characteristic aspects of Suprematism, its use of colour. Drawing from numerous discussions, in treatises about colour, of the fact that "two areas of different intensities, even when they are lying in one plane, are grasped by the mind as being at different distances from the eye", Lissitzky equates Suprematism with a positional system (the perceived 'distance' of a colour area from the stable zero of the picture-plane depends from its intensity, which is a function of its position on the colour scale): "These distances cannot be measured by any finite measure, as can the objects in planimetric or perspectival space. The distances are irrational; they cannot be represented as a determinate ratio of two whole numbers."
We then come to the third interpretation of the zero, and, finally, to the diagram of the absolute 'body of numbers', the continuum of numbers and the unbroken line. Reading from left to right, it proceeds from the notation of minus infinity, to negative numbers, then to the zero, to positive numbers, and finally to the notation of plus infinity. Earlier texts of Lissitzky, in which he uses the same series of numbers in a slightly different way, might cast some light on what is at stake here. Speaking of the

32

7. Ibidem, p. 344.
8. Ibidem, p. 26.

9. Cf. Leo Steinberg, *Other Criteria*, Oxford 1972, (Oxford University Press), p. 82-91.

series of positive numbers which follows the zero, he wrote in one of these essays:

"Certainly this series ascends, but on the other side of painting as such. If people once said that time had brought painting to a square in order that it would perish there (this is the theme of the black square as the last painting), we have said: if the slab of the square has blocked up the narrowing channel of painterly culture (perspective), its reverse serves as the foundation for a new, volumetrical growth of the concrete world."[10]

At this point, Lissitzky illustrated his text by yet another diagram, which refers to the *Proun* as an index of the world to come, as a theoretical model for the revolutionary reality which needs to be build. If the *minus* infinity refers to the absence of human point of view in axonometry, the *plus* infinity refers to the infinite potentiality of the material culture which has to be shaped once painting (the zero) has been overcome. In other words, if Lissitzky's *Prounen* are documents, it is because they are for him diagrams for action, operational charts for a strategy to adopt in order to transform society and to go beyond the picture plane. This metaphoric reading of the function of the zero in his text might seem contradictory to the two others, it is nevertheless in keeping with the final interpretation Lissitzky chose for his *Proun*, abandoning painting as such and dealing exclusively, at the end of his career, with architecture, typography and exhibition designs, that is, with practices engaged in the real space of material culture, rather than in the imaginary space of painting. As he wrote himself: "We begin our work on the two-dimensional surface, we then pass on to the three-dimensional model constructions and to the needs of life.... Through the *Proun* we have now come to architecture - which is not accidental".[11]

10. El Lissitzky, 'Prouns' (1921), in:
El Lissitzky, Galerie Gmurzynska, Cologne
1976, p. 64.
11. Ibidem, p. 70.

A new style

Three dimensional Suprematism and Prounen

S.O. Chan-Magomedov

While the figure of Lazar Markovich Lissitzky is a firm fixture in the art of the twentieth century, he presents scholars with a number of problems. The diversity of his talent reveals itself in the many fields of art in which his creativity flourished, including painting, architecture, typography, exhibition arrangement, and design. Lissitzky's superior artistic mastery, his skills and his excellent taste, are beyond challenge. Overall, then, we have the pictures of a great artist, one of the founders of modern art. And yet, Lissitzky's contribution to the emergence of the new style of art differs in an important way from that of most other pioneers of the new art. Lissitzky possessed no distinct, independent creative concept. He never claimed to possess one, either, nor did he attempt to formulate a theoretical construct in this direction. Such an assessment of Lissitzky's work may appear disturbing, perhaps even seem insulting to a master of such repute. And yet, it is valid, even though there are scholars today who claim otherwise and seek to glean a conceptual framework from out of Lissitzky's numerous texts. The absence of such a concept was a strong point rather than a weakness in Lissitzky's creativity. In the interplay of various forms of art and under the conditions of convergence of artistic and scientific-technical activities, a new style emerged during the first third of the twentieth century in the struggle against tradition-bound eclecticism and stylism. The goal was the development of a system of artistic presenta-tion capable of serving as the foundation of an enduring stylistic period. One may even be bold enough to assert that the quest involved the establishment of a style order comparable to the classical one, which fathered more than one style.

The quest for the foundations of the new style during the first third of the twentieth century availed itself of many approaches to form creation which were dramatically different from each other. All the same, the primary creative concepts of those years also exhibited similarities. Their creators strove to formulate primal foundations of form depiction in their quests for *style formulas*, foundations unencumbered by tradition. They more or less cleansed the language of art of its semantic additives and sought the primary mechanisms of form and style creation which lay beneath these.

With the style forms of the past overcome, creative concepts emerged during the formative period of the new style (especially in the representational arts) which were primarily rooted in fundamental impulses of creativity. The manner in which these impulses were approached in turn governed the content of the fundamental style-generating concepts. At the time, the main concern was the quest for the primary impulses of creativity on which, as a concrete style emerged, the entire artistic-compositional system of the means and methods of expression was to be erected.

Some sought this impulse in simple geometric forms and elementary colours, others in the functional-constructive fundamentals of buildings and objects, still others in the human need for spatial orientation. In Russia, the pursuit of these three elementary creative impulses led to the emergence of three independent style-generating concepts, Suprematism (Kasimir Malevich), Constructivism (Vladimir Tatlin, Alexander Rodchenko, Alexander Wesnin), and Rationalism (Nikolai Ladovsky). The fact alone that style-generating concepts of such a fundamental character emerged and developed within Soviet art represented a major accomplishment and important achievement, as well as a substantial contribution to the overall process of the development of the new style.

Assessing style-generating concepts of this kind is an extremely difficult undertaking. Thus, we often apply measures which really belong to formative concepts of the second or third generation, concepts in which the *style formulas* of the founders have already been fleshed out. The real goal, however, would be to determine and understand just why the particular creative concepts, both in their theoretical and in their practical dimensions, of artists such as Malevich, Tatlin, or Ladovsky were able to acquire such influence and impact on the style-generating processes of art in the 20th century. In our attempt to unearth the roots of their practical and theoretical creativity, we must quite possibly even be doing the founders of the new style a disservice insofar as these factors exerted their style-generating influence only in their most rudimentary forms.

By far not every leading artist present or past has influenced style-generating processes in direct relationship to the stature of his talent. An analysis of these processes valid for the 20th century clearly shows that style-generating influences are predicated on a special brand of talent, one that endows the overall work of the artist with a distinct touch, a rare gift which requires special circumstances for its full flowering. Malevich, Tatlin and Ladovsky, the founders of the most important style-generating concepts, possessed this rare talent, a key requirement in times of style transition and one that can only mature in such periods. You may ask what all this has to do with Lissitzky. It's well-known that, at the time of the style's emergence, each of the creators of formative concepts imbued with special and fundamental style-generating qualities conceived of it to be a self-contained creative concept incompatible with other concepts. It was hardly surprising, then, that Suprematism, Constructivism, and Rationalism each claimed a monopoly on the creation of the new style. Today, from the vantage point of time, we can recognize that each of these concepts represented but a part of the entire spectrum of means and methods of expression of the then emerging formative system of the new style. Back then, though, the representatives of the particular concepts polemically rejected the other parties even though reciprocal influences can be demonstrated. This mutual disdain is not only explainable in its essence, it is even necessary to the self-assertion and development of each particular concept, in short, a normal and predictable phenomenon.

In the formative phase of the new style, the basic style-generating concepts tapped creative impulses of such a fundamental character and expressed these in *style formulas* of such brevity that the continued development of the style necessitated an integration of the means and methods of expression involved. Only in this way would it be possible to hasten the process of crystallizing the full system of the new style's artistic creativity. Such a challenge called for integrative talents – talents such as that possessed by El Lissitzky.

At this point, it's worth distinguishing, albeit only schematically,

two types of talents which figure prominently, in a time when a new style emerges, in the hewing of its basic outlines. They are the style-generating talent and the integrative talent. When analyzing the role of the former, a number of general circumstances deserve consideration:

First, the process leading to the style-generating level of artistic activity is marked by an extreme formalization of the artistic means and methods of expression. Whereas subsequent users of a style generally elaborate and enrich the key means and methods of expression while adopting the style, this process moves in the opposite direction for the style generator: he aims for strict selection and sharp delineations. This was especially the case with Malevich, the creator of Suprematism.

Second, the influence of the style-generating artist on the overall process of form development proceeds in channels where the artistic calibre of his innovative works or that of his followers is not decisive. Herein lies a distinction between this type of influence and the kind involved in the conferral of artistic mastery.

Thirdly, such an extremely formalized style-generating concept of creativity generally embodies an equally cogent theoretical foundation that is easily passed on to others.

The artist with an integrative bent, by contrast, must exhibit other proficiencies:

First, the spirit of such an artist may not be keyed to a self-sufficient, personal concept of formative creativity, as such an orientation presumes the polemical exclusion of other concepts. His talent must be capable of embracing the most diverse style types and directions.

Second, the artistic liberties he takes in the impartial adoption of divergent style-generating concepts may not be boundless. Though he may not ensconce himself within the palisades of a single style-generating concept, he must honour style coherence all the same. This is a particularly difficult feat to undertake at the time of a style's emergence when it still lacks clear contours. The intuitive grasp of these contours places the integrative artist in a special role in the interactive process between the concepts existing at the wellsprings of the new style.

Third, he must exhibit exeptional artistic mastery and possess outstanding taste in order to create works which, despite the blending of means and methods of expression from disparate style-generating concepts, find the admiration of both the experts as well as the man on the street.

Fourth, the best integrative artists generally exhibit equal adeptness in different artistic fields. This is especially important during the phase of a style's gestation when the means and methods of the new artistic compositional system are in the process of emerging both through reciprocal influences between the individual style-generating systems as well as through the reciprocal influences among the individual fields of art.

During the twenties, Lissitzky was probably the most typical and clearest example of an integrative artist. With extreme sensitivity, he selected all the novel elements that furthered the emergence of the new style. The bent for polemical negativism typical of adherents of the individual approaches was alien to him. We can discover none of the traits of partisan exclusionism in him.

At a time when most artists faithfully adhered to a particular concept, the special nature of his talent engendered certain problems. Thus, on occasion he was seen as an indiscriminate stylizer or even as an eclectic who employed elements of the different style-generating concepts in an unprincipled fashion. At the time, the Suprematism of Malevich and the Formalism of the Ladovsky school were the object of severe criticsm on the part of the theoreticians of Constructivism. Rationalism supporters, in turn, berated the limitations of Constructivism, and so on. Lissitzky very much appreciated Malevich and made ample use of the formal and aesthetic accomplishments and discoveries of Suprematism in his works. At the same time, he retained creative contact to the thinkers and practitioners of Constructivism, such as Moissej Ginsburg, and he entertained close links to Ladovsky and the Rationalist direction.

Such an all-round orientation was close to impossible under the conditions of the times, and yet it was a fact. Today we can appreciate how much Lissitzky, all in all, accelerated the integrative processes during the phase of the new style's emergence through his organizational and theoretical activities as well as through his artistic work. Herein lies Lissitzky's major accomplishment, one that so far has not received the recognition it deserves. Indeed, in more recent publications, Lissitzky is portrayed as, among other things, a kind of jack-of-all-arts, undertaking forays into the most varied fields of art and using the methods and discoveries of Suprematism, Constructivism, and Rationalism indiscriminately.

To understand the place and role of the works of Lissitzky in modern art, one must take him for what he was, a person who was in creative touch, in an organic fashion, with the leading representatives of the different style directions, an artist who

borrowed his means and methods of expression from different style-generating concepts without regard for the boundaries between them. It is exactly this disrespect that enabled the integrative element in Lissitzky's talent to achieve maximum effect. The thinkers and practitioners of the different concepts of creativity strove primarily to elucidate the creative formulas of their particular schools and to propagate these as the sole and all-embracing foundations of the new style. Lissitzky, by contrast, sought primarily to clarify which elements in the various avant-garde creative concepts could be merged to contribute to the unity of the new style.

Perhaps one other reason why Lissitzky possessed such keen awareness of the processes of artistic form-creation is the circumstance that he often observed the development of Soviet art during the first years following the revolution from abroad, where he worked together actively with many Western European artists. Returning home, he saw more clearly than those directly embroiled in the polemics of creativity that it was their joint, active contribution to the emergence of the new style and not the battling between the avant-garde directions which counted. To him, the shared elements of the various schools were more important than their limits – an approach not typical for those years.

Let us compare two statements from the same year (1922) about the interrelationship between Suprematism and Constructivism, one by Boris Arvatov, the thinker of the Constructivists, the other by Lissitzky. Arvatov distinguishes two lines of leftist art development, the line Cézanne-Picasso-Tatlin, and the line Van Gogh-Matisse-Kandinsky-Malevich, and goes on to write that there is at present no greater enemy than the nonobjective,nonrepresentational Tatlin and the nonobjective Malevich[1]. Proceeding from the position of Constructivism, Arvatov delivers a very negative assessment of Suprematism. In polemical hyperbole, he describes Suprematism as the vilest reaction under the flag of the Revolution, that's to say a doubly dangerous reaction. Leftist art as expressed in the form of its truly revolutionary groupings (Constructivism) must mercilessly sever links to Suprematism[2]. Lissitzky, by contrast, in the lecture *Neue Russische Kunst* (New Russian Art), emphasizes Tatlin's role in the establishment of a constructive form of art and writes: "Two groupings have furthered Constructivism, the *Obmochu* (the Stenberg brothers, Medunezki, Joganson, etc.) and the *Unowis*... The first group has worked in materials and space, the second in materials and planes."[3] Constructivism inter-   37

1. *Srelisca* (1922) no. 8, p.9.
2. *Pecat i revoluciia* (1922) no. 7, p. 343-344.
3. *El Lissitzky*, Dresden 1967, p. 336.

ested Lissitzky, as we can see, not as a self-contained system but as an important element of a new style to whose emergence the supporters of both Suprematism (Unowis) and Constructivism (Obmochu) contributed. The integrative features of Lissitzky's talents expressed themselves not only in his autonomous posture toward the various currents of the avant-garde and the different artist groupings, but also in his efforts to transfer the achievements of a particular creative thrust from art field to art field. His role in the expansion of Suprematism from the two-dimensional into the three-dimensional, one which has preoccupied scholars for so long, is characteristic of this feature.

On the one hand, there appears to have been general agreement that the Vitebsk collaboration between Lissitzky the architect and Malevich the painter clearly influenced the ensuing re-orientation of formal esthetic experiments in the direction of three-dimensional subjects and architecture. On the other hand, applying in-dept studies, scholars have also found spatial elements in the works of Malevich that predated the Vitebsk period. They concluded that Malevich had preprogrammed the expansion of Suprematism to architecture already at the very beginning of Suprematism. Let us assume that this opinion is justifiable. After all, Suprematism as a style-generating concept of form creation had the genuine potential of being expanded into the entire domain of representational art. Even then, a careful study of Suprematism's development from the two-dimensional into the three-dimensional reveals that, without Lissitzky, an important link in the sequence of formal esthetic transformations would have been missing.

We do in fact find compositions which depict simple geometric bodies during the gestative phase of Suprematism, when it was just emerging from Cubism. The main concerns of Suprematism during its early stages of development, however, involved planes and their dynamics. The two-dimensional increasingly became the visual form of space depiction.

The white background of Suprematist picures introduced by Malevich symbolized an infinite space in which the two-dimensional elements floated. Malevich shifted completely from his early spatial compositions, which were still tied to Cubism, to two-dimensional elements. The planar Cubism he developed was no random phase: it amounted to the stylistic governance of his formative concept. He also systematically simplified the means and methods of expression within the context of Suprematism by repeatedly introducing new limitations until the sim-

plification process culminated in the laconism of his style formula.

Whereas Cubism and Futurism proceeded toward a growing complexity of image composition, including diversity of form and the depiction of spatial elements, all this vanished from the repertoire of means and methods of expression of the emerging Suprematism. The students under Malevich in Vitebsk, too, passed through the rigorous sequence of development of the latest art – from Cézanne via Cubism and Futurism to the black-white two-dimensionality of Suprematism.

Already by the Vitebsk phase, Malevich's intensive efforts at formulating the style formula had for all practical purposes come to a conclusion. It had focussed exclusively on the surface of the two-dimensional suprematist image, with its very restricted possibilities of varying image structure. Some outside observers at the time construed this as a crisis for Suprematism. What in fact was the case was that Suprematism, having reached its style formula, was now ripe to influence other areas of representational art productively. Suprematism entered the object-world not by going from being two-dimensional to three-dimensional, but by breaking through the frame of the painting. Though the introduction of the colour white (after it had destroyed, as he put it, the blue colour of the sky), Malevich expanded, so to speak, the space in which the flat elements floated into the infinite. But this space was essentially imaginary: any white (or as good as white) plane became an infinite space for the two-dimensional suprematist elements. They left the painting and went into the world of objects, but they did not (at any rate not necessarily) enter real space, but an imaginary space which could be formed by the surface of random objects. This expansion did not begin with the conversion of two-dimensional into three-dimensional elements. Instead, it involved the transfer of the two-dimensional suprematist elements from the canvas onto real objects. "All objects, our entire world," wrote Malevich, "must be garbed in suprematist forms – fabrics, tapestries, jars, plates, furniture, signs, in short, everything requires the signature of Suprematism as the new form of harmony."[4] What Malevich had in mind was a two-dimensional suprematist adornment of real objects – and that is how Suprematism embarked on its mission to conquer the real world. Not just objects were painted, even the houses and streetcars of Vitebsk were painted. Figuratively speaking, the two-dimensional suprematist elements, as it were, flew out of the painting and attached themselves to any random surface

4. M. Kunin, 'Ob UNOVISe'. In: Iskusstvo, Vitebsk 1921, no. 2-3, p. 15-16.

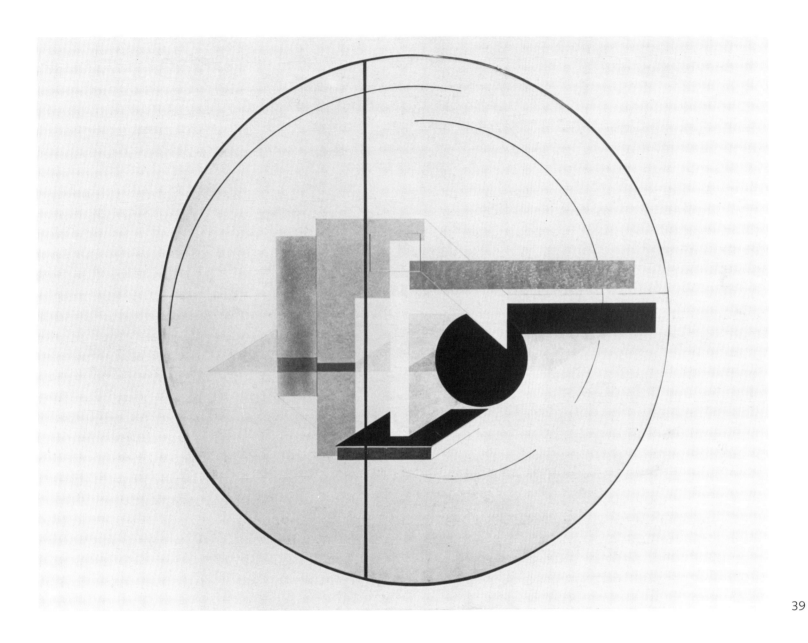

ill. 6
Round Proun, 1926
Photograph of the gouache. On the
back in Lissitzky's handwriting:
Proun.ist.die.Umsteigestation.von.
Malerei.nach.Architektur. (Proun is
the transition from painting to
architecture.)
Municipal Van Abbemuseum,
Eindhoven

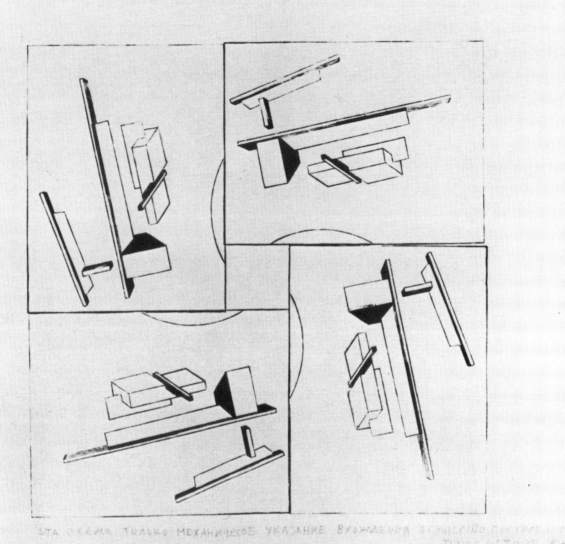

ill. 6A
Construction floating in space,
ca. 1920
Photo: Lissitzky catalogue, Harvard
1987

(the wall of a house, a poster, a vase, a tram, etc.). They created a fairy-tale setting of simple, brightly decorative elements, which stylistically linked everything that they adored.

This expansion of ornamental two-dimensional elements escaping from suprematist paintings is well conveyed in a description by S. Eisenstein:

"A singular provincial town. Built, like so many of the towns in the west of our country, of red brick. Begrimed with soot and depressing. But there is something very odd about this town. In the main streets the red bricks are painted white. And over this white background there are green circles everywhere. Orange squares. Blue rectangles. This is Vitebsk in the year 1920. The brush of Kasimir Malevich has gone over the brick walls... You see orange circles before your eyes, red squares and green trapeziums... Suprematist confetti strewn about the streets of an astonished town."[5]

Suprematism entered the real (three-dimensional) world along a broad front in 1920 and not just via the flat ornament. During that year, the idea of introducing Suprematism into the world of architecture was given clear formulation. In this way, the apparent demise of Suprematism from the exhaustion of its developmental possibilities on canvas was averted. New fields of creativity were made accessible to Suprematism. How did Malevich himself see this important phase in the development of Suprematism, its transition into the object world? How did he perceive his own involvement in this new three-dimensional, object-oriented Suprematism?

In a publication written in December 1920 and entitled *Suprematism*, he summerized the course Suprematism had taken up till then, outlined its latest phase, and related his own plans: "Suprematism has passed through three stages in its historical development: the black, the color, and the white phase. All these phases honored the significance of the two-dimensional and more or less gave expression to the dimensions of the prospectively spatial bodies: we are in fact seeing Suprematism at present arise in the space-time of new architectural design... We cannot speak of painting in Suprematism. Painting has long since been abandoned. With specific foundation having been laid in the suprematist system, I entrust the further development of what is now already architectonic Suprematism into the hands of... speaking most broadly – you architects, as only in them do I see an era of new architecture arising.

I myself have dared to enter a new field of thought and will report, should the opportunity be granted me, what I see in the infinite space of the human head. Long live the unitary system of world architecture!...
Vitebsk, 15. December 1920."[6]

Barely more than a year had passed since Malevich had published a declaraton, also entitled Suprematism, in the catalogue of the 10th official Exhibition in Moscow in 1919 – and yet so much had changed. In 1919, Malevich had written: "I have destroyed the blue background of the colour barrier and proceeded to the colour white. Soar along with me, comrade aviators, into the unfathomable! I have set up the semaphores of Suprematism."[7]

As one can see, by 1920, Malevich is already speaking of something completely different – about the final end of painting and about Suprematism's shift to architecture. In issuing this clarion call, he's no longer thinking of himself but rather of his successors, for whom he points the way into the unknown land of architecture, a way he will no longer be going himself. To all appearances, Malevich in 1920, at the point when Suprematism entered the object world, seems inclined to see his artistic work as having ended. He decided to withdraw into the field of reflection. Just how did this rapid evolution of Suprematism take place?

By scrutinizing the works of Malevich, the entire process of form development can be followed in his creations. It is possible to see how he arrives at Cubism and thereafter at Futurism, and how all three stages of two-dimensional Suprematism arise. In his painting, Malevich works through practically all the basic variations of image structure, always leaving the detail work to his followers. The stage marking the transition to three-dimensional Suprematism, however, is not documented by such exploratory works in his paintings, and the time after Vitebsk is already marked by intensive work on architectones and planites. Thus, between the final stage of two-dimensional Suprematism and the period of the architectones and planites, there is a gap: that of spatial image creation. This situation is puzzling, as Malevich had already intuitively engineered the transition to the object and architecture in 1920, during the Vitebsk days. Nor did Malevich's art instruction in Vitebsk entail such exercises among his students. Conversations with three Malevich students in Vitebsk, the subsequent architects F. Belostozkaya, M. Lerman, 41

5. S. Eisenstein, *Notes on V.V. Mayakovsky. V.V. Mayakovsky in the memory of his contemporaries*, Moscow 1936, p. 279-280.

6. Kazimir Malevich, 'Suprematism'. In *Vytvarné umeni* (1967) no. 8-9, p. 385-386.
7. *10-aja Gosudarstvennaia vystavka. Bezpredmetnoe tvorcestvo i Suprematizm*, Moscow 1919, p. 20.

and L. Chidekel, made this evident. Their statements are all the more significant because, as architects, they clearly appreciated the difference between two-dimensional and three-dimensional Suprematism. Their time in Vitebsk coincided with the transition from plane to spatial Suprematism, and they themselves, as students, participated in this process through their world.

They reported that, under the direction of Malevich, works were done at the school in the spirit of Cézanne, Cubism, Futurism, and two-dimensional Suprematism. Solid forms were produced, such as interiors, ceramics, and the like, and were painted, but planeness ruled in both the image as well as the solid forms. For the sake of instructional purposes, though, spatial-flat Suprematist compositions were also prepared under the guidance of Malevich. In the words of Malevich, two-dimensional black-white Suprematism consisted of regular geometric planes floating in an infinite space of white. It was decided to transform this concept into spatial terms. Under the direction of Malevich, Ilia Tsyasnik and Nikolai Suetin produced a work in which painted rectangular elements were situated at various heights in front of a background with depth. They created the impression of planes floating in space. This production again demonstrated that tabular images of two-dimensional Suprematism displayed planes and not solids projected orthogonelly onto a flat surface. The spatial-flat works of the pupils of Malevich thus represented "layerings", that is, they belonged to two-dimensional and not three-dimensional Suprematism.

This gap between the final developmental stages of flat Suprematism and the spatial works of the group around Malevich in Leningrad (beginning 1923) was filled by Lissitzky's *Prounen*, produced between 1919 and 1921, as well as by the student productions prepared at the Vitebsk school under his guidance. The cross-influences between Malevich and Lissitzky, the one a painter, the other an architect, were without doubt very complex during the formative phase of three-dimensional Suprematism. Lissitzky came to Suprematism at a time when leftist painting had already passed on the leadership in the development of the new style to architecture. At the time, he saw himself practically alone with Malevich in Vitebsk. Together, they devised a system by which Suprematism proceeded along a zigzag course of creative dialogue to reach the materiality of architecture. Being a painter as well as an architect, Lissitzky accelerated the process of developing three-dimensional Suprematism. He didn't undergo an apprenticeship as painter with Malevich. Instead, he learned from him only in his capacity as the creator of Suprematism.

Resolutely and quickly, Lissitzky acquired the wherewithal of Suprematism, to which he subscribed fully as a painter. Others did so, to be sure, but the key element that made Lissitzky different was that, once he arrived in Suprematism, he began functioning as an architect rather than as a painter. That's how he was able to become the catalyst of the rapidly accelerating development of three-dimensional Suprematism.

It's worth reiterating at this point that the talents of Malevich and Lissitzky were quite obviously different. Suprematism as a style-generating concept was clearly the creation of Malevich. Lissitzky did not function as producer of formal ideas in the process of style generation. Instead, he played an important role in the transition to the spatial, to architecture. In 1919-1921, Lissitzky created his *Prounen* (*projekty utverzhdeniya novogo*, or projects for the affirmation of the new). These are axonometric projections of assorted kinds of geometric forms in equilibrium, sometimes resting on a firm base, sometimes floating, as it were, in a cosmic space. Lissitzky's *Prounen* were highly individual models for a new architecture, experiments in architectonic design, a landmark in the search for new geometric-spatial ideas, a kind of compositional preparation for future buildings. Lissitzky deliberately took architecture as his model and regarded the *Prounen* as *the station where you transit from painting to architecture*. It is no accident that several of his *Prounen* have titles like *Town* or *Bridge* etc. [repr. 21, 15]. He later used a number of them while working on actual architectural projects (horizontal skyscrapers, a housing block, a watersport clubhouse, a bridge, interiors of exhibition pavilions, etc.) [repr.125-140]. Without a doubt, the *Prounen* originated in two-dimensional Suprematism with its white background and in the cosmic Supremes of Malevich. In contrast to the planar elements of other suprematist works, the cosmic Supremes are easiest to conceive of as orthogonal projections of solid elements in a setting of infinite space. To Lissitzky the architect, these suprematist designs by Malevich were fully comprehensible in this particular sense.

Lissitzky's role as catalyst in the formative phase of three-dimensional Suprematism proceeded along two paths: in the elicitation of the plastic character of the elements floating about in space in the works of Malevich, who knew no top or bottom, and in teaching draftsmanship to students at the Vitebsk school. Initially, the *Prounen* enabled him to pursue the theme of elements floating in space. But, by seeing the elements of two-dimensional Suprematism in a spatial setting, he engineered a transformation. Being an architect, he drew objects with a top and a bottom, thereby giving them association to the ground, even when they floated on a white background. They became architectonic figures, even when Lissitzky had them circling about in various ways (that is how round *Prounen* arose) disconnected from the ground. It was no different when Lissitzky directed students of the Vitebsk school to prepare sketches and architectonic drafts. These were strictly architectonic compositions. The subsequent work at the *Ginchuk* proceeded in the same direction.

Already during its early phase, Suprematism as an overall style-generating concept of creativity was endowed with an inclination to move from the canvas to the real world. Malevich was clearly aware of the universal validity of the *style formula* he had developed. This formula, however, had needed the protective shielding of the two-dimensional up to a certain stage of its development. It sort of underwent a certain embryonal phase of development, a time of clarification and maturation. In the Vitebsk phase, Suprematism appears to have already exhausted the possibilities of the two-dimensional image and was ripe for the transition to the object-spatial world. As already mentioned, Suprematism did not at first proceed / move directly from the image to the three-dimensional object. Rather, it moved to the two-dimensional ornament. It dealt solely with surfaces and not with the volume characteristics of bodies and objects. Earlier developmental stages had paved the way for the ornamental transition to the object-spatial environment during the Vitebsk period. The Vitebsk period, though, deserves the credit for ushering in the transition to three-dimensional Suprematism, to object and architecture, a transition in which Lissitzky was actively involved and one which found rapid expression in the architectones, planites, etc. of the period after Vitebsk. Lissitzky's *Prounen*, thus, were one of the media through which the three-dimensional stage of Suprematism crystallized. They are well known and do not require a detailed review here, their emergence is self-explanatory. They are expressions of a form of Suprematism perceived through the eyes of an architect used to thinking in terms of the three-dimensional and the spatial. Lissitzky's interest in Suprematism did not embrace colours. What fascinated him were the spatial possibilities of its *basic formula*. Already in its early developmental stages, artists intuitively saw Suprematism as a distinct outline for the stylistic organization of the object world. This element was visible in the Suprematist pictures of Malevich from the outset, affecting the three-dimensional object world as a whole rather than in terms of individual objects. The spatial depth of the picture backgrounds and the diagonal positioning of rectangles emphasized the extent of these projections. They more or less constitute the core elements of the intended stylistic portrayal of the real world. The transfer, in the form of decoration, of this two-dimensional suprematist stylism onto the surfaces of objects (houses, purses, ceramics, tribunals, streetcars, etc.) diminished the sweep of the suprematist projective claim. The idea lost in size, and there arose the impression of "confetti", to cite Sergei Eisenstein, who had seen the suprematistically painted Vitebsk firsthand. To some extent, albeit in miniature, the grandeur of the idea again found expression in suprematist adornments of porcelain with a white background. Here, the legitimacy of the design found qualified application.

The attempt on the part of suprematist artists to transfer Suprematism into the real world by and large led to a diminution of the style-generating idea (see, for instance, the purses and garments of Olga Rosanova and Nadyeshda Udalzova). Lissitzky proved to be the first adherent of Malevich capable of doing justice to the requirements of suprematist stylistics. He found a way to transfer Suprematism from the two-dimensional into the object-spatial world without suffering lossage in the process. The *Prounen* became the links between the tabular forms and the scale requirements of architecture and city.

Let us look briefly at the influence of Lissitzky's instruction-methods in Vitebsk on Suprematism's transition to the three-dimensional. Lissitzky taught technical draftsmanship to the students of Malevich. It was something of a novelty bordering on the sensational for the instruments of draftsmanship to crop up at a school of art. Students were eager to engage in this activity, which was new to them. To be sure, even before Lissitzky's time, there had been spatial figures in Malevich's own work. In his system of instruction, though, he had proceeded with his students only to the final stage of two-dimensional Suprematism. Lissitzky, by contrast, taught his students of technical draftmanship to perceive two-dimensional suprematist compositions merely as projections of spatial constructions. This was unexpected and fascinated the students of Malevich. Under the influence and direction of Lissitzky, they began to transform their suprematist exercises spatially. In conversations with me, F. Belostozkaya, M. Lerman and L. Chidekel unanimously declared that they associated the rapid shift to three-dimensional Suprematism primarily with Lissitzky. Under his auspices,

43

Malevich's students began to create three-dimensional models in the basis of suprematist compositions. This occurred as follows: at first, conventional two-dimensional suprematist compositions were prepared: then, under the guidance of Lissitzky, axonometric drafts were prepared; these, in turn, served as the basis for the three-dimensional models. The archive of L. Belostozkaya contains two such drafts for axonometric designs from the year 1920 which could serve as the basis for three-dimensional models. She herself prepared no such models, but she recalls such work being done by other students working under Lissitzky. M. Lerman also confirmed this.

The axonometric creations derived from planar suprematist compositions were called *Architectonic Investigations* in Vitebsk. F. Belostozkaya recalls first having heard the word *architectonics* at the Vitebsk school. Source of all this was Lissitzky. The focus on architectonic investigations, F. Belostozkaya felt, was informed by the conviction that architecture very much deserved treatment. Belostozkaya left Vitebsk for Moscow in 1922, and had no more contact with Malevich after that. Her statements thus definitely refer to the Vitebsk phase of Suprematism, from which the axonometric sketches must stem. The dates of Chidekel's student productions and experimental drafts present more problems. Chidekel completed his Vitebsk studies as painter in 1922 and stayed in touch with Malevich in Leningrad. He, too, believes that the influence of Lissitzky very much helped Malevich recognize the significance of his abstract compositions for architecture. Although their chronology isn't always precise and clear, the Vitebsk works of Chidekel help to provide an idea of how two-dimensional Suprematism proceeded first to the spatial-planar phase and then to the graphic-objective and from there to spatial-objective Suprematism. Already the two-dimensional suprematist compositions by Chikedel give the impression of being outlines of architectonic facilities. According to him, he had had the intention of producing some of them as spatial-planar models, that is, to layer the rectangular planes that at present intersected each other. One can detect in the designs a kind of layering of the plane elements involved in an imaginary space. What's more, the ground has replaced a sense of infinite space as the background of these compositions. These works already point to a fundamentally different approach to the compositional projective possibilities inherent in Suprematism. One can clearly see in these compositions by Chidekel how, out of the layered planes, a massive and complex body resting on the ground emerges in an axonometric

fashion, presumably created as an exercise in technical draftsmanship.

The axonometric drafts of the students of the Vitebsk school combined numerous graphic and theoretical concepts of Malevich with the architectural experience of Lissitzky.

Also worth noting is that Lissitzky spent much attention to teaching axonometrics at a time when architecture (even at the universities) focussed far more on drawing facades and perspectives. Axonometrics figures prominently where a basic outline already exists which then needs spatial elaboration. As a result, the student practicing this develops a special kind of corporeal-spatial way of thinking.

Lissitzky taught axonometrics to retain the basic contours of two-dimensional suprematist creations in the spatial-objective domain. His *Prounen* gave body to the Supremes floating in space.

Many leftist painters rapidly moved on to architecture during the years from 1919 to 1922, including Tatlin, Rodchenko, Gabo, Koroliov, Shevchenko, Lavinski, Klucis, and others. Malevich took this step much later, in 1923-1924. Thus, in Vitebsk, in the time from 1919 to 1922, a time when other painters were working on architectural experiments, Malevich did not occupy himself with architecture. Lissitzky, too, (if we assign him to the leftist painters), shifted to architecture in the years from 1919 to 1921 with his *Prounen* and the sketches of his students at the Vitebsk school. This means that the contact between the painter Malevich and the architect Lissitzky during the Vitebsk phase of Suprematism did not take place in the manner that Malevich first moved on to architecture, with Lissitzky then beginning to experiment in the domain of the new architecture (the way it generally went during the founding period of the new architecture). Instead, Lissitzky rapidly acquired the basics of Suprematism and then moved on, almost without stopping in the two-dimensional stage, to space and architecture. Suprematism's base of spatial painting was, thus, not so much a stage in the painting and drawing of Malevich than the route over which Lissitzky found his way to Suprematism. Other painters coming to Suprematism proceeded by the conventional way of planar Suprematism and worked accordingly. Lissitzky, by contrast, moved immediately to the spatial stage of Suprematism after acquiting all the stages of two-dimensional Suprematism and attempted to apply Suprematism to architecture. At the same time, he also devoted himself to the practical applications of Suprematism, as in the design of posters and book graphics.

In the ensuing period, Lissitzky applied three-dimensional Suprematism to architectonic design such as the horizontal skyscraper (*Wolkenbügel*) [repr.125]. Within the style-generating processes of architecture in the twentieth century, Lissitzky plays an important role as catalyzer in Suprematism's transition to space and architecture, a role that has been insufficiently appreciated to date.

Pan-Europe and German art

El Lissitzky at the 1926 Internationale Kunstausstellung in Dresden

Kai-Uwe Hemken

"The art of the twentieth century is the only provisional proof of the real existence of a Pan-Europe and its supremacy in the world. Whilst an apparent shift of emphasis to new centres of the earth has taken place in all fields of spiritual and material life, the old continent holds its own in the fulfilment of an artistic mission and for the moment this is the only way in which Europe has moved from the stage of ideas into the reality of an international community of equal partners, or rather: the solidarity and leadership of Europe have been maintained."[1]

This was the evaluation made by the renowned art historian Will Grohmann with regard to the work which was presented at the *Internationale Kunstausstellung* (International Art Exhibition) in Dresden. In a special issue of the periodical *Cicerone* he gave a detailed report of the internationally recognized exhibition project, which was opened in 1926 as part of the *Jubiläums-Gartenbau-Ausstellung* (Jubilee Horticultural Exhibition). Grohmann's review was written by arrangement with the organizing committee of the exhibition, whose chairman was Hans Posse as director of the *Gemäldegalerie* in Dresden (Dresden

Picture Gallery). Thus it reflects not least the intentions of the organisers. In Dresden efforts were obviously being made to supply proof of the existence of a Pan-Europe through the modern painting and plastic art at the close of the 19th and beginning of the 20th century. Yet there can be no question of "equal partners" in a European community, about which Grohmann had spoken. Nor did he fail to mention the different cultural achievements of the individual nations: "It is not as though every country has made an equally valuable contribution to Western art – the degree and the quality of participation vary enormously and are by no means constant in the different epochs (...)"[2] Thus the 1926 *Internationale Kunstausstellung* in Dresden saw itself as a balance of the cultural level of the individual European nations and was ultimately a contest between the countries involved.

In the midst of this extensive exhibition El Lissitzky designed and arranged his *Raum für konstruktive Kunst* (Room for constructivist art) [repr.120-121]. It is known from letters that the commissioning of Lissitzky by Posse and the architect of the exhibition, Heinrich Tessenow, caused a certain amount of friction. It was only through the initiative of Sophie Küppers and the well-known Dresden collector Ida Bienert that Tessenow and more particularly the sceptical Posse could be persuaded to allow the Russian artist to design a room for constructivist art.
The constructivist art assembled in this room was of Pan-European origin, i.e. in contrast to the other exhibition rooms it did not represent a nation. Thus alongside work by Lissitzky, Piet Mondrian there were also exhibits by Laszlo Moholy-Nagy, Francis Picabia, Willy Baumeister and Oskar Schlemmer. So from the very start Lissitzky's room managed to elude the exhibition concept of organizing a contest of nations.

According to remarks made by Sophie Lissitzky-Küppers the idea of "designing a special space in the exhibition for non-representational pictures (...)"[3] originated from Lissitzky. Through the intermediary of Ida Bienert Sophie Küppers was able to put this idea to Posse and Tessenow and in the following months she carried out the business side of the assignment.[4] Lissitzky, who moved to Moscow in the spring of 1925, left the negotiations on the spot to Sophie Küppers. Not until the end of May 1926 did he arrive in Hanover, and subsequently got to work on setting up the exhibition space in Dresden.[5] In January 1926 it was still not clear, whether Lissitzky would be given the

1. Will Grohmann, 'Die Kunst der Gegenwart auf der Internationalen Kunstausstellung Dresden 1926'. In: Will Grohmann, Gustav Allinger and Georg Biermann, *Internationale Kunstausstellung, Jubiläums-Gartenbau-Ausstellung*. In: *Cicerone* (special issue) 18 (1926), p.377. The *Internationale Kunstausstellung* lasted from June to September 1926 and was held in the Dresdener Ausstellungshallen.

2. Idem.
3. Sophie Lissitzky-Küppers, *El Lissitzky, Maler, Architekt, Typograf, Fotograf. Erinnerungen, Briefe, Schriften, übergeben von Sophie Lissitzky-Küppers*, Dresden 1967, p.60.
4. Up to his arrival in Dresden Lissitzky had no direct contact with Ida Bienert, as appears from a letter of Lissitzky's to Posse of 29.4.1926. Archives of the Staatliche Kunstsammlungen Dresden, Kupferstichkabinett, No.16, vol.16, *Internationale Kunstausstellung Dresden 1926*, fol.343. During their stay in Dresden (to set up the exhibition room) Lissitzky and Sophie Küppers lived with Gret Palucca.

5. Lissitzky wrote in a letter to Posse of 25.5.1926: "[...] At last I've happily landed in Germany and hear from Dr. Sophie Küppers that the exhibition is supposed to open on 15 June. If that is indeed so, may I perhaps stay on here this week to have a good rest and then next month I'll get to work in Dresden? I'll bring my two works for the exhibition with me [...]". Ibidem, fol. 344.

space assignment for the Dresden exhibition.[6] In a letter to Sophie Küppers of 8 February Lissitzky was nevertheless already asking for technical and organizational details about the intended space and indicated his basic concept: "The space must be a kind of showcase, a stage, on which the pictures make their appearance as actors in a drama (or comedy). It should not imitate a living space."[7]

Lissitzky compared his exhibition space with a stage, whose form would provide the "best visual effect."[8] It is therefore not surprising that for his design Lissitzky obviously oriented himself to stage projects. In 1923 in his lecture Neue Russische Kunst (New Russian Art) he had already described a stage curtain which closely resembled the determining wall form in Lissitzky's room: "The latest work of the Constructivists, the Sterenberg brothers and Medunezki, is very interesting – it is something new in stage design. They constructed a curtain of vertical wooden strips (venetian blind type), which divided as it opened, folded itself back in a semi-circle and formed the backdrop. The surfaces were not painted, but illuminated by coloured light sources as needed."[9] This description could also apply to Lissitzky's spatial and wall form. In front of a generally grey wall surface and perpendicular to the wall Lissitzky mounted narrow wooden slats, whose sides were painted either black or white.[10] Wall by wall he changed the black-white painting, so that "optical dynamics were created by the changing human standpoint".[11] The works of art hung in front of the slats thus acquired a threefold background. The space was illuminated by a top source of light, which occupied the entire ceiling. Lissitzky used this great expanse of even light covering the whole surface as an additional means of creating form by fitting muslin, through which the light now fell indirectly into the room, and 'overlaying' it along one end wall with blue and along the other with yellow. This resulted in one half being "coldly lit, the other warmly".[12] For this effect the hangings at the entrance and exit were certainly necessary to keep out the bright light from the neighbouring rooms.

Lissitzky further installed five wall display cases, in which paintings were to be placed.[13] By means of sliding metal panels the pictures, which were hung on top of each other, could be concealed or exposed to view. Through this system the impression of overcrowded display cases was avoided. The restrained presentation of works of art was a distinctive characteristic of Lissitzky's concept of space: "The great international picture

parades are like a zoo, where the visitors are roared at by a thousand different animals at the same time. In my exhibition space the objects will not all pounce upon the viewer at the same time. If he was usually lulled into a certain passivity as he filed past the picture-filled walls, in our arrangement he will be activated. This is to be the objective of the room."[14] [ill.8].

An eyewitness observed precisely this dynamic effect, which emanated from this special form: "The constructivist Lissitzky has been given his own room; they are not pictures which are hanging there, but geometrical compositions alternating with slats and wooden panels, which can be turned, so that the red power centre, which was originally on the left, now shifts to the upper right, whereby the source of energy, expressed in shafts of light, gushes forth in another direction."[15]

In fact the room for constructivist art differed fundamentally with regard to the hanging method from those arranged by Posse and Tessenow. Inspite of occasional solemn, almost sacral rooms, the arrangement of the Internationale Kunstausstellung was characterized by the closely packed hanging of the exhibits. From the point of view alone of the abundance of the works exhibited the fundamental differences between Posse and Lissitzky are perfectly clear. Whilst Posse wanted to stage manage the Dresden exhibition into a comprehensive synopsis of international art, Lissitzky's intention was carefully to introduce the viewer to the not immediately comprehensible quality of constructivist art. The possibility of a step-by-step and partly independent selection of the works to be viewed was a means of interesting the observer in abstract art. To a certain extent the visitor embarked on a voyage of discovery, but one which did not by any means take place unguided. Through the different widths of the wall display cases, which were to evoke a certain spatial asymetry, and through the change of 'colours', Lissitzky stimulated the viewer to make a tour, whose course was directed in rhythm and speed by the different methods of presentation (slatted wall or display case).[16]

Nevertheless the reactions to Lissitzky's spatial form were in general extremely sceptical. Thus, for instance, Conrad Buchwald described the Constructivist Cabinet as "half operating theatre, half padded cell, the whole an object of dalliance."[17] J. Becirka even spoke of a 'curiousity': "A sort of strong room, but laminated from wooden strips and metal surfaces riddled with holes."[18] Walter Schmits 'acknowledged' for his part the systematic ele-

6. Lissitzky in a letter to Sophie Küppers of 30.1.1926. Sophie Lissitzky-Küppers, op. cit. (note 3), p.70. Moreover up to the end of March 1926 it was not settled whether the space Lissitzky was designing was to include abstract art exhibits. Lissitzky in a letter to Posse of 30.3.1926. Ibidem, fol.342.
7. Lissitzky in a letter to Sophie Küppers of 8.2.1926. Sophie Lissitzky-Küppers, op. cit. (note 3), p.60. The Raum für konstruktive Kunst is entered in the catalogue under number 31, had an area of 6x6 sq.metres and two means of access.
8. El Lissitzky, Demonstrationsräume. Typed manuscript. Archives of the Sprengel Museum Hanover. Ibidem, p.362.

9. El Lissitzky, Neue Russische Kunst. Lecture. Typed manuscript. Central State Archives for Literature and Art, Moscow. Sophie Lissitzky-Küppers, op. cit. (note 3), p.339. He means the Stenberg brothers.
10. The grey tone presumably originated from Tessenow, who as the exhibition architect had all the exhibition rooms painted in this sort of tint. The slats were placed at intervals of 7 cm. and were also 7 cm. in depth.
11. El Lissitzky, op. cit. (note 8), p.362.
12. Idem. Lissitzky presumably bases himself again on the stage curtain of the Stenberg brothers, who also provided for different coloured lighting.
13. Idem. The display cases were of different widths, from 1.10 m. to 1.80 m.

14. El Lissitzky, op. cit. (note 8), p.362. Cf. also Wulf Herzogenrath: 'Bewegung, Zeitablauf, Realitätsbilder, Ausstellung und Medienkunst'. In: Stationen der Moderne. Die bedeutenden Kunstausstellungen des 20. Jahrhunderts in Deutschland. Exhibition catalogue Berlinische Galerie, Berlin 1989, p.53-57.
15. Emil Waldmann, 'Ein Gesamtbild europäischer Kunst auf der Internationale Kunstausstellung in Dresden'. In: Bremer Nachrichten of 27.6.1926.
16. Cf. also Beatrix Nobis: 'Das Abstrakte Kabinett in Hannover und andere Demonstrationsräume El Lissitzkys'. In: El Lissitzky 1890-1941. Retrospective. Exhibition catalogue Sprengel Museum, Hanover 1988. Frankfurt, Berlin 1988, p. 220-223 and Jean Leering, 'Lissitzkys aktuelle Bedeutung'. In: El Lissitzky. Exhi-

bition catalogue Galerie Gmurzynska, Cologne 1976, p.34-46. According to Lissitzky's own statements the two access points to the room had been distinguished as an entry and an exit. The form of the sculpture stand indicated this distinction. There was thus a fixed direction for the tour of the room, as there had also been in Lissitzky's Prounenraum at the Grosse Berliner Kunstausstellung of 1923.
17. Conrad Buchwald, 'Die Internationale Kunstausstellung in Dresden'. In: Schlesische Zeitung of 19.6.1926.
18. J. Becirka, 'Die internationale Kunstausstellung in Dresden'. In: Prager Presse of 7.8.1926.

ment in Lissitzky's spatial form: "The Russian Lissitzky has designed a Room for constructivist Art: there may be madness, but there is certainly method."[19]

Through the didactic structure of his space Lissitzky planned step by step not only to introduce the viewer to the unaccustomed metaphor of Constructivism, but at the same time also to convey to him the notion of modern abstract art. The changing play of black, white and grey gave rise to the impression that the materiality of the walls ceased to exist.[20] "In the space allotted to me I have not conceived the four walls as retaining or protective walls, but as optic backcloths for the works of art. That is why I decided to dissolve the wall surfaces as such."[21] With the 'dematerialization' of the walls Lissitzky reflected the constructivists' comprehension of space, which the viewer could find in the works of Moholy-Nagy, Naum Gabo or Lissitzky exhibited there. In the form of the walls he oriented himself to the use of form by the constructivists. He indicated this step with the *sculpture stand* [repr.120-121], which as a pedestal for small sculptures makes in the first instance an unpretentious impression.[22]

The form of the sculpture stand was an unambiguous adoption of the constructivist sculptures of the Stenberg brothers, which were on show at the 3. *Obmokhu Exhibition* in Moscow in 1921 [ill.7]. At this already legendary exhibition the constructivists manifested themselves for the first time as a group. The sculptures of the Stenbergs were dominantly to the fore there.[23] For Lissitzky they represented the embodiment of constructivist sculpture. In 1925 in his historical survey *Die Kunstismen. Les Ismes de l'Art. The Isms of Art. 1924-1914*, which he had edited jointly with Hans Arp in Zürich, he had published a photo of the 3. *Obmokhu Exhibition* under the keyword *Constructivism*. The obvious adoption of this form in the Dresden sculpture stand must be judged as a demonstration by Lissitzky with regard to West European Constructivism, which was represented in the Dresden exhibition room by works of Moholy-Nagy, Schlemmer or Baumeister. In this way Lissitzky referred to the history of Constructivism, which as far as he was concerned was clearly indigenous to Russia. He claimed to represent the original Constructivism. The position of the sculpture stand in the middle of the room is thus to be interpreted as a clear gesture vis-à-vis the constructivists assembled there, to whom in 1926 Lissitzky was not always kindly disposed. In his opinion they laid claim to a monopoly on Constructivism, whose real aim was internationality.[24] Thus he complained in a letter to Sophie Küppers in 1925:

"I hope I'm proved wrong, but we shall live to see how Burchartz, Schlemmer, Röhl will appear as national Constructivism and national Bauhaus."[25]

With his spatial form Lissitzky went beyond a mere introduction to Constructivism. The spatial assignment forced him not only to bring the different trends in Constructivism under one denominator, but at the same time to declare his position with regard to his fellow artists. Lissitzky was already faced with this problem in 1924, when he and Kurt Schwitters jointly edited the special issue *Nasci* of the periodical Merz, and even more so in 1925, when he published *Die Kunstismen* with Hans Arp.[26] In both publications Lissitzky had concerned himself intensively with the development of modern art and had determined his own status within this development. Only a year after these reflections around 1924/25 Lissitzky took on the task of designing an exhibition space, which was to combine all the constructivist trends. Whereas *Nasci* and *Die Kunstismen* were more in the nature of private publications, the *Raum für konstruktive Kunst* possessed infinitely more publicity value in the framework of the exhibition. Nevertheless, the idea of presenting modern abstract art as an entity came from him. In this context the sculpture stand makes it clear that, just as in *Nasci* and *Die Kunstismen*, Lissitzky had an art-historical demonstration in mind, which would stress the status of Russian Constructivism.

Whilst in the room for constructivist art in Dresden Lissitzky still emphasized the Constructivism of the brothers Stenberg, in the following, almost identical project, the *Abstraktes Kabinett* (The abstract cabinet) in Hanover, he put his own share in the spatial design to the fore. In the Hanover cabinet, which was designed and arranged – with changes – in 1927/28 on the initiative and under the direction of the chief curator of the Provinzialmuseum, Alexander Dorner,[27] Lissitzky included a sculpture stand [ill.11], which just as in Dresden had a sort of programmatic function. He painted the two visible and square sides of the corner platform with black and red. From the red plane a red line led through the whole room and finally returned to the platform. The red and black sides of the platform represented the red and black squares, which are regarded as symbols of Lissitzky's *Proun* art as well as of Suprematism. He thus laid claim to a superordinate position for his art with regard to the kindred abstract geometrical Isms, which were to be seen in the Hanover exhibition room. Through the red line and the square he proclaimed that with this spatial form his art was capable of embracing all constructivist Isms.

19. Walter Schmits, 'Internationale Kunstausstellungen II'. In: *Kölnische Zeitung* of 18.7.1926.
20. Lissitzky's theories on colour, which he formulated in Moscow in 1921 in his *Proun* lecture, confirm this assumption. In this context black, white and grey are colours, which according to Lissitzky are to be designated as pure energy. The way in which the Dresden exhibition space was painted should therefore be in keeping with the "representation of energy" and the "dematerialization" of the wall surfaces. See El Lissitzky, *Proun*. Lecture. In: Sophie Lissitzky-Küppers and Yen Lissitzky, *Proun und Wolkenbügel. Briefe und Schriften*, Dresden 1977, p.21-34. Cf. also Kai-Uwe Hemken, 'Proun, Proun und nochmals Proun. El Lissitzky - die Technik und die Mittel der Kommunikation'. In: *El*

Lissitzky 1890 - 1941, op. cit. (note 16), p. 44-53.
21. El Lissitzky, op. cit. (note 8), p. 362.
22. On the stand was a sculpture by Naum Gabo: *Modell für 'Rotierender Brunnen'*, 1925, metal, celluloid and other materials, c. 54 x 35 cm. Family collection. My thanks to Mrs. Andrea El Danasouri for this information.
23. In the periodical *Veshch-Gegenstand-Objet*, published in 1922 in Berlin, which Lissitzky edited jointly with Ilia Erenburg, he included a photo of this exhibition, so that it is quite certain that he was acquainted with the exhibition.
24. In this context it is not without significance that Lissitzky was represented by two works in the *Raum für konstruktive Kunst*, including a preliminary study for a self-portrait *The Constructor* of 1924. For

Lissitzky this self-portrait was an expression of how he saw himself, with his architectural project *Wolkenbügel* and the *Lenin Tribune*, which he designed in 1924, as counting as a constructivist.
25. Lissitzky in a letter to Sophie Küppers of 12.12.1924. In: Sophie Lissitzky-Küppers, op. cit. (note 3), p. 53.
26. Cf. Kai-Uwe Hemken, 'Zwischen Solidarität und Konkurrenz: El Lissitzky und Kurt Schwitters'. In: *El Lissitzky 1810-1941*, op. cit. (note 16), p. 202-204 and Kai-Uwe Hemken, *El Lissitzky. Revolution und Avantgarde*, Cologne 1990.
27. For Dorner's museum activities see also Monika Flacke-Knoch, *Museumskonzeptionen in der Weimarer Republik. Die Tätigkeit Alexander Dorners im Provinzialmuseum Hannover*, Marburg 1985.

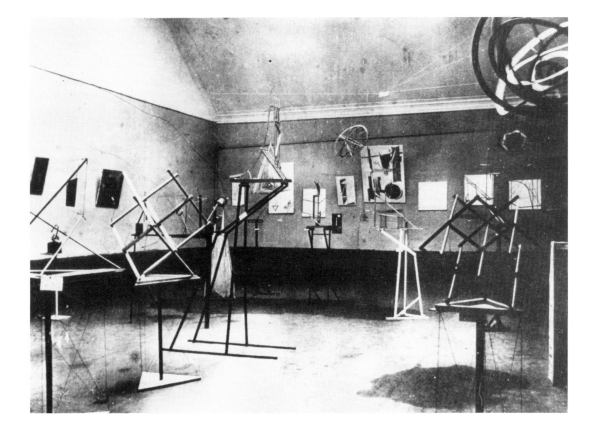

ill. 7
Obmochu exhibition, Moscow
1921
In front: constructivist objects by the
Stenberg brothers.
Photo: Kai-Uwe Hemken, Marburg

ill. 8
Internationale Kunstausstellung,
Dresden 1926
In the back, the curtains mark the
entrance of the *Raum für
Konstruktive Kunst* by Lissitzky.
Photo: Kai-Uwe Hemken, Marburg

ill. 9
Piet Mondrian, **Design of a salon for Ida Bienert,** 1925/26
Photo: De Stijl: 1917-1931, New-York 1988

DIE ABSTRAKTEN

ill. 10
Grosse Berliner Ausstellung (Great Exhibition of Berlin), 1926
Members of Die Abstrakten are photographed in front of their section.
Photo: Hüdrun Schröder-Kehler, Frankfurt

ill. 11
Abstraktes Kabinett (The abstract
cabinet), Hanover 1930
Sculpture stand.
Photo: Sprengel Museum Hanover

ill. 12
Kasimir Malevich, **At the harvest
(Marfa en Vanka),** 1928/32
Photo: Malevich catalogue,
Amsterdam 1989

ill. 13
Franz Wurbel, **Olympische Spiele**
(Olympic games),poster, Berlin 1936
El Lissitzky, **USSR Russische
Ausstellung** (USSR. Russian
exhibition), poster, Zürich 1929
Photo: Catalogue Die Axt hat
geblüht, Düsseldorf 1987

With his spatial form in Dresden Lissitzky entered into competition with spatial projects, which were designed at the same time and had partly been executed. He urged Sophie Küppers to push the negotiations with Posse and Tessenow to get him the commission for the design and lay-out of a room at the Dresden exhibition. He was particularly afraid of the competition from Piet Mondrian and from the Dessau Bauhaus: "Or do they think (=Posse and Tessenow, K.H.), that I am doing it (=the design and arrangement of the room, K.H.) out of my own pocket? Then we shall be bankrupt. Especially with the competition of 2 other champions – Mondrian and the Bauhaus [...]"[28]
In 1925 Mondrian had already designed the form of a private salon for Ida Bienert [ill.9]. The Dutchman treated the six surfaces of the room as projection planes which were to be painted in the neoplastic style. This form linked up with the wall painting of the *De Stijl* group, which had already been developed further in the architectural projects conceived in 1922 by Theo van Doesburg and Cornelis van Eesteren and in particular in the spatial design of Vilmos Huszar and Gerrit Rietveld for the 1923 *Juryfreie Kunstausstellung* (Open Art Exhibition) in Berlin. Lissitzky did not find Mondrian's designs for Bienert very convincing: "Thanks for the Mondrian photos. I had expected something more distinctive. It's more reminiscent of the earlier than of the later work. It's another spatial still life to be viewed through the keyhole."[29] However, it was just at the time of the preparations for the Dresden exhibition that Lissitzky had heard of, or seen these Mondrian designs for the first time, so that Mondrian's concept was undoubtedly of importance in clarifying his ideas for the Dresden exhibition space.
Whilst Mondrian conceived space through the eyes of a painter, Lissitzky planned his Dresden room from the perspective of the architect: "The creative material of the new painting is colour. The colour is an epidermis over a skeleton. According to the construction of the skeleton the epidermis is pure colour or tone."[30] And further: "One can try to find the best background for the pictures using painting itself as a means. One paints a rectangle on the wall in a corresponding colour – and there you are. There I have the wall itself facing me as a picture, and it really is absolute nonsense to nail a Leonardo onto a fresco by Giotto."[31]
Lissitzky's criticism was probably directed not only at Mondrian's use of wall painting, but also at the painting of the rooms of the artists' group *Die Abstrakten* at the *Grosse Berliner Ausstellung* (Great Berlin Exhibition) of 1926. This work was carried out by

the Dessau Bauhaus under the direction of Hinnerk Scheper. Scheper painted the walls to correspond with the exhibited works of Wassily Kandinsky, Paul Klee, Laszlo Moholy-Nagy, Oskar Nerlinger and Kurt Schwitters amongst others.

Competition between Lissitzky and the Bauhaus had indeed existed. The Bauhaus professor Kandinsky had approached Posse, about the possibility of an extensive presentation by the Dessau art school, which would be on an equal footing with Lissitzky's, presumably even with a separate spatial form. Posse wrote to Kandinsky in answer to his letter: "I hope that the design and arrangement of a small room by Mr. Lissitzky will materialize. As this time we have in principle only asked individuals and not groups etc. and have even excluded all groups in Dresden, we cannot in this case invite the Bauhaus as such to a closed exhibition."[32]
Thus Lissitzky's fears that the Bauhaus would compete with him in Dresden were well-founded. His criticism of the use of pure wall painting was therefore certainly also directed at the spatial project executed by the Bauhaus in Berlin. However, Lissitzky's criticism was presumably not just limited to the purely aesthetic dimension, but also concerned the policy aspect of the exhibition. At the time of the Berlin exhibition of 1926 *Die Abstrakten* group had just taken shape as an organization.[33] Their presentation in Berlin therefore had an explicit programmatic character. The section of *Die Abstrakten*, which altogether comprised four exhibition rooms, had as its motto 'knowing about Expressionism' [ill.10] and represented an attempt not to classify Expressionism as an art trend limited to a certain metaphor, but to characterize it as a general phenomenon in modern art. In this context the expressive-emotional factor was defined as the foundation of the 'creative act', which was even supposed to underly the constructivist works. *Die Abstrakten* thus devised another 'version' of Constructivism, which was not developed on a scientific and rational basis, as represented by Tatlin, Rodtschenko and Lissitzky. The expressionist Constructivism must be judged as a German variant of this trend, since it was based on the Expressionism indigenous to and fostered in Germany. Thus the whole programmatic aspect of the Berlin exhibition of *Die Abstrakten* was a counter-manifestation to Lissitzky's room for constructivist art, which at the *Internationale Kunstausstellung* in Dresden demonstratively displayed scientific-rational Constructivism of Russian origin.

28. Lissitzky in a letter to Sophie Küppers of 23.3.1926. Sophie Lissitzky-Küppers, op. cit. (note 3), p.72.
29. Lissitzky in a letter to Sophie Küppers of 2.3.1926. Ibidem, p.71.
30. Lissitzky, op. cit. (note 8), p. 362.
31. Idem.

32. Posse in a letter to Kandinsky of 5.5.1926. Archives of the Staatliche Kunstsammlungen Dresden, Kupferstichkabinett, no.16, vol.14, *Internationale Kunstausstellung Dresden 1926*, fol.32.
33. For the history of *Die Abstrakten* see Heidrun Schröder-Kehler, *Vom abstrakten zum politischen Konstruktivismus: Oskar Nerlinger und die Berliner Gruppe Die Abstrakten (1919 bis 1933)*. Thesis. Heidelberg 1984.
I want to thank Dr. Heidrun Schröder-Kehler for the sending of a photograph of this exhibition.

With his *Raum für konstruktive Kunst* Lissitzky clearly offered opposition not only to the Berlin exhibition of *Die Abstrakten*, but also to the policy of the *Internationale Kunstausstellung* in Dresden. It is conspicuous that 24 of the in total 56 rooms were reserved for art from Germany and Dresden, whilst foreign countries, such as Russia, America, Switzerland, Scandinavia etc. had to be packed into 32 rooms. Moreover, the German and in particular the Dresden art at the *Internationale Kunstausstellung* was stage managed to represent the end and climax of the exhibition.[34] Posse thus endeavoured to place German, and especially Dresden art at the centre of attention in his international art parade. This exhibition policy is to be explained by the economic and cultural policy of the former provincial capital of Saxony. As part of the *Jubiläums-Gartenbau-Ausstellung*, the *Internationale Kunstausstellung* was an event in the so-called *Jahresschau deutscher Arbeit* (Annual Show of German Labour), which had been initiated in 1922 by the city of Dresden with the massive support of Saxon industry. Publicity in the form of regular exhibitions and trade fairs was needed to promote the economic regeneration of the region, whose trade and industry had been seriously affected by the war. In the Twenties there were numerous trade fairs throughout Germany, but the city of Dresden with its series of events in the framework of the *Jahresschau deutscher Arbeit* created the impression that it was representing the whole of Germany.[35] Dresden tried hard to maintain its position in the competition between German municipalities and at the same time to bear witness to the fact that 'products of German origin' were of world class.

Thus at the *Jahresschauen* from 1922 onwards only industrial products were exhibited, until in 1924 it was decided to organize a *Gartenbau-Ausstellung*. This exhibition was intended to satisfy idealist rather than commercial interests. Professor Sterl of the Dresden Academy of Arts suggested that the horticultural exhibition should be accompanied by an international art exhibition, which would constitute a representative cross-section of contemporary art. In 1925 Hans Posse, the director of the *Gemäldegalerie*, took on the management and changed the concept.[36] Posse attached less importance to a cross-section of contemporary art and the reciprocal stimulus which it would generate within international art. He was much more interested in using the exhibition to provide evidence of the cultural traditions and the artistic potential of the city of Dresden and also of Germany. Here was a definite need to catch up lost ground. For whilst trade and industry were recuperating, not least on

account of the 'Annual Shows', and were even planning non-commercial exhibitions such as for horticulture and the visual arts, the Dresden artists' community saw its influence waning. This loss of esteem for Dresden art was in stark contrast with the economic strength of Dresden in around 1926, with the result that a cultural vacuum developed. The *Internationale Kunstausstellung* thus provided a welcome opportunity to redress this clearly unbalanced situation. The strong presence of German and Dresden art in the *Internationale Kunstausstellung* cannot therefore be attributed solely to the arrogance and presumption of the exhibition organizers, but is also to be explained by the urgent necessity of looking after Dresden's image as a city with an artistic tradition. Judged from this viewpoint, Posse displayed German and Dresden art to the world public as a high-quality proprietary article. This art was regarded as proof of the quality of German culture and thus formed the equivalent of the German products, which were otherwise on view at the *Jahresschauen deutscher Arbeit*. The exhibition organizers had hereby arranged the cultural contest of the nations in favour of German and Dresden art. Grohmann's reference to the different achievements of the participating nations at the Dresden exhibition had already been decided by the organizers respectively the exhibition policy. It is especially clear here that Grohmann's prophesy, quoted at the beginning, of a Pan-Europe with equal partners was heavily imbued on the part of the exhibition organizers with the idea that Germany had a claim in the heart of Europe to the position of a leading power in the economic, political and cultural field.

The *Internationale Kunstausstellung* had a strongly nationalistic character, which was in glaring contrast to the conception of Lissitzkys exhibition space. For the underlying concept of Constructivism was an Internationalism, which was based amongst other things on the rational-scientific and the functional. Evidence of this programmatic aspect was also to be seen in the efforts of Lissitzky, Hans Richter and Theo van Doesburg in 1922 to set up a 'Constructivist International'. This Internationalism is reflected in Lissitzky's room for constructivist art in his reference to Russian Constructivism. In so doing he rejected not only expressionist Constructivism, but also the ambitions of Posse, who stirred up competition amongst the nations with the *Internationale Kunstausstellung* in Dresden and tried as well to decide it in favour of Dresden and of Germany. In his *Raum für konstruktive Kunst* Lissitzky opposed the policy of cultural Nationalism and demonstrated in favour of cultural Internationalism.

54

34. Cf. *Internationale Kunstausstellung Dresden 1926. Jahresschau deutscher Arbeit*. Official guide and catalogue of the exhibition, Dresden 1926.
35. This is borne out in particular in the members of the committee of honour. As well as the German Minister of Foreign Affairs, Stresemann, the German President, Paul Hindenburg, was also represented.
36. Sterl withdrew from the organization of the exhibition for reasons of health.

Inspite of this Lissitzky could not avoid being considered by the press as representing Russia. Lissitzky had by no means been invited as a representative of Russia, nor had the Russian authorities regarded him as their representative and certainly not in the vanguard,[37] and yet Lissitzky's exhibition space was reviewed as the "only Bolshevik work". The reasons for this lay on the one hand in the unimpressive Russian section and on the other hand in the public's special expectations of Russian art. Speaking for many Walter Preusser summarized his impression of the Russian section at the Dresden exhibition in these words: "For many people the Russians are particularly disappointing. Above all for many of our young artists, who expected so much of the art of Bolshevism. This hope has been shattered. The Russians live and create completely under the influence of the French, though one experiences the intention of reason more strongly with them than with their examples. Even Chagall and Segall are on the decline. The only artist who behaves like a Bolshevik is Lissitzky with his constructivist cabinet."[38]

The special expectations with regard to Russian art were formulated right at the beginning of the plans for the *Internationale Kunstaustellung*. From the outset Professor Sterl, the initiator of the exhibition, was convinced that contemporary Russian art must form a central theme of the exhibition. To achieve this goal he even made use of the diplomatic machinery.[39] At the *Ministry of Education and Culture* his interest was reciprocated, with the result that the authorities lent their support to Russian participation. Posse, Sterl's successor, had less interest in contemporary art from Moscow, but tried to get the museum stocks of Russian and French art of around 1900 from Russia for the Dresden exhibition. Whilst Sterl attached importance to the 'exchange' of contemporary international art, for Posse it was clearly a question of documenting the strong adoption of Western European models in Russian art. Russia therefore gave general consent to participating in the exhibition, but insisted that they only wanted to send contemporary art to Dresden.[40] Eventually a compromise was reached, which was nevertheless certainly detrimental to the contemporary relevance of Russian art. This was not the least of the reasons why the Russian section gave the impression of a parade of old acquaintances.

With his unusual spatial form Lissitzky could attract the attention of the press, since he was able to fulfil the public's expectation of the new Russian art. In a letter to Ilia Erenburg he proudly reported: "This summer at the *Internationale Kunstaustellung* in Dresden I have designed and arranged a small room, which the press has designated as the only Bolshevik work in the exhibition."[41]

In Lissitzky's oeuvre the *Raum für konstruktive Kunst* and the follow-up project in Hanover, *Abstraktes Kabinett*, were the last projects which, inspite of the dissociation from expressionist Constructivism, from Piet Mondrian, from the Bauhaus amongst others, were characterized by Internationalism. This Internationalism was aimed at a cultural exchange, at the conveyance and demonstration of artistic ideas, which was to provoke an examination of the works presented and of their theoretical basis. Together with the *Prounenraum* (Proun Space) [repr.60] designed and arranged in Berlin in 1923, the two spatial projects in Dresden and Hanover represent the last work of Lissitzky, which in this sense can be designated as demonstration rooms. In comparison the subsequent exhibition projects in Cologne, Stuttgart, Dresden and Leipzig, carried out under state direction, prove themselves to be presentations which bore the stamp of national self-manifestation.

37. Lissitzky even had great problems in obtaining a visa from the Russian authorities to travel to Dresden officially to realise his exhibition space. But when he returned to Moscow, the Russian authorities entrusted him with a state exhibition project, presumably the International Press Exhibition *Pressa* 1928 in Cologne. See note 41.
38. Walter Preusser, 'Internationale Kunstausstellung Dresden'. In: *Meissner Tageblatt* of 24.7.1926.
39. Cf. State Archives Dresden, Ministerium für Volksbildung, no. 14923, Internationale Kunstausstellung Dresden 1926, I 1924-1928. Sterl even consulted Wassily Kandinsky, to whom he presumably sent a list with his proposals. Kandinsky corrected Sterl's proposals, when he proposed Kasimir Malevich and Gustav Kijun

under the heading Suprematism and Vladimir Tatlin, Alexander Rodtschenko and the Stenberg brothers under the heading Constructivism. Kandinsky called Lissitzky "amongst others". Kandinsky to Sterl on 1.11.1924. Archives of the Staatliche Kunstsammlungen Dresden, Kupferstichkabinett, no.16, vol.16, *Internationale Kunstausstellung Dresden 1926*, fol.580/581.

40. The compromise provided for fewer of the older works than in Posse's request, which were then exhibited together with contemporary works. In the preparations for the Russian participation there was even a meeting between the German state art counsellor, Erwin Redslob, and the director of the People's Commissariat for Enlightenment, Anatoli Lunatscharski, who was staying in Western Europe in 1926.
41. Sophie Lissitzky-Küppers, op. cit. (note 3), p.119-120.

Lissitzky's dilemma

With reference to his work after 1927

Jean Leering

Last year the large Malevich retrospective came to the Stedelijk Museum in Amsterdam after being seen at museums in Leningrad and Moscow. This was the first opportunity to view Malevich's cubo-futurist and suprematist work, which is so well represented in the Stedelijk Museum's collection, in relation to the work which preceded and followed it. We are now in a similar situation with this Lissitzky exhibition.

What I am particularly curious about is how the post-1927 work will strike me. This is the part of Lissitzky's oeuvre which, as in the case of Malevich, is barely if at all represented in Western museums and other collections.
This in part explains why relatively little of the late work was to be seen at the first retrospective which I organised in 1965 for the Van Abbemuseum in Eindhoven, the Kestner Gesellschaft in Hanover and the Kunsthalle in Basel. The later period was mainly represented by the typographical work done for the magazine *USSR im Bau* (USSR in construction), which the authorities published largely to serve propaganda purposes abroad [repr.106-107]. In all honesty I should add that the choice of what was to be given prominence from this material (specifically, which pages from the various magazines lay open in the show cases, which photographic enlargements were hung on the walls) was guided more by the aesthetic standards of the day than by the desire to deal objectively with the various facets of this work (the different styles and methods, but also the choice of subject and content, etc.). Such a choice, whereby the work of

the artist is presented as forcefully as possible in accordance with the view that the exhibition organiser has formed of the work as a whole, was not unusual, certainly not at the time.
I well remember how Sandberg, the director who obtained the Malevich collection for the Stedelijk Museum in the late fifties, then regarded this artist's later work, i.e. the work which was not to be found in the Stedelijk's collection. He believed it to be far inferior to the cubo-futurist and suprematist paintings, and was not alone in this belief. It was widely assumed that political pressure was to blame for the 'decline' evident in this work. This was the pressure applied by the Soviet leaders from the adoption of the first Five-Year Plan in favour of Socialist Realism and against the avant-garde, particularly the suprematist and constructivist movements and everything in between. An important point in this connection is that people like Sandberg had personally experienced during that war how political pressure could turn into repression to achieve certain aims. So they had little need to ask themselves questions about the reasons behind this 'decline'.

This is something that later exhibition organizers, who can benefit from the material now made available, must do. If only as a courtesy to the lenders, these questions must be dealt with in a different way.
This is indeed what happened in the case of the Malevich exhibition, as is evident from the catalogue, which was prepared jointly. With all the openness made possible by perestroïka, many questions about both the work and the artist as a person were raised, but they were only partly answered. The Russian contributors to the catalogue point in no uncertain terms to the historical events which created the extremely difficult circumstances in which Malevich had to work as an artist and particularly as a teacher at and later director of the *Ginkhuk* (Institute of Artistic Culture). For his part Wim Beeren, the present director of the Stedelijk Museum, championed the cause of the artistic quality of the later work in a lecture given as part of a programme of talks accompanying the exhibition, thus leaving aside the judgement of his predecessor.
During repeated visits to the Malevich retrospective I found my reactions to the later work varied. At first I was very moved by the failure which I read into it. I did not and do not agree with Beeren's positive assessment. But I do regard it – particularly the group of works shown under the heading 1928-1932 in the exhibition – as an heroic attempt to retain all the insight that he

acquired through Suprematism and his architectural studies, while at the same time creating a figural art which would solve the problem of the reception of the painting in a different way to Suprematism. I use the term figural rather than figurative because, both in the making and the reception of such a painting, the emphasis is on a different view than is generally the case with a 'figurative' work. Both in making and looking at this kind of painting, it is its 'made-up' quality – something which is taken for granted with an abstract work – which stands out. In the case of a figurative painting, because of its mimetic or imitative character, this quality tends to retreat behind what is portrayed. The difference manifests itself primarily on the part of the viewer: to perceive the painting requires a greater effort from his consciousness in order to convert what is seen into meaning. This converting of the seen into meaning on the part of the viewer must always take place, but in his reception of the painting the 'figural' can give a helping hand. Indeed, the problem which I have with most of these paintings is not to do with their concessions to the reception, but with how they are made. I believe that Malevich's heroic attempt to add to his development another chapter of equal value to Suprematism – since that is what it is based on – almost always comes to grief in the realisation of his artistic vision. In the main lines of his peasant men and women, etc., usually seen from behind, one is often struck by the strong plasticity, the progress and direction of the contrast between light and dark, the colour, etc., but these large forms must be given hands and feet or similar details for the sake of the figural [ill.12]. This is where, in my view, the conversion of the seen (or the intended) into art fails, and unity of artistic vision is not realised.

Malevich set himself a huge task, and two comparisons may illustrate its severity. The first concerns Cézanne and his problem of 'réalisation'. Should not Malevich follow the same path as he but in the opposite direction, i.e. going back from abstraction – which Cézanne rejected but which was the basis of Malevich's painting – to reality?

The second, more contemporary, comparison relates to Duchamp's ready-mades. The task Malevich set himself after 1927 was comparable in difficulty with the problem Duchamp would have faced had he attempted to take one of his ready-mades (e.g. the coat stand), which had acquired the aura of art in the eyes of the viewer by being transferred from everyday reality to the museum, and restore it to that everyday reality. The new task Malevich faced had everything to do with the

changes in meaning involved in the comparisons I have drawn, from the point of view of both the maker and the reception.

However, respecting the courage required to take on such a task is one thing, and assessing whether the results represent success or failure is another.

During my first visit to the retrospective I experienced very emotionally what I saw as a sickening spectacle. You felt how seriously the artist took his intended aim, how bravely he embarked on this seeming reversal of his awe-inspiring adventure with painting (and architecture), the total commitment he gave to it, and at the same time the utter failure of the enterprise.
On later visits this general judgement lost its sharp edges and I discovered paintings which could be regarded as more or less successful. Then various questions arose. What did Malevich himself think? Was it his own, free decision or did he feel compelled by circumstances? How did those close to him react to this change in his work, and did they discuss it with him? To none of these questions does the catalogue provide an answer. This is quite deliberate, because does it not say in several places that the retrospective marks the first step towards further, joint research?

We do at least know of one reaction from a contemporary who is the main subject of interest here.
On 19 July 1930 El Lissitzky wrote from Moscow to his wife (in German): "At *Voks* (the Society for Foreign Contacts, J.L.) I met Malevich. We talked just as though nothing had happened between us, and he has invited me to come and visit him in the country. He's getting old, and a difficult situation, plans to go abroad again in the autumn, and paints, paints representational art and signs 1910 etc. Pathetic affair. Does it very seriously and thinks he can fool people...".[1] The quotation ends abruptly here in the book about her husband which Sophie Lissitzky-Küppers published in 1967 in East Germany. We would like to know more, but this is typical of his style, certainly in German.
Right up to his death Lissitzky told everyone who was ready to listen how much of a debt he owed to meeting Malevich and his friendship with him. People who knew Lissitzky here in the West in the twenties, such as Nelly van Doesburg, have often told me how in the heat of discussion, when he was struggling to find the words in German to win a point, he would exclaim: "But

1. "In *Woks* habe ich Malewitsch getroffen.
Die Unterhaltung war, als ob nichts zwischen uns passiert ist, und er hat mich eingeladen zu ihm aufs Land zu kommen. Alt wird er, und schwere Situation, soll im Herbst wieder ins Ausland, und malt, malt darstellende Kunst und unterzeichnet 1910 etc. Jämmerliche Geschichte. Macht es sehr ernst und denkt Dumme zu fangen …".

Malevich says...". He revered Malevich as if he were a prophet, and I do not believe there was anything dubious behind what he said in the letter quoted above: it was his honest opinion. But times had changed.

In his work Lissitzky had chosen a path different to that of Malevich. It is quite conceivable that when at the end of 1923 he became severely ill with TB and had to go to southern Switzerland for a cure, he was forced by this illness to lay down his brush, which he was hardly ever to take up again.
Apart from typographical work, which paid for his treatment, he did some writing and editing. As soon as the treatment allowed, he also took up photography (e.g. his self-portrait *The Constructor* [repr.117]) and architectural work (his *Wolkenbügel* project for Moscow [repr.129]). When he returned to Moscow, in the middle of 1925, he found that the latter work was a good preparation for the changed situation in the visual arts since he had left the country (in late 1921 or early 1922). This change was, although not directly, in part a result of the New Economic Policy which Lenin had introduced in 1921 in response to the growing unrest throughout Russia caused by the shortages of food and other necessities. Lenin and his advisors wanted to stimulate production, and that meant that less money was available for the arts. The newly established cultural institutions had to be self-supporting as far as possible, and artists were forced to obtain their income through the old market principle. Many, now famous, artists such as Kandinsky and Chagall, who had contacts in the West before the war, now left, and others followed their example. Many of them belonged to the avant-garde and had played a leading role during the Revolution and afterwards in setting up and running the new institutions. This is why it might seem as if the avant-garde was already at this stage suffering the effects of ideological prejudice on the part of those in power. This was not the case: the reason for their departure was that they had a better chance of making a living in the West. However, Lissitzky's reasons for leaving were entirely different: he was despatched as a kind of cultural ambassador and indeed later returned.
It was, however, true that priorities in cultural policy were modified. During and immediately after the Revolution, the various avant-garde movements had been given ample scope – aware as they were – to participate in finding new forms for the new society being constructed. But they now had to share this support with those organizing literacy programmes for the vast backward areas of the country (so that the people there could also contribute to increasing production).
Since the late seventies a great deal of research has been done on the effects of the political and economic conditions on cultural attitudes among both the Russian leaders and artists during those years. A good survey of this research is given in a publication by Jeroen Boomgaard,[2] which also seeks to determine the theoretical position of Lissitzky's later work.

Returning to the path which Lissitzky - unlike Malevich - chose for the development of his work, we see him following his 1922 motto "Not world visions, but world reality"[3] while busily occupying himself with architectural competitions and interior design, and teaching furniture design at *Vkhutemas*. He put into practice what he had written for a questionnaire shortly before leaving Switzerland: "The easel painting has run its course as a work of art, and all the creative energy which was generated here must create a new work of art (not an easel painting). All plastic creativity is realised in and around architecture. This architecture is my goal."[4]
However, his architectural designs (on which he continued to work well into the thirties) were never to be built. But, in addition to his typographical work, from 1926 onwards he began to receive commissions in the new field of exhibition design. No doubt the fact that he received such commissions regularly, partly because of the international success he achieved in this field, goes some way to explain the following remark in his autobiography: "1926 saw the beginning of my most important artistic work, the design of exhibitions."[5] I think that here he also had in mind the content of the different way he had chosen.

To understand this we must consider another factor which was of great importance to Lissitzky as an artist. He was truly inspired by the Revolution and by its promise of building a new society. However utopian and idealistic that may seem to us with hindsight, and I shall return to this point, in my opinion until well into the thirties he cherished the belief that the difficulties of carrying out the Revolution would eventually be overcome and that a truly socialist state would be created. Intelligent and naive at the same time, he viewed the new developments in art in close relation to this social struggle.
In his remark about designing exhibitions I sense the influence of both these elements: his preoccupation with architecture and his deep-seated wish to contribute to building the new society.

58

2. Jeroen Boomgaard, *Theorie en praktijk van de russiese avant-garde*, Den Helder 1981, Talsma & Hekking Uitgeverij.
3. "Nicht Weltvisionen, sondern – Weltrealität"
4. "Das Staffeleibild hat seinen Lebensgang als Kunstwerk abgeschlossen, und alle schöpferischen Energien, die hier ihren Ausgang hatten, müssen ein neues Kunstwerk (nicht ein Staffeleibild) schaffen. Alles plastische Schaffen realisiert sich in und um die Architektur. Diese Architektur ist mein Ziel".
5. "1926 beginnt meine wichtigste künstlerische Arbeit, die Gestaltung von Ausstellungen".

At first this was not immediately apparent because his services were required for an art exhibition. In 1926 the Committee of the *Internationale Kunstausstellung* (International Art exhibition) in Dresden invited him to take charge of the presentation of non-figurative art [repr.119-121]. In the light of his views quoted above on the position of painting in 1925, Lissitzky must have felt this commission was of limited significance. But what he did with it went much further than the original task he was set. Through his design he made a statement not only about the form of the space, not only about the arrangement of the works and thus the relations between them, but also about the role of the viewer in the process we call art. His arrangement of the space and the paintings in it – there was an abstract sculpture in the middle – was such that the viewer was given opportunities to take action: to see all the works he had to move panels which screened one painting in one position and another in the next.[6] The entire design of the space is directed towards activating the viewer in this way. The walls are covered with slats which provided a light or dark background to the paintings depending on the position of the viewer. This device can of course be assessed according to its effect on a painting, but also according to its effect on the consciousness of the viewer – which would probably be more in line with Lissitzky's intentions. It is the viewer, and he alone, who with every step brings about a change in the viewer-painting-background relation. Lissitzky called the Dresden space a *Demonstration Space*, a term he was also to apply two years later to his most celebrated exhibition design: the Soviet pavilion at the *Pressa* in Cologne, where the theme was communication [repr.155-158]. In contrast to abstract art, this was a subject that was comprehensible to a wide audience. For the purpose of communication, special techniques were developed to give the visitor the same opportunities to take action. Because of the originality and effectiveness of these techniques and the way they were applied on a large scale, the design was the subject of admiring articles in the international press. This was the first time that photomontages had been used on such a scale and in such a spatial manner in an exhibition. Moving transmission belts with examples of the Soviet press provided a cinematic image of distribution, which plays such an important role in communication. etc. etc. At the same time, specially made sculptures with inscriptions were used which were figural in a similar way to the paintings Malevich did at this time – the very paintings Lissitzky had condemned in the letter quoted above. So here again questions are raised. To begin with, one can ask

whether there is such a thing as continuity in Lissitzky's work. In other words, can we who admire his *Proun* paintings so much find a link with them in his various exhibition designs? Is there a principle which is common to both? To answer this question we must consider the *Proun* paintings in greater detail.

As examples I will take the paintings *Proun 12E* and *Proun 30T*, both from around 1920. [repr.27 and 29] We see flat, i.e. two-dimensional, forms and three-dimensional bodies with a geometrical look floating in space. We also get the impression that these forms or elements may start moving at any moment and change their position relative to each other: like the pendulum of a clock they hang from the top edge of the painting in the space depicted.

Looking more closely, we see that the elements are spatially related: the planes in which they lie change direction, sometimes parallel to the picture plane and sometimes at an angle to it. Looking even more closely, we discover that flat, two-dimensional elements suddenly become three-dimensional. In other words, one and the same form can be perceived as both two- and three-dimensional. From this we can conclude that the elements painted on the canvas are not only in motion but also in the process of developing. This motion and development is spatial and is concretely depicted – unlike in Futurism: as you follow a particular form or constellation, changes take place within it; its character changes, and hence its meaning.

Putting it yet another way, during the process of looking changes take place in the consciousness of the viewer, which is itself set in motion. The viewer embarks, so to speak, on a journey through the (imaginary) space: in this process he is like someone passing through a large city and seeing the prominent towers and bridges from a constantly shifting point of view, and thus in a constantly different relation to each other, as he strolls from street to street and from square to square.

So what is involved is a conception of space which is clearly different to that in traditional painting. Lissitzky does not just open a window so that the viewer can look outside, into space; no, Lissitzky takes him by the hand, so to speak, and goes into the space with him.

Participation by the viewer is essential to Lissitzky. Actively involving him in the dynamically conceived art process is at the heart of Lissitzky's work. This is also the principle behind his typographical work, demonstration rooms and exhibition designs. As he said himself on more than one occasion, the painting – the art of painting – was not for him an end in itself,

59

6. See also the article by Kai-Uwe Hemken in this catalogue.

as it was, for example, for Mondrian and Malevich. For him every result of artistic action was "only" "movement frozen for a moment". The real action still had to take place, on the part of the viewers who must absorb the work and its content creatively, or rather 're-creatively', and carry it further.

All this has to do with Lissitzky's conception of reality and his hopes as regards building a new society. It is clear that the paintings, in their aims and visual techniques, are also given an "opportunity to take action",[7] as he put it. This participation is worked out in more detail in the demonstration rooms and exhibitions.

The first step in the transition from the one category, *Proun* paintings, to the other, *Demonstrationsräume* and exhibition designs, was the *Prounenraum* (Proun Room) [repr.60] which he created in 1923 for the *Grosse Berliner Kunstausstellung* (Great Berlin Art exhibition) in the Lehrter Bahnhof. This was a space measuring 3 x 3 x 2.5 metres which was to express the spatial concept of the *Proun* three-dimensionally.

In this space the viewer was offered a visual experience in which, while walking round, he was shown the essential directions in space and plane – a horizontal, a vertical and a diagonal, with the squared as the basis and thematic link – through the paintings and reliefs mounted on the walls. If we were to encounter this work today, we would call it an "environment". It was more or less similar in character to the demonstration room in Dresden discussed above. This idea was later perfected in the *Abstraktes Kabinett* (The abstract cabinet) at Alexander Dorner's museum in Hanover [repr.122-124]. A fundamental change took place in 1928 when in the case of the *Pressa* exhibition the theme had to do with society rather than art.

Other commissions followed the one for the *Pressa* exhibition, which had been such an international success. He designed the Soviet stands at the *Internationale Werkbundausstellung Film und Foto* (International Trade Union Exhibition Film and Foto) [repr.165] in Stuttgart (1929), the *Internationale Hygiene-Ausstellung* (International Hygiene Exhibition) [repr.162] in Dresden (1930), and the *Internationale Pelz-Fachausstellung IPA* (International Fur Trade Exhibition) [repr.166] in Leipzig (1930). But after that there were fewer commissions. The new techniques – the photo collages and montages filling whole spaces, the moving mechanical or electrical components, the abstract and figurative sculptures which carried short texts that could be

absorbed at a glance – were all perfected and their design refined with the same aim: activating the viewer and intensifying communication of the message.

But here again a question arises: who was the viewer?

The answer was the kind of people who went to such international exhibitions. In other words, foreigners who probably took little notice of the message from the Soviet Union and came for reasons of business, public relations or recreation. This is why this kind of exhibition soon acquired an air of inflated propaganda, with the design suffering as a result.

The people with whom Lissitzky was concerned were certainly not there. And this brings us to another question: why were such exhibitions not held in the Soviet Union? I suspect that the authorities used these exhibitions to create a favourable image abroad (to show that they were also progressive as regards culture), while at home they preferred to put the emphasis on literacy programmes, etc.

After 1932 Lissitzky earned his living mainly by teaching and doing typographical work. His work on the magazine *USSR im Bau* took up a good deal of his time [repr.106-107]. Here we can see how decline set in, despite the fine examples of photomontage and typographical composition – in the latter the typography plays the same role in relation to reading as the reciter does in relation to listening to poetry. The propaganda aspect became dominant (as it had not in Malevich's work), particularly in the special issues devoted to such topics as the Red Army. Increasingly often the tone was one of unshakable optimism which completely ignored the dark side of the methods used to build the new society – the inhuman sacrifices which these methods demanded of the people. This tone can be seen in the faces of the two boys in the poster Lissitzky designed for the Russian exhibition in Zurich (1929), but it did not really become familiar until the Nazis began to adopt a professional approach in their propaganda (and this certainly affects how we now look at such a poster by Lissitzky) [ill.13].

In the formal structure of both the typography and his later designs for demonstration rooms, such aspects as the return of symmetry as the ruling principle raise many questions. Had he not attacked Le Corbusier's design for the League of Nations Palace on this very point in his 1928 article *Idole und Idolenverehrer* (Idols and idol worship) [repr.147]? When we also look at his incomplete design of 1934 for a housing block, we see an intact formal structure. In my view, these questions indicate that

7. "Anleitung zum Handeln".

ill. 14
El Lissitzky, Vilmos Huszar, **4 i Lampe (Heliokonstruktion 125 Volt),** 1923
Photo: Merz, 1923

ill. 15
Five Year Plan Architecture, 1931
Fotomontage, showing Lissitzky's 1930 model for the House of heavy industry.
Photo: private archives

ill. 16
Soviet pavilion at the International Press Exhibition Pressa, Cologne 1928
Photo-frieze by El Lissitzky and Sergei Senkin.
Photo: private archives

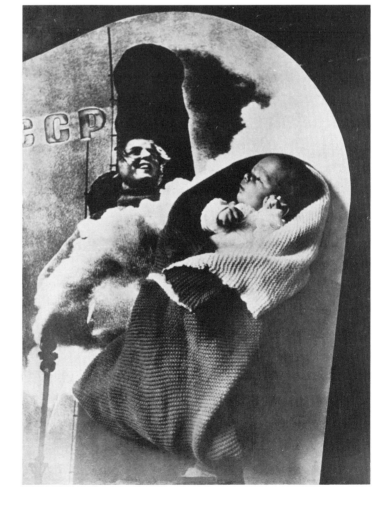

ill. 17
Untitled (Sophie Lissitzky-Küppers and boys), ca. 1923/25
Photo: Berlinische Galerie, Photographische Sammlung, Berlin

ill. 18
Birth announcement of the artist's son, 1930
Photo: Robert Shapazian, New York

in the late twenties and early thirties, like Malevich and many other artists in and outside Russia, Lissitzky was facing a dilemma.

In the article just mentioned he goes into this, although only if you read between the lines. The article is about the situation of architecture in the Soviet Union. He criticises the fact that Russian architects are too inclined to look admiringly at the work of their colleagues in the West, which is then imitated in an almost academic fashion. This had been a sensitive point in Russia since the time of Czar Peter the Great and the building of Petersburg in the neo-classical style. Lissitzky's specific question is: can we find examples in Europe for what we in the Soviet Union need in the fields of architecture and town planning? His answer is no. This is all quite explicitly stated. He arrives at this conclusion by analysing Le Corbusier's work and its relation to the building and housing culture which a country such as France produces. Lissitzky puts it as plainly as this: "All this (the conflicting interests of the architect, the owner/developer and the user, J.L.) compels us to turn our attention not to individual architects but to the country which produces them."[8]
Between the lines Lissitzky is talking about his problem: the dilemma in which art and culture find themselves, the dilemma that the creativity of the individual artist is no longer in touch with the collective creativity of the society in which he works. The only thing is that Lissitzky does not see this as a dilemma but as a problem to be solved. He evades this problem by simply arguing that in the West the collective housing culture has been lost – partly as a result of the political (capitalist) system which encourages speculation for profit. In the West the artist (or architect) claims without being sufficiently self-critical to be able to provide a solution based on his individual creativity as a replacement. At the same time, Lissitzky is absolutely convinced that the political (socialist) system in his own country provides guarantees of achieving a collective culture. All what is needed is some adjustment of the conditions: more notice should be taken of what is valuable in all kinds of designs and experiments in Russia which were not realised, and there should be sharper criticism of the projects of little architectural value which have been carried out.
But what happened to Lissitzky himself – and to Malevich and Tatlin and many others – proves that the dilemma he describes existed in Russia too...as it still does.

It is a dilemma in the true sense of the word: there is no satisfactory solution. This is because the mentalities behind both capitalism and socialism are too closely related. It is a dilemma encountered both here and there, everywhere where Western ideas have influenced the shape of society. Michel Foucault referred to it in a philosophical and historical context in discussing the subject, "the fundamental postulate which French philosophy from Descartes to today has never abandoned"[9] But to indicate the anthropological nature of this dilemma, and so link up with what has been said above, I will quote some passages from an article Martin Buber published in 1947 under the title *What is Man?*:
"But if individualism only comprehends a part of man, collectivism only comprehends man as a part: neither penetrates into the totality of man or man as a totality.
Individualism only sees man in reference to himself, but collectivism does not see man at all, it only sees 'society'. Both views of life result from or are expressions of the same human condition. This condition is characterised by the confluence of cosmic and social homelessness, of fear of the world and fear of life, in an existential state of loneliness, such as has probably never been known to this extent before.
In order to save himself from the despair with which his isolation threatens him, man sees no other solution than its glorification. Modern individualism has in essence an imaginary basis. This is where it fails: for the imagination is not capable of dealing with the given situation in reality.
Modern collectivism is the last barricade, which man has erected against the confrontation with himself...; in collectivism, through the relinquishment of the immediacy of personal decision and responsibility, this confrontation of man with himself becomes impossible.
(...)
The fundamental fact of human existence is neither the individual as such nor the collective as such. Neither, considered on its own merits, amounts to more than a powerful abstraction."[10]
Buber also tries to outline a way based on the interpersonal. But he is not very specific and, pursuing his own argument, this probably cannot be expected of any one individual.
What seems to me important is the place he gives to responsibility – responsibility which an individual must always give as an answer when the question is put to him by a known community. In the development which the concept of art has gone through in the last few centuries, the one pole – the artist and the viewer

8. "All dass zwingt uns, unsere Aufmerksamkeit nicht auf die einzelnen Architekturpersönlichkeiten zu richten, sondern auf das Land, das sie hervorbringt".

9. In an interview with Duccio Trombadori published in *Ervaring en Waarheid* (Experience and Truth), Ter Elfder Ure, 1985.
10. Martin Buber, *Das Problem des Menschen*, 1947.
"Wenn aber der Individualismus nur einen Teil des Menschen erfasst, so erfasst der Kollektivismus nur den Menschen als Teil: zur Ganzheit des Menschen, zum Menschen als Ganzes dringen beide nicht vor.
Der Individualismus sieht den Menschen nur in der Bezogenheit auf sich selbst, aber der Kollektivismus sieht den Menschen überhaupt nicht, er sieht nur die 'Gesellschaft'.
Beide Lebensanschauungen sind Ergebnisse oder Aeusserungen des gleichen menschlichen Zustands.

Dieser Zustand ist durch das Zusammenströmen von kosmischer und socialer Heimlosigkeit, von Weltangst und Lebensangst, zu einer Daseinsverfassung der Einsamkeit gekennzeichnet, wie es sie in diesem Ausmass vermutlich noch nie zuvor gegeben hat.
Um sich vor der Verzweiflung zu retten, mit der ihn seine Vereinsamung bedroht, ergreift der Mensch den Ausweg, diese zu glorifizieren.
Der moderne Individualismus hat im wesentlichen eine imaginäre Grundlage. An diesem Charakter scheitert er; denn die Imagination reicht nicht zu, die gegebene Situation faktisch zu bewältigen.
Der moderne Kollektivismus ist die letzte Schranke, die der Mensch vor der Begegnung mit sich selbst aufgerichtet hat ...; im Kollektivismus gibt sie, mit dem Verzicht

auf die Unmittelbarkeit persönlicher Entscheidung und Verantwortung, sich selber auf.
Die fundamentelle Tatsache der menschlichen Existenz ist weder der Einzelne als solcher noch die Gesamtheit als solche. Beide, für sich betrachtet, sind nur mächtige Abstraktionen".
Later published in: *Forum. Maandblad voor Architectuur en Gebonden Kunsten* 14 (1959), no. 8, p.249.

as individual – has been established, but the 'known community' is a more difficult matter. Hasn't the commercialised and consumerist treatment of art turned this into a neutral audience? This is why Lissitzky's idea of activating the consciousness of the viewer was an excellent starting point, and he succeeded in giving it shape in a completely new way. But he was overtaken by propaganda whose aims and content were dictated by others, and this conflicted with the freedom required to set consciousness in motion. The viewers became a neutral audience.

In the case of Lissitzky, the political pressure which was undoubtedly brought to bear on him was not the main reason for the evident decline in his work. After all, he himself believed in the building of a socialist state, which was the purpose of that political system. It was this belief, his own utopian idealism, of which he was the victim.

What Martin Buber says about despair and the glorification of it seems to me well worth thinking about when trying to evaluate what is presented to our consciousness through the Malevich retrospective and the present exhibition of Lissitzky's work. Does it not indicate the course museums should follow in organizing such retrospectives? Mindful of the warning Lissitzky gives in his article *Idole und Idolenverehrer*, museums should not set up 'idols' before the public in these exhibitions, but make tangible through the works presented and the catalogue, etc. the dimensions of strength and weakness, of undaunted courage and anxious recoiling; in short, the dimensions of success and failure which are present in all of us, artist and viewer, as well as in every age and in the culture which takes shape within it.

Lissitzky and photography

Peter Nisbet

In a 1921 lecture, Lissitzky wrote dismissively about photography, according it barely a single sentence. "The (painted) picture fell apart together with the old world which it had created for itself. The new world will not need little pictures. If it needs a mirror, it has the photograph and the cinema."[1] A few years later, in 1929, he devoted an entire essay to the creative and expressive possibilities of the medium, illustrated with examples of his own photographic work. The essay ends:

"The language of photography is not the language of painting, and photography possesses properties not available to painting. These properties lie in the photographic material itself and it is essential for us to develop them in order to make photography truly into an art, into fotopis'. When we enrich ourselves through a language of special expressivity, we enrich ourselves with one more means of influencing our consciousness and our emotions."[2]

The rapid progression of Lissitzky's ever deeper involvement with photography between 1921 and 1929 can be traced over a year-by-year survey of his activities: in 1922, he used some fragments of photographs in the collages which were the basis for his illustrations to Ilia Erenburg's *Shest povestei o legkikh kontsakh* (Six stories with an easy ending) (N 1922/12) [repr.11-12].[3] In autumn 1923, he published a curious photogram, co-created with Vilmos Huszar and entitled *4/i/Lampe Heliokonstruktion 125 Volt* [ill.14] in the pages of Kurt Schwitters' periodical *Merz*.[4]

The following year he used double-exposures or multiple negatives to make the series of three portraits of Hans Arp, Schwitters [repr.111] and, most famously, himself as *The Constructor* [repr.117]. 1925 saw the continuation of his experiments with photography in commercial advertising for the Pelikan office-supply company (N 1924/7-9 and 1925/6).

After his return to Moscow, he began to investigate the application of photography to the decoration of a sports-club which his colleagues were designing. This resulted in the *Runner in the City* image in 1926 [repr.114]. In 1927 he exhibited his photographic work and wrote an essay *The Artist in Production* which included comments on the use of the photograph, the photomontage and the photogram in typographic design.[5] The following year, he was able to implement some of his ideas in the design of the Soviet Pavilion at the *Internationale Presse-Ausstellung Pressa* (International Press exhibition Pressa) [repr.101] in Cologne, and in the accompanying catalogue (N 1928/6). (In 1928, he was also on the selection committee for the all-Russian exhibition of photography, though he showed no work.) By 1929, he was using his own photographic experiments for posters and book-covers, and as illustrations for the essay translated on p. 70. 1929 also saw a broad representation of his photographic work at the *Film und Foto-Ausstellung* organised by the *Deutscher Werkbund* and shown in Stuttgart and elsewhere.[6] [repr.165].

Clearly, by 1929 Lissitzky had become converted to the value and importance of photography as a medium. In this, he was in many ways entirely typical of the European avant-garde of which he was so integral a member. However, for Lissitzky's career in photography to be fairly assimilated to this broader story, we must have a clear sense of its particular character and achievement. By this, I do not mean that we must urgently resolve the disputes over the invention of certain photographic methods or unravel the precise techniques used for some of Lissitzky's images (however important those will be to any fully satisfying account). Rather, I want to point to three aspects of Lissitzky's photographic work which seem decisively important, and which also cast some light on the still problematic subject of Lissitzky's work for Stalin's propaganda press, after the 'high-water-mark' of 1929.

Firstly, Lissitzky's increasing attention to photography through

1. El Lissitzky, 'The Conquest of Art', *Ringen* (Warsaw), (1922), no. 109, p. 32-34, translated from the Yiddish by Michael Steinlauf in: Peter Nisbet, *El Lissitzky (1890-1941)*. Exhibition catalogue. Busch-Reisinger Museum, Harvard University 1987, p. 59-61, here p. 61. Some of the points in my present contribution receive fuller treatment in this earlier publication, especially in 'An Introduction to El Lissitzky', p. 13-52.
2. El Lissitzky, 'Photography (Fotopis')', *Sovetskoe foto* (15 May 1929) no. 10, p. 311. Since this important latter essay, a key document in understanding the evolution of his views, dating from the period of his own most intense involvement with the experimental resources of the medium, has remained unknown to scholarship on Lissitzky, I have appended a

translation of the text, omitting the brief comments by the editors of the magazine. For the two illustrations Lissitzky published with this essay, see notes 6 and 7 below.
3. Throughout this essay, numbers following an upper-case N refer to my 'catalogue raisonné' of Lissitzky's typographical work, published in the catalogue cited above Peter Nisbet, op. cit. (note 1), p. 177-202.
4. *Merz* (October 1923) no. 6, p. 62. The photogram uses two glasses and a Philips light-bulb, and other unidentified materials. In its multiple references to and uses of light, it is a sophisticated work.
5. N 1927/7, sec. II, p. 3-8. The essay is translated into German as 'Der Künstler in der Produktion' in Sophie Lissitzky-Küppers and Yen Lissitzky, *El Lissitzky:*

Proun und Wolkenbügel. Schriften, Briefe, Dokumente, Dresden 1977, p. 113-117. Careful study of the installation photograph of this 1927 exhibition, published in Sophie Lissitzky-Küppers, *El Lissitzky. Maler. Architekt Typograf. Fotograf*, Dresden 1967, fig. 197, reveals that *The Runner in the City* was included in that exhibition, reinforcing my suggested date of 1926 (Peter Nisbet, 'An introduction to El Lissitzky,' op. cit. (note 1), p. 51, n. 95. Several other photographs are also identifiable.
6. Recently published installation photographs from the Berlin presentation of this exhibition (*Stationen der Moderne.* Exhibition catalogue. Berlinische Galerie, Berlin 1989, p. 241, together with the well-known photographs of Lissitzky's design for the Stuttgart installation,

Sophie Lissitzky-Küppers, op. cit. (note 5), fig. 210-211, may lead us to hitherto unidentified photographs by Lissitzky. In our context, it is interesting that a prominent place in the exhibition was given to the photogram of a curiously posed mannequin (reproduced in reverse and in negative by Sophie Lissitzky-Küppers, op. cit. (note 5), fig. 166. This image was precisely one of two which Lissitzky chose to illustrate his 1929 essay, translated below. Could other unattributed photographs in the so-called *fifo* exhibition be by Lissitzky. I am thinking of images such as the two workers in a sphere of scaffolding (used by Lissitzky as part of the cover for an exhibition catalogue, N 1930/5) or the frontal portrait of a man pointing a camera directly at the viewer. Both of these originally appeared without attribu-

the 1920s is inextricably linked with his growing dissatifaction with, and eventual abandonment of, abstract painting. Second is the closeness of much of Lissitzky's work in photography to his interest in architecture. And finally, I cannot overlook the apparent connexion of his photography to his family life, to a private sphere of personal satisfactions. I hope that it will become clear that there are no absolute lines of demarcation among these three topics.

Although Lissitzky liked to claim that his *Prounen* were a link between painting and architecture, his own pronouncements about the future of art (his own included) indicated that this future lay more in photography and film than in construction and building. The two major publications which he prepared in 1924 both argue a privileged position for photography and film. *Die Kunstismen* (N 1925/2), his survey of the art-isms of the decade since 1914, culminates with Vicking Eggeling and the abstract film (before the final concluding question-mark, which characterises the future). And the theoretical essay *K. und Pangeometrie* (A. and Pangeometrie) (a chapter of a proposed book), while being mainly an analysis of the changing role of perspective in art, ends with an examination of the way that movement of real bodies can create imaginary bodies (which in turn create a new perception of space). Effects of light, as recorded and even prompted by photography and film, are clearly central to this state of what Lissitzky calls "a-material materiality".

Photography may even have seemed to have far greater potential to evoke that indefinite, irrational, complex and dynamic space at which the *Prounen* aimed. For example, a virtually indecipherable photograph [repr.109] from the mid-twenties is inscribed by Lissitzky with the evocative equation which alludes both to his multiple sources and to his wish to transcend them: N^2ature + T^2echnology + A^2rt $= -1$. Doubt about the efficacy of abstract art alone was, to a greater or lesser degree, always inherent in Lissitzky's *Prounen*. An early manifestation of this doubt was the incorporation of photographic fragments into *Proun* compositions for book illustrations in 1922 (just as in 1923 Lissitzky introduced real humans by building a *Proun*-space on an architectural scale) [repr.60]. These doubts perhaps reached their extreme when Lissitzky exhibited, alongside a *Proun*, a painting-sized enlargement of a photograph (showing his hand holding a pair of compasses and drawing a curve) at

the *Internationale Kunstaustellung* in Dresden in 1926[7] [repr.120].

Nevertheless, if photography increasingly attracted Lissitzky as the inadequacies of his *Proun* work became more and more evident, it was to architecture that he turned most of his professional attention – at least in the second half of the 1920s. Important for this context, however, are the ways in which Lissitzky tentatively sought points of contact between photography and architecture. A nice instance of this overlap is given by some of the photograms which he produced in the middle of the decade, presumably as exercises in the newly fascinating medium. These are rather simple efforts involving glasses, lace or gauzy material, tools and similar objects (and they are not always ascribed to Lissitzky with absolute certainty). But a couple of photographs preserved among the Lissitzky papers in Moscow are particularly interesting, as they are apparently produced directly as cyanotypes, that is as blue-prints in a procedure familiar in architectural drafting.[8]

This link at the level of material and technique between Lissitzky's photography and his architecture finds its equivalent elsewhere.[9] Some of his most pertinent criticism of photography concerned Erich Mendelsohn's book of architectural photographs, *Amerika* [repr.104].[10] He often manipulated photographs of his own architectural projects, either montaging a proposal onto a photograph of its projected site, as with the *Wolkenbügel* [repr.129],[11] or superimposing a photograph of a model of a competition entry onto a heroic image of monumental workers, as he did with *Asnova's* project for a *House of heavy industry* [ill.15].
Three of his most manipulated photographs were made in 1929 for the dust-jackets for books on modern architecture (N 1930/1-3).[12]

More interestingly still, Lissitzky attempted a functional convergence of these two spheres of activity. He was quite explicit about expecting that some of his photographic work was intended for execution at an architectural scale, as a mural. The photographic *Pelikan* advertisements [repr.95] were to be produced at poster size; he envisioned a photo-frieze for the sports-club in Moscow, and collaborated with Sergei Senkin to produce such a building-scaled image for the *Pressa* exhibition hall [ill.16]. Even the poster for the 1929 Zurich exhibition [repr.102] (N 1929/3)

tion in *Sovetskoe foto* vol. 3, (November 1928) no. 11, p. 491, and vol. 4 (January 1929) no. 1, front cover.
7. See the installation photographs in Sophie Lissitzky-Küppers, op. cit. (note 5), fig. 186-187. The image, one of the components of *The Constructor* self-portrait, was also exhibited by Lissitzky in several later exhibitions and used for the cover of a book about architecture at *Vkhutemas* (N 1927/2).
8. I know of two such cyanotypes, one showing a pair of tweezers, the other a piece of chalk and a torn scrap of paper (TSGALI 2361/1/21/10 and 11). Related photograms (perhaps prints from negatives produced by rephotographing a unique image) include two in the Museum Ludwig, Cologne [repr.108] and two recently offered at auction (Christie's,

New York, 23 April 1990, lots 36 and 37). Although I suggest that these are all relatively minor works, it is interesting that Lissitzky chose a similar image, showing a pair of pliers, gauze and a glass, to illustrate the 1929 essay translated here. In fact, the 1929 illustration was clearly produced at the same time as one of the Cologne images: the position of the gauze is identical (though printed in reverse and in negative), the pliers have been slightly moved and the glass added [repr.108].
9. I am leaving out of account Lissitzky's use of photography to document his own architectural projects. Two interesting instances are: the composite panoramic photograph (by Lissitzky?) of the *Prounenraum*, published in *G* in mid-1923 [repr.59] (and also exhibited in an enlarged format at the 1929 *Film und*

Foto-Ausstellung); and Lissitzky's letter to Albert Renger-Patsch (now in the Getty Center for the History of Art and Humanities, Santa Monica, CA), asking him to photograph the Soviet pavilions and exhibition stands of the two trade-fairs in Germany which Lissitzky directed in 1930, the *Internationale Hygiene-Ausstellung* in Dresden and the *Internationale Pelz-Fachausstellung* in Leipzig. It is not clear whether Renger-Patsch accepted the commission.
10. This text is now available in English translation by Alan Upchurch with helpful commentary of Christopher Pillips, ed. and intro., *Photography in the Modern Era. European Documents and Critical Writings*, New York 1989, p. 221-226.
11. See the photomontage illustrated in Peter Nisbet, 'An Introduction to

El Lissitzky', op. cit. (note 1), p. 33, fig. 21.
12. The cover for his own book about architecture in Russia is particularly interesting. Once again, Lissitzky feels it necessary to merge one of his *Prounen* (the lithograph of the image known at *The Town*) with a photograph of similar spatial and visual complexity, appropriately showing workers on construction scaffolding, seen from below. The photograph was published in *Sovetskoe foto* (22 September 1929) no. 18, p. 554 with an attribution to V. Borisov. Is this a pseudonym for Boris Vsevolodovich Ignatovich, to whom the photograph (printed in reverse and in a different orientation) is given in Grigory Shudakov et al., *Pioneers of Soviet Photography*, New York 1983, p. 160, no. 176?

implies a truly monumental scale for the photomontage of fused heads of a male and a female youth looming over an architectural element (actually the exhibition stands probably designed by Lissitzky for the 1927 *Polygraphic exhibition* in Moscow).

Of course, the most famous point at which Lissitzky the photographer and Lissitzky the architect intersect is precisely the photomontage of himself as architect-constructor. In these few lines, I cannot adumbrate all the possible meanings of this resonant image. Here I want only to indicate that it is one of a series of photographic works concentrating on the artist, his closest family and immediate circle of friends and collaborators. Without counting the family snapshots (of which there are, significantly, also a good number among Lissitzky's papers), we have manipulated photographs of friends in Hanover, of his wife Sophie, of her two sons by a previous marriage [ill.17], of the artist in various situations, and of his own son Yen. In part, this reflects Lissitzky's own most attractive side as a devoted friend, husband and father. It also reflects the availability of those close to him for such photographic experiments, especially at a time when such activity was becoming increasingly suspect.

The 1929 essay translated below specifically uses the example of the 'manipulated' portrait to elucidate the value of some of these experiments. When Lissitzky writes of the expressive potential of photographically adding objects associated with the sitter, it is difficult not to recall the portrait of Arp against the page from a Dada magazine with the text "Here comes the great Pra", or the use of Lissitzky's own sketches for a child's mathematics book as the back-drop for a double portrait of his two step-sons, or the image of himself at the centre of a kaleidoscope of images from the *Pressa* installation [repr.118].[13]

One especially powerful example of this side to Lissitzky's photographic work is the 1930 multiple exposure now known as the *Birth Announcement of the Artists Son* [ill.18]. Here we see Lissitzky's infant child, superimposed on a photomontage of two images: a standard-bearing woman worker melded with Dimitrii Georgievich Debabov's photograph of a smoking factory chimney and steaming factory whistle.[14] Here Lissitzky melds the most personal and the most public, the beginning of new life and the onrush of triumphant industrialisation in the middle of the first Five-Year Plan. The symbol of the factory is the symbol also of functional architecture, here layered with Lissitzky's pri-

vate hopes for future improvement. The image exploits all the spatial ambiguity and almost surreal dematerialisation which the artist discovered in the medium during the 1920s, it invokes the grand public building projects on which Lissitzky still hoped to be engaged; and it is a moving private homage to the wonder of birth and natural growth which had so long fascinated the artist.

This image can also help us to understand the subsequent ten years of Lissitzky's career. The passionate identification of his own son with the fortunes of the young socialist state must have reinforced both the artist's intellectual commitment to the success of the Revolution (as he understood it) and his eagerness to provide an adequate income for his family.

The decade of the 1930s saw extensive work for various propaganda organs of the Stalinist state. After about 1932, there is little or no evidence that Lissitzky continued to experiment with the photographic medium himself. His earlier practice of using and manipulating the work of others now became his exclusive manner of working. His inventiveness is restricted to juxtaposition, layout, paper folds and materials, concentrating the form, sequence, look and feel of the printed page. Certainly, the 1930s were not simply years of artistic sterility for Lissitzky and he maintained a measure of aesthetic and moral integrity not common in his generation. I have argued elsewhere for the importance of some of his achievements.[15] And the photograph plays a central role in many of those achievements. Typical for the publications for which Lissitzky worked (usually as a free-lance) was *USSR im Bau* (USSR in Construction) [repr.106/107], whose first issue had proudly announced that the publisher "has chosen the photograph as a method to illustrate socialist construction, for the photograph speaks much more convincingly in many cases than even the most brilliantly written article". That these publications were produced largely for export (or for consumption by the party elite) makes it difficult to situate this creative work within politically inflected analysis of the development of Soviet art and society. (The same, of course, is true of Lissitzky's work for the *Pressa* exhibition in Germany in 1928 and other, relatively early work of this kind).[16]

Lissitzky's later work, I propose, is more appropriately seen in the context of his ongoing 'debate' with the reality of the given world. As an artist, Lissitzky constantly renogiated the terms of the relationship between the status quo and its possible trans-

13. The Arp portrait was also used later for the cover of a book of poetry, N 1928/1. Sophie Lissitzky-Küppers, op. cit. (note 5), fig. 168 illustrates the double portrait of the two brothers. A print is now in the Berlinische Galerie, Berlin (*Photographie als Photographie*. Exhibition catalogue by Janos Frecot, Berlinische Galerie, Berlin 1989, p. 25-26, 175). The portrait of the artist at *Pressa* is illustrated in Sophie Lissitzky-Küppers en Yen Lissitzky, op. cit. (note 5), pl. 18.

14. The photograph originally appeared in *Sovetskoe foto* vol. 4 (February 1929) no. 3, p. 79. Reversed, it served as the frontispiece to the first issue of *USSR im Bau* (January 1930). Lissitzky first combined the chimney and woman. A print is in TsGALI (2361/1/21/7) and illustrated in Sophie Lissitzky-Küppers, op. cit. (note

5), fig. 183. One print of the photograph with the baby carries the typed inscription 'Klein el' and the date October 12 1930, Sophie Lissitzky-Küppers and Yen Lissitzky, op. cit. (note 5), pl. 20. It worth noting that a German communist designer, Max Gebhard, used Debabov's photograph and a similar image of a heroic standing woman seen from below, in a poster for the 1930 election campaign in Germany, appealing to working women to vote for the KPD (*Künstler im Klassenkampf*. Exhibition catalogue, Museum für Deutsche Geschichte, Berlin 1988, p. 32). Did Lissitzky influence Gebhard or vice versa? The interaction between German and Soviet design in these years has not yet been sufficiently explored.

15. See the concluding sections of my essay, 'An Introduction to El Lissitzky', op. cit. (note 1) and the relevant entries in the 'catalogue raisonné' of typographical work.

16. Failure to recognise this is one of the weaknesses of Benjamin D. Buchloh's article 'From Faktura to Factography, *October* (Fall 1984) no. 30, p. 82-119.

formation. More than most, he seems to have accepted (however reluctantly) the given situation as the material with which he had to work in his efforts to effect positive change. This given situation, these 'data', could include political reality, the ideas of others, and, importantly for us in the context of the 1930s, photographs by others.

Yet photography itself, as an art medium, encompasses precisely this tension between accepting and transforming the outside world. A photograph can accept (even affirm) external reality, yet it can also manipulate it (through effects of light and material) to achieve an expressive effect. In his 1921 lecture, Lissitzky had acknowledged photography's role as a 'mirror'; by 1929 he was emphasizing photography's other potential as an expressive "means of influencing our consciousness and emotions" (presumably with a view to instigating action). This dual aspect, inherent to photography and central to Lissitzky's entire creative oeuvre, explains why his use of photography, while not the most prominent or original of his many contributions, may be the most typical and the most revealing.

Appendix

El Lissitzky, **Photography** *(Fotopis')*

Photography is today the most widely accessible means of achieving an image. The basis of photography is the activity of light on a surface sensitive to light. I propose to direct attention to the fact that it is possible to achieve an image on a light-sensitive layer not only by means of a photographic camera, and, moreover, even with its help, not only by means of the generally-known negative and positive processes.

By means of the camera we gather rays reflected from the object through the lens onto a light-sensitive film, and we get a negative.
But we can place the object directly, without a camera, on to a light-sensitive layer of film, or, more conveniently, of paper, and, exposing it to light, get an image corresponding to the system of its shadows, of its traces. When we work with a camera, we construct our shot on the varying illumination of the object - from full light to full shadow. Without a camera, we use the varying degree of translucency of the object, and, most importantly, through the conscious organisation of the light sources and the direction of their rays, we seek the construction of shadows which would render the object most characteristically. The technique of achieving the image by these means is very simple, but precisely because of this, it demands profound skill, clarity of the task set and an accurate planned approach to execution.

The following stage in the expansion of photography's possibilities is the exclusion of the negative from the automatic contact process. From one and the same negative it is possible to achieve various impressions – depending on the angle of its placement in relation to the paper, on the direction, strength and number of light sources. Thus, for example, I can, from a negative, print a portrait as a full characteristic of the given face, but I can strengthen certain features (I elongate the skull), achieve a second, accompanying image, include a series of objects which have productive associations with the given face. Such a result can be achieved through the conjunction with the negative of a series of objects of varying translucency, set at an angle to the paper. This is all lit from two light sources, one direct, the other reflected.

Several of these examples show that photography cannot be reduced to getting into focus and releasing the shutter. The language of photography is not the language of painting, and photography possesses properties not available to painting. These properties lie in the photographic material itself and it is essential for us to develop them in order to make photography truly into an art, into fotopis'. When we enrich ourselves through a language of special expressivity, we enrich ourselves with one more means of influencing our consciousness and our emotions.

The work of L.M. Lissitzky in the Tretiakov Gallery

M.A. Nemirovskaya

To mark the centenary of the birth of Lazar Markovich Lissitzky (known as El Lissitzky), an exhibition of his work is being held at the Tretiakov Gallery and the Van Abbemuseum. It presents work from the collections of both museums.

The Lissitzky exhibition in Moscow is part of a series held in recent years at the Tretiakov Gallery which is devoted to the work of the great masters of the Russian avant-garde of the early twentieth century: P.N. Filonov, K.S. Malevich, V.V. Kandinsky and L.S. Popova. Among these courageous reformers and explorers of new avenues in art, L.M. Lissitzky occupies a position of special distinction. He left his brilliant mark on the most varied fields.

In a questionnaire for an encyclopaedia Lissitzky listed his activities in the following order: 'Engineer-architect, painter, photographer, typograper.'[1] By training and inclination Lissitzky was primarily an architect. But he was also an interesting painter, and a remarkable draughtsman and lithographer. Behind the modest description 'photographer and typographer' lie Lissitzky's fundamental innovations in the design of books, newspapers and posters. He was a craftsman who exploited to the full the expressive possibilities offered by modern printing and photographic techniques, and he brought about a revolution in book design. Another, equally important part of his oeuvre was the design of large exhibitions or, more correctly, the discovery and development of this art form. Among Lissitzky's best works in this field were the Soviet pavilions at the *Internationale Presse-Ausstellung Pressa* (International Press Exhibition Pressa) in Cologne and the *Internationale Hygiene-Ausstellung* (International Hygiene Exhibition) in Dresden. They attracted attention through their originality and daring, and incorporated remarkable innovations in the use of the most diverse techniques and materials.

Lissitzky was a very active and successful teacher. From 1919 to 1920 he taught at the People's Art School in Vitebsk, and in the second half of the twenties he lectured at *Vkhutemas* (Higher State Technical-Artistic Studios) as a member of the wood- and metalwork department. Here he was appointed professor of interior design and thus pioneered this field in the USSR. He gave special attention to furniture construction.

Even this necessarily brief summary of Lizzitzky's wide range of activities shows their undeniable importance and value to art. Both during his years as a student (before the First World War) and later on (in the twenties), Lissitzky spent long periods in Western Europe, where, apart from his work as an artist, he published theoretical articles and took an active part in the artistic life of the time.

He was a friend of many of the leading figures in the arts in Europe and collaborated with them. His work always attracted great interest in other countries. In the twenties and above all between 1970 and 1980, exhibitions devoted to Lissitzky were held in various European countries and in the United States, and a great many articles and books were published.[2] But in his native country Lissitzky's work, together with that of other members of the Russian avant-garde, was long forgotten. Still today the most authoritative book on the artist, written by his wife and loyal helper S.C. Lissitzkaya-Küppers, has not been published in Russian. It first appeared in East Germany in 1967 and was later published in many other countries.[3]

This Lissitzky exhibition at the Tretiakov Gallery is the first to be held in the Soviet Union.[4] The Gallery possesses almost all the artist's works which have remained in his native country. They could not be seen today in the leading national museum were it not for the determination and selflessness of S.C. Lissitzkaya-Küppers, who preserved her husband's work despite many obstacles. We regard it as our duty to say something about this remarkable woman.

Sophie Küppers, artist, connoisseur and director of a gallery in

71

1. Central State Archive for Literature and Art in the USSR, File 2361, Register I, Storage Unit 58.

2. Works by Lissitzky from the collection of the Tretiakov Gallery were seen in Halle and Leipzig in 1982 at an exhibition devoted to the artist.
The catalogues of the Lissitzky exhibitions held in Cambridge, Mass. from 26-10 to 29-11-1987, in Hanover from 24-1 to 10-4-1988 and in Halle from 7-5 to 3-7-1988 are unusually comprehensive. Several works from the collection of the Tretiakov Gallery were shown in Hanover and Halle.

3. *El Lissitzky. Maler, Architekt, Typograf, Fotograf. Erinnerungen, Briefe, Schriften, übergeben von Sophie Lissitzky-Küppers*, Dresden 1967, Verlag der Kunst, (Second edition 1976). Excerpts from this book, chiefly Lissitzky's letters in a translation by his son, Y.L. Lissitzky, were published by S.O. Chan-Machomedov in the collection *Zodchestvo* (Architecture), no. 1 (20), Moscow, Stroyizdat, 1975.

4. On 18 and 19 November 1960 an exhibition of work by Lissitzky untitled 'Printing, drawing, photographs and architecture' (no catalogue but a poster and an announcement) was held at the Mayakovsky museum cum library at the Taganka (Mayakovsky cross-street, no. 15/13). This was one of a series of exhibitions entitled 'Artistic design in the books of V.V. Mayakovsky'. The Lissitzky exhibition was held at the initiative of N.I. Khardzhiev. See N.I. Khardzhiev, 'Memories of the artist Lissitzky' in *Dekorativnoe iskusstvo SSSR* (1961) no. 2, p. 29-31.

Hanover, first saw Lissitzky's work at the *Erste Russische Kunstausstellung* (First Russian Art Exhibition) in Berlin in 1922. Shortly afterwards she met the artist and became an active participant in all his artistic endeavours. In 1927 she moved to Moscow, where she again became his loyal helper and courageously shared all the problems of his difficult life. In December 1941 Lissitzky died of tuberculosis. In September 1944, like all other Germans, Sofya Christianovna (as she was known in the Soviet Union) was exiled from Moscow. All that her anxious friends (particularly E.D. Stasova) could do for her was to arrange for her place of exile to be the district of Novosibirsk instead of Kazakhstan. After the war Sophie Lissitzkaya-Küppers lived in the city of Novosibirsk. She was continually bombarded with offers to sell Lissitzky's works to foreign museums and private collectors. But she rejected even the most generous offers because of Lissitzky's desire for his work to find a place in a museum in the Soviet Union. It was not until 1958 that she was able to return to Moscow and fulfil her husband's deepest wish.[5]

The Tretiakov Gallery purchased over 300 graphic works by the artist. These drawings, watercolours and lithos are held in the department of Soviet graphics. Valuable archive material, rare editions of Lissitzky's books and photographs were also acquired.[6]

The earliest work by Lissitzky in the Tretiakov Gallery consists of books he designed. *Sikhes Khulin. A Prager Legende* (An Everyday Conversation. A Legend of Prague) by the symbolist poet M. Broderzon dates from 1917 [repr.8]. The influence of the tradition of Jewish religious manuscripts is immediately evident in this book's design. It takes the form of a roll, consisting of pages glued together, inside a special case with brocade cords. Each page is a separate, independent work and at the same time part of a larger whole which is unrolled as one reads. The text in black and white, which is done like a manuscript made by a professional copyist, is framed by fanciful, coloured decoration full of traditional signs and objects of symbolic significance. The entire edition of *Sikhes Khulin. A Prager Legende* consists of 110 copies, of which twenty were coloured in Indian ink.[7] The unusual form of the book and the very limited edition make it clear that it was intended for a small circle of bibliophiles and connoisseurs. It was printed by *Shomir*, a publishing house in Moscow which supported a group active in the revival of Jewish art and culture after the February Revolution.[8]

The design of *Sikhes Khulin. A Prager Legende* clearly shows the influence of the style and methods of the *Mir Iskusstva* (World

of Art) group. It also reflects the enthusiasm for the revival of book-making as a craft which was shared by Russian artists and poets during the first five years of the century.

The Gallery's collection includes a slim volume from 1917 entitled *Khad Gadya* (One billy goat) with watercolour illustrations which is closely related to this interest in the book as a craft product [repr.6]. This handmade book can be seen as the original of the edition published in Kiev in 1919, but at the same time it is an independent work. The clarity of the watercolours is somewhat reminiscent of a child's drawing, but their inventivity, the wealth of detail in the composition and the subtle interaction of illustration and text on the page show that *Khad Gadya* is less a fairy tale than the kind of wise story told at Passover. The originality of the genre is reflected in the design of the book and the expressive illustrations, which show a remarkable purity and cohesion. All this makes *Khad Gadya* one of the finest books from Lissitzky's early period.

A collection of Ukrainian and White Russian tales with illustrations by Lissitzky was published in Berlin in 1922 [repr.10]. They were in Yiddish, in verse translations by L. Kvitko. The originals of some of the illustrations are in the collection of the Tretiakov Gallery.

In 1922 and 1923 Lissitzky was very busy with graphic work for magazines and newspapers. He had gone to Berlin at the end of 1921. The purpose of his journey was to restore the links between artists in Russia and the West which had been disrupted by years of war and revolution. As Sophie Lissitzkaya-Küppers writes, "His perfect knowledge of German, high intelligence, lucid mind and ability to articulate his thoughts precisely made him the obvious person to carry out this mission."[9]

There were many Russian artists and writers in Berlin at the time, among them A. Bely, V. Mayakovsky, B. Pasternak, N. Aseyev, V. Shklovsky, A. Tairov, N. Altman and A. Archipenko. One of the important events of this period was the *Erste Russische Kunstausstellung*, which opened in Galerie Van Diemen in Berlin in 1922 and was later seen in Amsterdam. Lissitzky showed work at this exhibition and designed the cover for the catalogue.

The various designs for this cover, in different colours, are only part of the large collection of Lissitzky's graphic work from the twenties in the Tretiakov Gallery. This also includes different versions of the covers for the magazines *Wendingen* [repr.84] and *Broom* [repr.87 and 90], the cover design for *Das Entfesselte Theater. Aufzeichnungen eines Regisseurs* (Theatre Unbound.

5. Information obtained in a conversation with Y.L. Lissitzky on 24 April 1989 in Moscow. Some of the circumstances surrounding the Tretiakov Gallery's acquisition of work by Lissitzky were clarified in a conversation between the author and P.L. Telingater, the widow of the eminent artist S.B. Telingater, a pupil of Lissitzky.
6. A very interesting part of Lissitzky's archive, which includes his graphic work, also came into the hands of the Central State Archive for Literature and Art (File no. 2361) at this time.
7. In the copy in the Tretiakov Gallery, only eight of the fifteen pages are coloured.

8. The other members of the group apart from Lissitzky included M. Chagall, N. Altman, A. Efros and Y. Tugendkhold. See A. Kandtsedikas, *El Lissitzky* (typescript, being prepared for publication by Sovyetski Khudozhnik [The Soviet Artist], Moscow). See also *Tradition and Revolution: the Jewish Renaissance in Russian Avant-garde Art 1918-1928*, Jerusalem 1987.

9. S.C. Lissitzkaya-Küppers, op. cit. (note 3), p. 19. Quoted in the translation by Y.L. Lissitzky. He generously made the Russian manuscript available to the authors of this catalogue.

Notes of a Director) by A. Tairov and other works. During this period Lissitzky made several illustrations for I. Erenburg's book *Shest povestei o legkikh kontsakh* (Six stories with an easy ending). One of these, the *Footballer* [repr.12], can be regarded as the artist's first attempt to use photomontage in a book. Later on Lissitzky was to make frequent and highly successful use of the expressive possibilities of photographic techniques in his graphic work, exhibition designs and architectural projects.
The high point of Lissitzky's work in book design is the volume of poems by Mayakovsky called *Dlia Golosa* (For the voice) published in Berlin in 1923 [repr.80].[10] The originality and clarity of the design is achieved solely through printing and setting techniques: the form of the individual letters, their relation to the typeface as a whole, the use of a thumb index, the free and yet finite placing of all the elements of the sentence on the page, interacting with the rhythms of the poems, and finally the use of the colour red in the columns of text. All the components of the design clearly embody the expressive symbolism and stylistic idiosyncracy of Mayakovsky's poetry. *Dlia Golosa* became the embodiment of Lissitzky the master printer's credo: 'Our palette is modern typographical techniques.' With this and other outstanding typographical work in the twenties, Lissitzky put into practice the principles of the 'visual book', in which 'the form of the book was assigned a special task in accordance with its specific function".[11]
Looking at Lissitzky's graphic work from the twenties as a whole (and here we must also mention his strikingly clever and inventive design for a group exhibition by himself, Mondrian and Man Ray [repr.98]), it is impossible to ignore the obvious influence of Suprematism. The theory and practice of Suprematism, which he learned from K.S. Malevich at Vitebsk in 1919-1920, played a large part in shaping Lissitzky's creative ideas.
The Tretiakov Gallery's collection contains examples of his graphic work from the thirties and the beginning of the fourties in a wide range of genres of varying artistic value: covers for film scenarios, illustrations for I. Erenburg's novel *Padeniie Parizha* (Fall of Paris), different versions of designs for Mayakovsky's books.
Lissitzky's skills as a layout man were employed during the thirties in his work as the main artist involved with the magazine *USSR im Bau* (USSR in Construction) [106-107]. He himself was particularly proud of the issues devoted to the building of a dam in the Dnieper, the polar region and the Soviet constitution.[12] However, there are no original designs or alternative versions

relating to this side of Lissitzky's work in the Gallery's collection. His last works were also in the field of graphic design. When the Second World War broke out, Lissitzky was mortally ill and confined to his bed. He designed two anti-fascist posters in crayon, and one of these, *Give more tanks!*, was printed in November 1941 shortly before his death [ill.15].
But perhaps the most important part of Lissitzky's artistic legacy is what he called *Prounen* (proyekty utverzhdeniya novogo: or 'projects for the affirmation of the new'). The origins of the *Prounen* have to do with his time in Vitebsk in 1919-1920 and his part in the celebrated *Renaissance of Vitebsk*, as E.F. Kovtun called it. Marc Chagall had set up the People's Art School in Vitebsk and invited Lissitzky to join him there. From the summer of 1919 Lissitzky was in charge of the architecture department at this school and also gave lessons in graphics and printing. Malevich, whom Lissitzky had met earlier in Moscow, arrived in Vitebsk in the autumn of that year.[13] His suprematist ideas had already had a considerable influence on Lissitzky. This influence was all the greater because these ideas corresponded completely with both his revolutionary outlook and the development of his creative methods. Another important factor was Malevich's personality: his imperious attitude, his energy and his unshakable faith in the new horizons opened up by Suprematism, the art of the new, revolutionary age.
Early in 1920 the group *Unovis* (Advocates of the new art) was formed within the collective of students and teachers at the school. The aim of *Unovis* was a complete renewal of the world of art on the basis of Suprematism and the transformation of the utilitarian social aspect of life by means of new forms.[14] The group's emblem became the red square, and on the back was one of Lissitzky's first *Prounen* dating from 1919. The typed, richly illustrated *Unovis* almanac designed by Lissitzky is in the manuscripts department of the Tretiakov Gallery. The wealth of material it contains (including theoretical articles and memoirs) gives an accurate picture of the group's turbulent and wide-ranging activities in the 1919-1920 academic year. Malevich and Lissitzky collaborated on the so-called *Design for a curtain* to decorate the room where the 'Committee on the struggle against unemployment' met, and several lithos by Lissitzky formed the basis for suprematist compositions by Malevich.
In our opinion the term *Proun* can be taken to refer not only to the individual works but to a special world, the art of special forms and the relations between them. The artist's own definition is well known: "The *Proun* is the station where one changes

73

10. Some proofs of this book, which were acquired from S.C. Lissitzkaya-Küppers, are in the library of the Tretiakov Gallery. A facsimile edition of *Dlia Golosa* was published by Khudozhnik RSFSR (Artist of the Russian Federation) in Leningrad in 1987.
11. N.I. Khardzhiev, 'L. Lissitzky. The book from the point of view of visual observation – the visual book' in: *The Art of the Book*, Moscow 1962, third edition, p. 167. See also L. Oginskaya (one of the finest artists to take an interest in printing), *Dekorativnoe iskusstvo SSSR* (1973) no. 6, p. 33.

12. See the form 'Information about the artist of the book' (Manuscripts Department of the Tretiakov Gallery, File 76/4; Central State Archive for Literature and Art, File 2361, Register I, Storage Unit 58). See also his autobiography: "The magazine *USSR im Bau* took me on in 1932 and my first job was the issue devoted to the dam in the Dnieper. I did this work with great enthusiasm. The word 'design' does not by any means cover all the creative content of our work. I would go as far as to say that one illustration in one issue, for example 'The population of Cape Chelyuskin' or 'The constitution of the USSR', was just as exacting as working on a map. And the social reverberations were just as wide." (Manuscripts Department of the Tretiakov Gallery, File No. 76/2).

13. A. Shatskich, 'K. Malevich in Vitebsk', *Iskusstvo* (Art) (1988) no. 11, p. 38.
14. A. Kovtun, 'The way of Malevich' in: *Kasimir Malevich (1878-1935).* Exhibition catalogue Stedelijk Museum, Amsterdam 1988, p. 161. Exhibition in Leningrad, 1988; Moscow, 1988-1989; Amsterdam, 1989.

from painting to architecture." In the world of Lissitzky's *Prounen* the suprematist planes acquire depth, architectonic dimensions and a value in cosmic space. "At the last station on the suprematist journey we have torn up the old painting (...) and turned it into a world which floats in space. We have placed it (the painting, ed.) and the viewer beyond the limits of the earth and he must turn the painting and himself on its axis like a planet in order to understand it."[15] Some *Prounen* actually foreshadow, as it were, the view of space which man did not obtain until he journeyed into the cosmos. The view of space as cosmos involves new correlations between objects and the world surrounding them, a new awareness of being in motion or at rest. The *Prounen* have no fixed top or bottom; their inner balance depends on the very strong force of attraction between the different geometrical bodies. Lissitzky himself repeatedly underlined the possibility that his *Prounen* were equally valid when seen from different angles and at different levels. This applies, for example, to the *Proun floating construction in space* [repr.14], which is known in several versions, and to the *Round Proun* [repr.24].

Experiments and solutions in the field of space and volume which were recorded in the *Prounen* became an inexhaustible source for many of Lissitzky's later works. They were a strong stimulus in his designs for books and magazines, exhibition stands and interiors. The thinking behind the *Prounen* was reflected in his theatre designs and photomontages. Finally, there is a close correlation between the *Prounen* and his architectural projects and ideas. Among a series of designs for the *Wolkenbügel* [repr.125], there is a *Proun* in the form of a collage on the theme of this project. The titles of some *Prounen* (*Town* [repr.21] and *Bridge* [repr.15]) immediately make clear their connection with architecture. The project for a speaker's rostrum, which was developed in 1920 by Lissitzky and his pupils and later became known internationally, also began as a *Proun*. But it would be a mistake to see the *Prounen* only as plans and sketches for future buildings or as drafts for cover designs, like a sort of building kit of elements that can be taken out and combined as required. The *Prounen* are a method of creative thinking. Essentially, this is an anti-dogmatic method characterised by daring and freedom but also by pliability and clarity of structure. As a whole, it may represent a utopian world, but it is based on the laws and objects of the real world. The Tretiakov Gallery has a broad and varied collection of *Prounen*. It must be said that the larger part consists not of the finished, painted *Prounen* (as

in other, mainly private and museum, collections), but of the many sketches, drafts and variants. These preliminary sketches in pencil or Indian ink are invaluable because they illustrate how the artist's expressive ideas were born, developed and realised. Together they form a creative laboratory that is especially interesting for those wishing to study Lissitzky's art.

The *Prounen* in the form of collages and lithos are more finished in character. There are two series (portfolios) of lithographed *Prounen*. One was printed in Moscow in 1921 (the Tretiakov Gallery has nine of these). The other, known as the *1° Kestnermappe Proun* (First Kestner Portfolio Proun), was printed in Hanover in 1923 at the initiative of the leaders of the Kestner Society group of artists [repr.13-24].[16]

The spatial ideas embodied in the *Prounen* undoubtedly influenced another of Lissitzky's projects which originated during his short but extremely productive period at Vitebsk. This was the figurines for the opera *Victory over the Sun*. The libretto was by A.E. Kruchenykh, the music by M. V. Matyushin, and the verse prologue by V.V. Khlebnikov. There have been several studies of the origins of this futuristic opera and the various productions.[17] It was first performed in Petersburg in 1913 with sets and costumes by Malevich. In 1920 it was staged in Vitebsk by members of the *Unovis* group with costumes by V.M. Ermolaeva. Lissitzky's 1920-1921 costume designs for the opera take the form of watercolours, gouaches and pen-and-ink drawings. They are preserved in the Tretiakov Gallery. He used these designs as the basis for a series of coloured lithos, the so-called *Figurinenmappe Sieg über die Sonne* (Figurine portfolio Victory over the Sun) [repr.61-71], which he produced in Germany in 1923 (a copy is in the Gallery). In figurines such as *Neuer* (The New) [repr.70] and *Zankstifter* (Troublemaker) [repr.67], and the design of the whole stage spectacle (the so-called *Schaumaschinerie*) [ill.20], the link with the *Prounen* is immediately apparent. According to the explanatory text in the portfolio, the figurines were conceived as characters in a kind of 'electro-mechanical show' – a stage spectacle based on a synthesis of modern art and the latest technology. However, this project was never realised.

There is a fundamental difference between Kruchenykh's libretto and the visual effect of Lissitzky's figurines. The libretto has to be 'deciphered', but once one has struggled through the obscure combinations of words and deliberate illogicalities, the *Sieg über die Sonne* turns out to be the enthronement of anarchy, the irrational, and the victory over the past. The New:

74

15. L. Lissitzky, 'Suprematism in World Reconstruction', *Unovis* (1920) no. 2. Manuscripts Department of the Tretiakov Gallery, File 76/9, p. 13.

16. "...the leader of the group, Von Züdow, and Dr. Dorner suggested to Lissitzky that the portfolio of lithos should be printed as the annual gift to the members. The printing was to be done in the graphic studio of Leonis and Chapman", S.C. Lissitzkaya-Küppers, op. cit. (note 3), p. 24.
17. E. Kowtun, *Sieg über die Sonne. Materialen*, Berlin 1983, p. 27-52. B. Nobix, 'El Lissitzky und das Theater' in: *El Lissitzky. Retrospective*, 1987-1988, p. 178. A. Shatskich, op. cit. (note 13).

ill. 19
El Lissitzky, Kasimir Malevich,
Suprematism, curtain design, 1918
Photo: M. Guerman, Art of the
October revolution, New York 1979

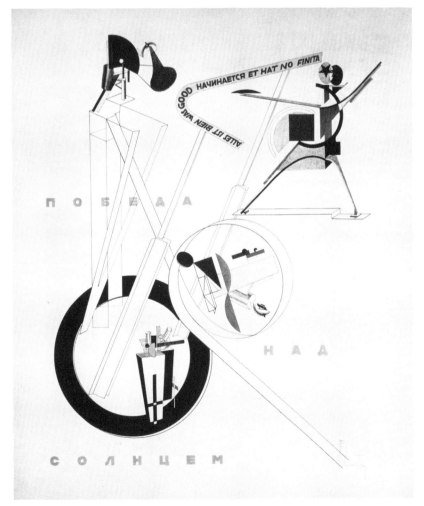

75

ill. 20
Schaumaschinerie
(Show-machinery), 1923
Litho from the Figurinenmappe Sieg
über die Sonne (Figurine portfolio
Victory over the sun).
State Tretiakov Gallery, Moscow

ill. 21
El Lissitzky exhibition, Dresden
1925
Photo: Private archives

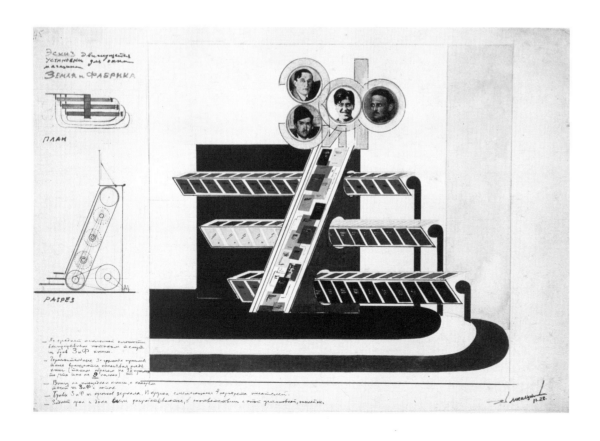

ill. 22
**Rotating bookdisplay for the show-
window of the bookshop of the
publishing-house Land and Factory,**
design, 1928
State Tretiakov Gallery, Moscow

"We have fired at the past." The Cowards: "What! Has nothing survived? Not a trace." The Reader: "Freed from the earth's gravity, we dispose freely of all we possess." Etc. Lissitzky's figurines tell their own story. They are a triumph of vivid local colour, gay rhythms, and clear, meticulous composition. In characters such as *Neuer* and *Globetrotter in der Zeit* (Globetrotter in time) [repr.65] an obvious revolutionary pathos can be felt, and there are even elements of the symbolism of 'reds' and 'whites' (the red star of *Neuer*, the red stripes in the costume of the *Sportsmänner* (Sportsmen) [repr.66]). There are clear stylistic similarities between the figurines and Lissitzky's propaganda work from the time of the Revolution – his posters and murals for holidays.

Vitebsk also played a part in the origins of one of Lissitzky's most interesting architectural constructions – the mobile speaker's rostrum. As stated above, the project was developed by the students in his studio in 1920. In 1924 he made some changes and improvements to it, and added a photograph of Lenin.[18] The model for the *Lenin Tribune* [repr.152] caused a sensation at the *Internationale Ausstellung für Theaterkunst* (International Exhibition of Theatrical Art) in Vienna in 1924, where it was first seen.

Another of his major architectural projects, the *Wolkenbügel*, dates from the same year.[19] The Tretiakov Gallery has fourteen sheets of drawings related to this project, which was later given the more specific title of *Wolkenbügel on the square by the Nikitskii Gate*. [repr.125-133] There is a particularly fine *Proun* and a series of working drawings, plus views of the skyscraper as seen from various points in Moscow: the Kremlin, Kudrinskaya Square and Tverskoy Boulevard. Lissitzky worked on this project with enormous enthusiasm and saw it as a matter of principle. In the article 'A series of skyscrapers for Moscow', which appeared in the *Asnova* (Association of New Architects) bulletin in 1926 [ill.4], he discussed in detail both the technical aspects and the need to erect such buildings in Moscow. The skyscrapers were to be offices rather than housing. The location, determined by the plans for ring-shaped urban development, was to be at the points where the main radial routes crossed the A (Bulvarny) and B (Sadovy) ring roads. In order not to obstruct traffic, the skyscraper stood on three columns which contained the lifts. The horizontal floors were fixed to the central framework by means of consoles. There were to be underground stations beneath the columns. Although it was well thought out, this project for a 'horizontal skyscraper' was never to be realised, and nor were any other of Lissitzky's architectural schemes.[20] They

suffered the same fate as the innovative plans of other outstanding architects of the twenties, e.g. K. Melnikov, N. Chernichov and N. Ladovski.

Other architectural projects in the Tretiakov Gallery confirm Lissitzky's original approach and his urge to be innovative. There are sketches and designs for a textile factory, communal housing, a library cum reading room, etc. One of the most interesting is his design for a watersports club house for the International Red Stadium on the Lenin Hills. He began to work on this in the first months after he returned to Moscow in 1925. Despite persistent illness and the problems of daily life in the city, he worked with great concentration. From the very first sketches one can see how he aimed to reconcile the strictly functional building with the aesthetic effects of its various components. In a letter to S.C. Lissitzkaya-Küppers he wrote, "The basis of this work is a *Proun*, whose design I will draw for you later" [repr.134-135].[21] The contrast and interaction between taut, square forms (the blocks of the main building) and the advanced dynamics of lines like flashes of lightning (the ramps between the terraces) are indeed very close to the principles of the *Prounen*. The same qualities can be found in the designs for interiors: the theatres and cinemas (the so-called *Design for a cinema with two screens*), living quarters and libraries cum reading rooms.

The style of Lissitzky's architectural work has similarities with that of the constructivists, but he took a broader view of architecture. He never simply equated it with the technical aspects of construction. For him the aesthetic effect of a building always remained the most important criterion.

Perhaps this was one of the reasons for his success as a designer of large-scale exhibitions. He undoubtedly pioneered this art form. His innovative ideas, imagination and keen insight were best seen in the major international exhibitions held in Cologne, Dresden, Berlin and Stuttgart in the twenties [ill.21]. The design of the Soviet pavilions (of which the one at the *Pressa* exhibition in Cologne was the best) was discussed at length in newspapers and magazines and brought Lissitzky international recognition [repr.155-158].

The Tretiakov Gallery has examples of his work as a designer in many fields, from the initial sketches for a room with *Prounen* at his solo exhibition in Berlin in 1923 to his designs for an international exhibition which was to have been held in Belgrade in 1941. His talents were evident not only in large-scale projects but also in discoveries on a smaller scale. His design for a book-

18. From Lissitzky's letter of 16 May 1924: "I got a series of designs from the students I worked with in the studios at Vitebsk. From them I chose the project for a tribune from which Lenin speaks, and carried out the work for the book by A. Behne, *Tselevoye stroïtelstvo* (Functional construction). I think it's a pity that it's only to be published now, since it was done in 1920, when Tatlin was working on his tower and there were not yet any constructivist stage sets." S.C. Lissitzkaya-Küppers, op. cit. (note 3), p. 47.

19. From letters written by Lissitzky in 1924: "Work proceeds on my 'celestial flat-iron' (the 'horizontal skyscraper', M.N.), but I still have to do a lot to the foundations." "It stands on three legs and wobbles. Isn't that crazy?" S.C. Lissitzkaya-Küppers, op. cit. (note 3), p. 52, 55.
20. The present high-rise buildings stand where the radial streets intersect the B ring road: at Krasnye Vorota (Red Gate), on Ploshchad Vosstaniya (Revolution Square) and on Smolenskaya-Sennaya Square.

21. From a letter written by Lissitzky in 1925: "I have been working hard. I'm dead beat. I can't sleep. (...) The whole complex is located on the steep bank. Three large red horizontal lines, they are the terraces; a lightning-shaped zigzag of diagonals, that's the curve of the ramp joining the lower and upper terraces. At the bottom right is the main hall. The roofs can be used as stands for the spectators during regattas." S.C. Lissitzkaya-Küppers, op. cit. (note 3), p. 63.

display for the bookshop of the *Land and Factory* publishing house, for example, makes use of the effect created by the contrast between moving elements and fixed objects [ill.22].

In 1935 Lissitzky was appointed chief artist for the *All Union Agricultural Exhibition*. "But," writes S.C. Lissitzkaya-Küppers, "he felt obliged to abandon this project because his ideas aroused strong opposition from those in charge, and arguing with them would serve no purpose."[22] Only the plans for the main pavilion have survived. The material in the Gallery shows the enormous amount of work he carried out. He completed the plans for the pavilion, the various rooms and stands, and did designs for the ceilings, lighting, decorative sculpture, metal fences and many other things. In several of these drawings one can see traces of the inventivity which was so characteristic of his earliest work. But in general these designs bear no comparison to his previous successes. In the soullessly symmetrical overall concept and the meticulously drawn details, it is almost impossible to recognise the old Lissitzky of daring, revolutionary architectural ideas and brilliantly original expressive solutions. But even this design, although icily correct and balanced, was rejected. Tasteless extravagance and ostentation became the chief characteristics of exhibition buildings.

There is another sad aspect to Lissitzky's designs for the agricultural exhibition, since yet again this was a case of long, hard preparation for a project which was never to be realised. It provides depressing evidence of how the creative individuality of a great artist could be broken and deformed under the pressure of the exceptionally difficult social and cultural situation in our country in the second half of the thirties.[23]

Lissitzky's last designs were to be for the *Belgrade International Exhibition*. He began work in the autumn of 1940. But the exhibition material made to his designs was barely ready for shipping when German troops occupied Belgrade.

As S.C. Lissitzkaya-Küppers wrote, "The exhibition was cancelled because of the war". A few sheets in the Gallery's collection give us some idea of his plans. As already mentioned, the last work of the dying artist consisted of two anti-fascist posters. The designs for these are also in the Gallery's collection.

'Books have their fate'. Rephrasing this old Russian adage, one might say that works of art have their fate too. As early as the twenties many of Lissitzky's works shown in solo exhibitions in Europe ended up in foreign collections. The works which the artist himself had kept became part of the Tretiakov Gallery's collection. Some of these are finished and ready for exhibition, but the larger part consists of all kinds of preparatory material such as studies and sketches. These were often not intended to be seen by the public. This applies in particular to the *Prounen* but also to the architectural and design projects. The Gallery's collection also includes works from the second half of the thirties which have received little attention in the literature.[24] The combination of these works with those from other periods allows us to view the course of his career from an unusual angle. We then see his oeuvre not as a series of masterpieces, which are always rather static when seen out of context, but as a complex development within the dynamics of various plans and conflicting results and achievements at different times.

The abundance of preparatory material together with the sharp contrast between Lissitzky's best work and what he produced in the late thirties inevitably compels us to consider the origins of each work and the fate of the artist – and perhaps, in a broader sense, the fate of the movement of which he was such a brilliant representative. These are very complex issues on which there is unlikely to be unanimity.

There can be no doubt that the deformation of Lissitzky's art in his later works and their obviously lower standard was largely determined by the extremely difficult situation caused by the totalitarian regime which had established itself in our country. But it must also be said that there were signs of a crisis among other members of the avant-garde at that time – artists working under entirely different political, social and cultural conditions. The rationalism that is so characteristic of the avant-garde and the obsession with technological and social utopias evidently proved to be of little value in the light of the terrible conflicts in the real world of the twentieth century. In the work of Lissitzky, as in that of all other members of the Russian avant-garde, the clash with this reality took a particularly severe and sometimes tragic form.

The Russian public is only beginning to become acquainted with the world of the avant-garde of the early twentieth century. Thorough study and painstaking research into this world will be required to explain all its peculiarities, possibilities, losses and achievements.

The organizers of this centenary exhibition of Lissitzky's work hope that it will not only show the oeuvre of one of the outstanding members of the avant-garde, but also bring about a deeper understanding of this fascinating period in the history of art, both in the Soviet Union and elsewhere.

78

22. Ibidem, p. 96.
23. Apart from in the project for the agricultural exhibition, this can also be seen in the covers for film scenarios and the designs for books by Mayakovsky.

24. A few works by Lissitzky are in the Bakrushin Theatre Museum (Central State Museum of Theatre) in Moscow, and in the V.V. Mayakovsky State Museum in Tashkent in the State Museum of Art and in several private collections.

The Lissitzky collection at the Van Abbemuseum

Henk Puts

In 1965 Jean Leering, who was then director of the Van Abbemuseum in Eindhoven, came across a portfolio with eighty-five works on paper by El Lissitzky at the house of Mrs. Vordemberge-Leda in Stuttgart; two of his works hung on the wall in her home. In addition to drawings, gouaches and lithographs, this collection comprised a series of sketches, designs, working sketches and proofs which, as a whole, clearly depicted the developmental process of Lissitzky's work. It gave an idea as to the nature of Lissitzky's work up to 1923, particularly the last two of these years, which he spent in Germany. These eighty-five works are now part of the collection of the Van Abbemuseum.

Leering became interested in the artist and architect Lissitzky while studying in Delft; he wanted to make a retrospective exhibition of his work, which was still relatively unknown at that time. Various attempts to organize an exhibition failed, but when Leering discovered the Vordemberge-Leda collection it seemed to become possible. He had hitherto been able to acquire a copy of the *Figurinenmappe Sieg über die Sonne* (Figurine Portfolio Victory over the Sun) [repr.61-71] for the museum and was continuing his search for works by El Lissitzky; a great many letters in the archives of the Van Abbemuseum are evidence of this. Leering came in touch with many who knew Lissitzky, such as Zadkine, Berlewi and Erenburg, and with museums and collectors.

There were others who had an interest in Lissitzky. The typographic designer Jan Tschichold had been interested in Lissitzky's work since 1925 and had written various articles about him.[1] In 1965 he was working on a small monograph on Lissitzky which was to come out in 1971.[2] In Germany in 1958, Horst Richter had published a book about the *Figurinenmappe* in a limited edition.[3] Ella Winter had described, in several articles, how she purchased a number of works from Sophie Lissitzky while working as a war correspondent in Moscow.[4]

In the Soviet Union, too, there were still people who showed an interest in Lissitzky, despite the government policy which prescribed Socialist Realism. The Russian art historian Nikolai Chardzhiev had made a small exhibition at the Mayakovsky Museum in Moscow in 1960, dedicated to Lissitzky as the designer of two volumes of poetry by Mayakovsky[5]; in subsequent years he published two articles about him and one by Lissitzky himself in Russian magazines.[6] He had contact with Sophie Lissitzky-Küppers, the widow of El Lissitzky, who, as a German, had been transferred to Siberia during the war and had resided in Novosibirsk. All of Lissitzky's work, which he had left to her, was in turn donated to the Russian government. The greater part of this ended up at the Tretiakov Gallery in Moscow; documents and small drawings were housed in the State Archives for Literature and Art in Moscow.

When Jean Leering came into touch with Sophie Lissitzky, she was working on a book about El Lissitzky that was to be published in Dresden in 1967; this contact made it possible for a number of reproductions of works from the Vordemberge-Leda collection to be included in the book, such as the drawings from Lissitzky's student years in Darmstadt. No other works from this period are known to exist. The book by Sophie Lissitzky-Küppers became the most extensive source of information on Lissitzky to date.[7]

In addition to the drawings and lithographs from the Vordemberge-Leda collection, Leering nevertheless succeeded in bringing together a large number of paintings, typographic designs and other work from Europe and the United States; in December 1965 the exhibition in the Van Abbemuseum became a reality. The exhibition and catalogue[8] provided a complete survey of the many facets of Lissitzky's work, photography and architecture included. With the exception of a photograph of a design for the *Pressa* pavilion, only documentation pertaining to Lissitzky's later exhibition designs was missing. There were,

1. For example, the article 'über el lissitzky', for which he did the typographic design, *Imprimatur* 3 (1932), p.97-112.
2. Jan Tschichold, *Werkte und Aufsätze von El Lissitzky (1890-1941)*, Berlin 1971.
3. Horst Richter, *El Lissitzky. Sieg über die Sonne. Zur Kunst des Konstruktivismus*, Cologne 1958.
4. Ella Winter, 'Looking for Lissitzky', *The New Statesman* 54 (1957) no. 2, p.562-563; and 'Lissitzky: A Revolutionary Out of Favor', *Art News* 57 (April 1958) no. 2, p.28-64.
5. This exhibition took place on November 18 and 19, 1960.
6. Nikolai Chardzhiev, 'Pamjati Chudozhnika Lisitskogo', *Dekorativnoe iskusstvo SSSR* (1961) no. 2, p.29-31; and 'El Lisitskij - Konstruktor knigi', *Iskusstvo knigi* (1962) no. 3, p.145-161; and from Lissitzky 'Knigi s totsjki zrenya zritelnogo vospryatya - vizualnaya kniga', *Iskusstvo knigi* (1962) no. 3, p.163-168 (The Russian translation of 'Unser Buch').
7. Sophie Lissitzky-Küppers, *El Lissitzky, Maler, Architekt, Typograf, Fotograf, Erinnerungen, Briefe, Schriften*, Dresden 1967.
8. *El Lissitzky*. Exhibition catalogue Municipal Van Abbemuseum, Eindhoven; Kunstmuseum Basel; Kestner Gesellschaft, Hanover 1965-1966.

however, designs for the *Abstraktes Kabinett* (The abstract cabinet); Lissitzky's *Prounenraum* (Proun Room) was reconstructed specifically for the exhibition.

This reconstruction was possible due to the fact that the *Prounenraum* had been well documented by Lissitzky himself. Aside from numerous designs which are now in the Tretiakov Gallery and several photographs, we also know of a painting with the composition of the rear wall, *Proun GBA* [repr.31], a lithograph of the relief on the left wall [repr.55.6] and a lithograph which shows the wall in a fold-out form [repr.55.7]. Since the height of the door in this lithograph measures 10.5 cm, and that of a standard door is 210 cm, Jean Leering concluded that the lithograph had to be carried out on a 1:20 scale, which made an excellent point of departure for the reconstruction.

All eighty-five works from the Vordemberge-Leda collection were restored, framed, dated and catalogued for the exhibition at the Van Abbemuseum; the process took months. The works on paper looked neglected, with folded and wrinkled edges. Dating was a considerable problem, due to the lack of insight on the course of Lissitzky's development.

The exhibition made an important contribution to the knowledge on Lissitzky and gave rise to a substantial series of publications in the years to follow.

After the close of the exhibition, which was taken over by the Kunstmuseum in Basel and the Kestner Gesellschaft in Hanover, the collection remained on loan at the Van Abbemuseum. In 1968 Mrs. Vordemberge-Leda suddenly decided, however, to sell the entire Lissitzky collection and had received two offers of 100,000 dollars from individuals. The Van Abbemuseum had a right to match this offer, but 100,000 dollars, which was then 360,000 guilders, was far beyond the museum's budget. For a time, it looked as though the Lissitzky collection would be taken from the Van Abbemuseum, but soon the province and a private individual agreed to loan a total of 300,000 guilders. The mayor and aldermen of the city of Eindhoven, proprietors of the museum, managed to reach an agreement shortly thereafter with the *Coöperatieve Centrale Boerenleenbank,* which extended a long-term, low-interest loan for the entire sum, this being the fulfillment of a promise made at the opening of the bank's new office building in Eindhoven that a gift would be given to the municipality.

The purchase, however, still had to be approved by the city council, and this posed problems, as there were opponents who believed that the collection was second-rate and would be of little significance for art history; Lissitzky himself was to have attached no importance to the works and left them behind in his studio. After a long and bitter debate, the city council nonetheless voted, twenty-four to fourteen, in favour of the purchase. With this purchase the Van Abbemuseum had acquired, along with the collection in the Tretiakov Gallery, one of the most important collections of Lissitzky's work. Other fine but smaller public collections can now be found at the Busch-Reisinger Museum in Cambridge, Massachusetts, at the Sprengelmuseum in Hannover[9] and at Galerie Moritzburg in Halle.[10] The collections of E. Estorick in London and of George Costakis, who recently died, also contain a great deal of work by Lissitzky.

It became worthwhile to add to the collection at the Van Abbemuseum. But the sizeable encroachment upon the budget made it difficult to purchase a work on canvas or on panel; paintings therefore went to higher bidders. Documentary material and publications designed by Lissitzky were sought; a number of letters, books and photographs were purchased from J.M.A. Oud-Dinaux, widow of the architect J.J.P. Oud, with whom Lissitzky had corresponded for several years. Among these documents were a photograph of the painting *Round Proun* [ill.6], which Lissitzky had made in 1926 for the exhibition space in Dresden and which was later lost, the book *Suprematicheskii skaz pro dva kvadrata v 6ti postroikakh* (Suprematist story of two squares in 6 constructions) [repr.86], the catalogue of the *Erste Russische Kunstausstellung* (First Russian Art Exhibition) in Amsterdam [repr.78], *Dlia Golosa* (For the voice) [repr.79-80] which Lissitzky had given to Oud personally, the *Nasci-heft* issue of *Merz* [repr.93], *Die Kunstismen* [repr.96] and the *Asnova* Bulletin [ill.4] in which Lissitzky had published the plans for the *Wolkenbügel.* Just before his departure from Switzerland to Moscow, Lissitzky wrote the following to Oud: "As a salutation, I'm sending along a few photographs of a project that I was able to finish this year."[11] These photographs are now at the Van Abbemuseum; they were taken in 1925 from Lissitzky's designs, some of which no longer exist.

The example of the photographic self-portrait *The Constructor* [repr.117], now at the Van Abbemuseum, was discovered by Jean Leering in 1972 in the estate of Theo van Doesburg. In view of Lissitzky's autograph on the back, "For my colleague Syrkus in memory of our student days, El Lissitzky anno 1926 August"[12], Lissitzky gave this self-portrait to the Polish architect Szymon Syrkus, a fellow student of Lissitzky at the Polytechnic

9. Alexander Dorner, who had made an exhibition of Lissitzky's work in the Kestner Gesellschaft in 1923, had already begun to acquire work by Lissitzky as director of the Provinzialmuseum in Hanover. This collection was, however, largely confiscated by the Nazis. A newly assembled collection of paintings, drawings and graphic work can now be found at the Sprengelmuseum in Hanover; today the museum also houses a reconstruction of the *Abstraktes Kabinett*.
10. Galerie Moritzburg in Halle (Saale) had already purchased a series of works by Lissitzky in 1929; all but one of these was able to be preserved. For information on the fate of this collection, see: *Im Kampf um die moderne Kunst. Das Schicksal einer Sammlung in der 1. Hälfte des 20. Jahrhunderts.* Exhibition catalo-

gue Staatliche Galerie Moritzburg, Halle 1985.
11. Letter to Oud 14-5-1925, Van Abbemuseum archives.
12. Lissitzky wrote the inscription in Russian: Kollege Syrkusu v pamyati studentsyjestva.

Institute of Riga, which had been evacuated to Moscow during World War I. How and when this self-portrait left the possession of Szymon Syrkus and came into the hands of Theo and Nelly van Doesburg is not known. Lissitzky and Van Doesburg had already fallen out with each other long before.

The basis of the collection, the eighty-five works from the collection of Mrs. Vordemberge-Leda, was indeed once abandoned by Lissitzky in his studio but by no means because he regarded it as being unimportant, as opponents to the acquisition had claimed. In 1923 Lissitzky worked for a time in a studio set up for him at the Kestner Gesellschaft, until tuberculosis became manifest at the end of that year, with high fever and pneumonia, and the doctor forbade him to work. At the beginning of 1924 Lissitzky set off to Switzerland for a cure and left his work behind. The studio at the Kestner Gesellschaft was later occupied by Friedrich Vordemberge-Gildewart, who worked there from 1924 to 1930. It was with his widow, Mrs. Vordemberge-Leda, that Jean Leering found the work in 1965; she regarded the collection as a gift.
That so much preparatory work for the *Figurinenmappe* was left behind in the studio is not surprising; it is one of the last projects on which Lissitzky worked before becoming ill at the end of 1923. Lissitzky had to abandon at least nine of these works earlier, in 1914, when he left Darmstadt for Russia after the outbreak of World War I. It was not until 1923 that he visited the city again, shortly before his move into the studio at the Kestner Gesellschaft. His former landlady had kept an assortment of his belongings, including notes from his time as a student; on discovering these things, he wrote the following to Sophie Küppers: "I've found all of my works with a maid from the school. Drawings, watercolours 1909-1913. I'd like to save a few of these."[13] These few works are the only early works that are now known; they can be found in the collection of the Van Abbemuseum. [repr.1-5]

13. Sophie Lissitzky-Küppers, *El Lissitzky. Life, Letters, Texts,* London 1980 (second edition), p.35.

Travel sketches and Book illustrations

1
The Holy Trinity church in Vitebsk,
1910
30.0 x 37.7 cm

2
Tower of the fortress in Smolensk,
1910
24.0 x 32.0 cm

4
Ravenna, 1913
31.8 x 23.7 cm

3
Venice, 1913
26.6 x 34.5 cm

5
Italian town, 1913
24.0 x 32.4 cm

TRAVEL SKETCHES

6.1-4
Khad Gadya (One billy goat), 1917
30.0 x 26.0 cm

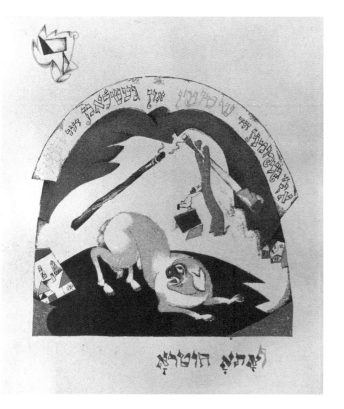

7.1-4
Khad Gadya (One billy goat), 1919
28.0 x 26.0 cm

6.5
Khad Gadya (One billy goat), 1917
30.0 x 26.0 cm

7.5
Khad Gadya (One billy goat), 1919
28.0 x 26.0 cm

8
M. Broderson, **Sikhes Khulin. A Prager Legende** (An everyday conversation. A legend of Prague), 1917
Scroll of 22.1 x 400.13 cm

9.1-3
R. Kipling, **Elfandl** (The little
elephant), 1922
28.7 x 27.5 cm

10.1-3
Vaysrusische folkmayses
(Belorussian folk tales), 1919/22
23.5 x 21.5 cm

BOOK ILLUSTRATIONS

11
Tatlin working on the Monument,
1921/22
29.2 x 22.9 cm

12
Footballer, 1922
33.0 x 24.3 cm

BOOK ILLUSTRATIONS

Prounen

13
Proun portfolio, cover design, 1920
49.7 x 38.0 cm

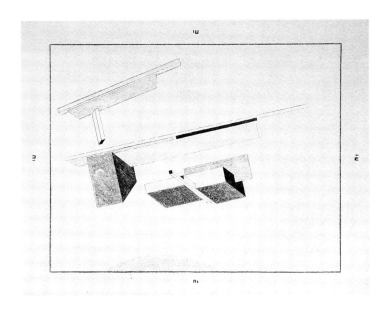

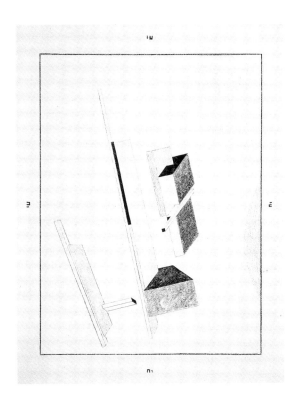

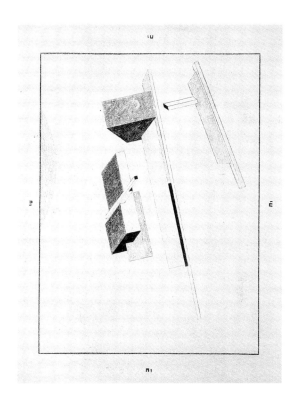

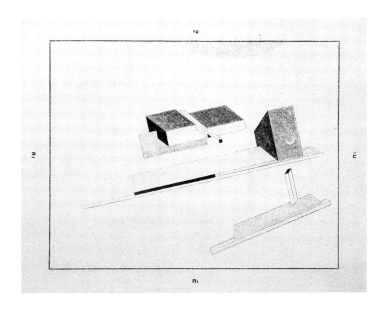

14
Proun 1, ca. 1919/20
25.6 x 27.5 cm

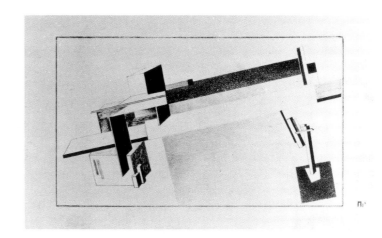

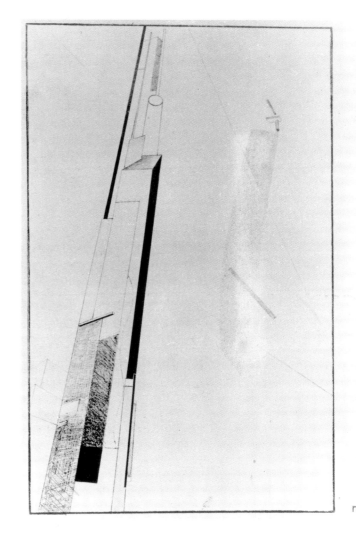

15
Proun 1A, Bridge, ca. 1919/20
17.0 x 30.0 cm

16
Proun 2C, ca. 1919/20
29.9 x 20.0 cm

18
Proun 2D, ca. 1919/20
35.7 x 22.5 cm

17
Proun 3A, ca. 1919/20
27.6 x 26.4 cm

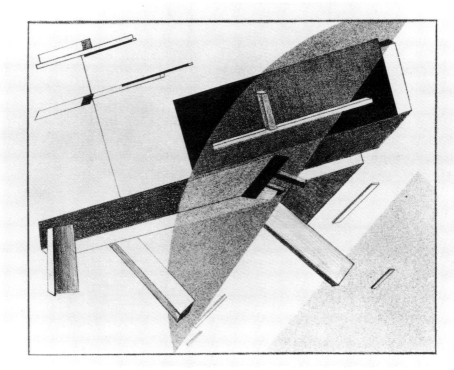

19
Proun 2B, ca. 1919/20
20.2 x 26.2 cm

20
Proun 1D, ca. 1919/20
21.5 x 26.9 cm

PROUNEN

21
Proun 1E, Town, ca. 1919/20
22.6 x 27.5 cm

22
Proun 1C, ca. 1919/20
23.2 x 23.3 cm

23
Proun 5A, ca. 1919/20
27.5 x 26.9 cm

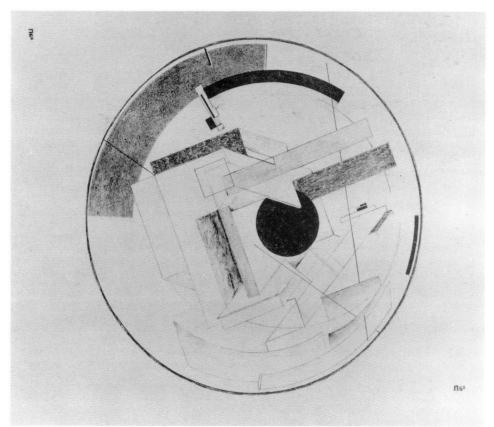

24
Proun 6B, ca. 1919/20
24.8 cm Ø

25
Proun P23, Würfel mit Hyperbel,
1919
52.0 x 77.0 cm

26
Proun 99, 1925
129.0 x 99.1 cm

27
Proun 12E, 1923
57.1 x 42.5 cm

28
Untitled, ca. 1920
73.5 x 51.5 cm

29
Proun 30T, 1920
50.0 x 62.0 cm

30
Proun 2C, ca. 1920
60.0 x 40.0 cm

31
Proun G.B.A., ca. 1923
77.0 x 82.0 cm

32
Proun R.V.N.2, 1923
99.0 x 99.0 cm

PROUNEN

33
Proun G7, 1923
77.0 x 62.0 cm

34
Proun G7, study, ca. 1922
47.9 x 39.0 cm

35
Proun G7, study, ca. 1922/23
78.2 x 62.7 cm

111

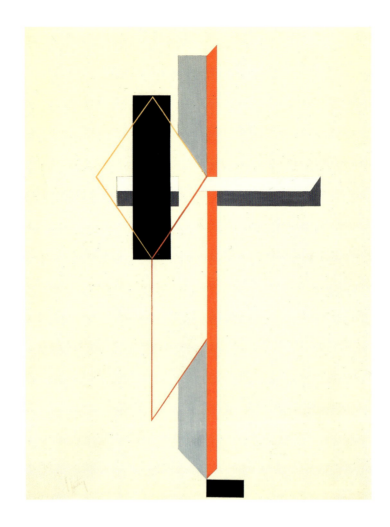

36
Proun, ca. 1922
50.2 x 40.0 cm

37
Proun, ca. 1923
45.1 x 41.5 cm

38
Proun, ca. 1923
35.9 x 27.5 cm

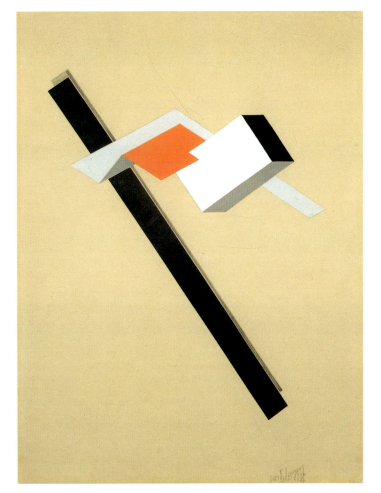

39
Proun GK, 1922/23
66.0 x 50.2 cm

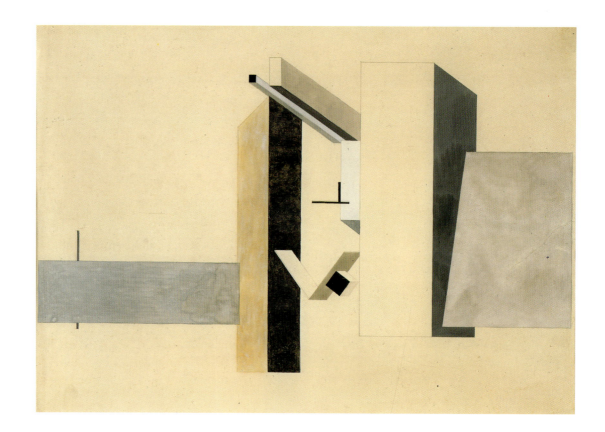

40
Proun, ca. 1919/23
49.0 x 68.0 cm

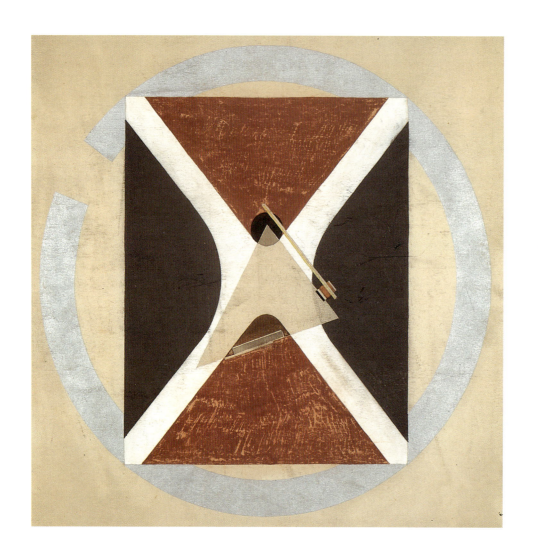

41
Proun 43, ca. 1922
66.8 x 49.0 cm

114

42
Proun, ca. 1921/23
46.5 x 39.0 cm

43
Proun, ca. 1922
24.0 x 22.0 cm

44
Gekläbtes Schwarzes, Proun 84,
1923/24
45.6 x 45.3 cm

45
Proun, ca. 1922/23
52.0 x 50.0 cm

PROUNEN

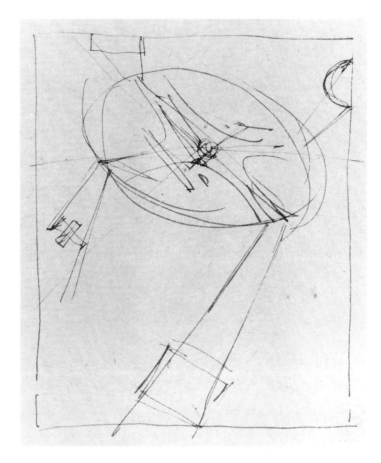

46
Proun G7, study, ca. 1919/20
13.1 x 8.9 cm

47
Proun, study, 1920/23
40.3 x 39.0 cm

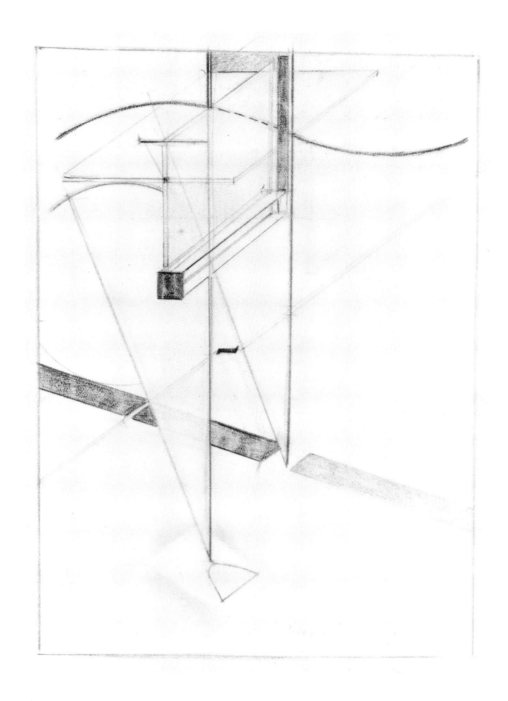

48
Proun LN 31, study Karton gross,
1922
21.7 x 16.0 cm

49
Proun, ca. 1924
45.5 x 45.5 cm

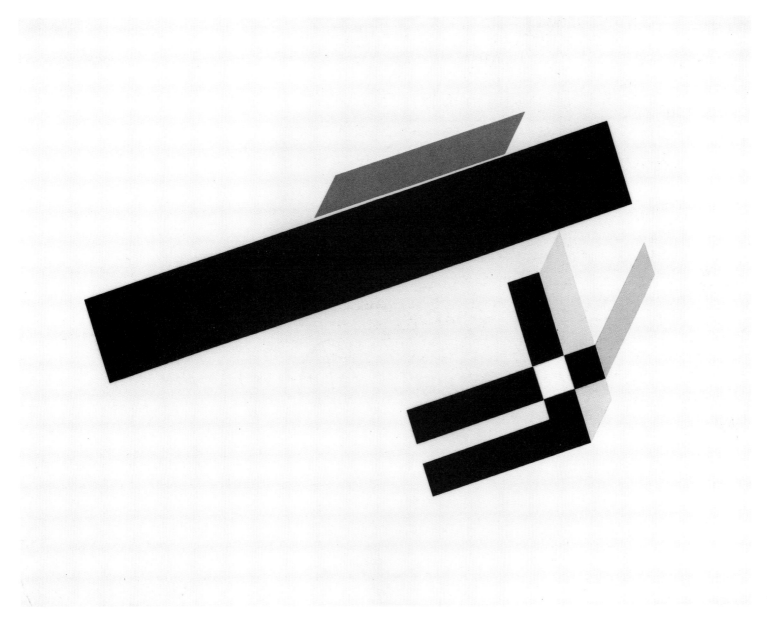

50
Proun 88, ca. 1923
49.9 x 64.7 cm

51
Kleiner grauer Karton, Proun 30,
ca. 1920
49.5 x 39.5 cm

52
Kylmansegg, Proun 1D, 1919
96.0 x 71.5 cm

53
Proun, ca. 1924
24.7 x 21.1 cm

54
Konischer, Proun 93, ca. 1923
49.9 x 49.7 cm

55.0
1° Kestnermappe Proun (First
Kestner portfolio Proun), cover,
1923
60.6 x 44.5 cm

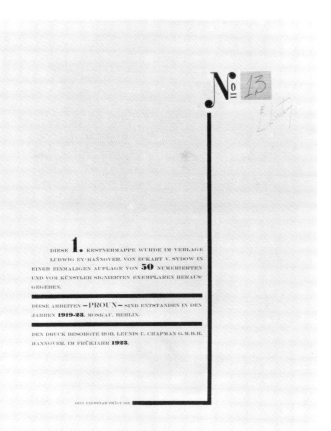

55.1
1° Kestnermappe Proun (First
Kestner portfolio Proun), title-page,
1923
59.8 x 44.0 cm

55.2
1° Kestnermappe Proun, (First
Kestner portfolio Proun), print nr.1,
1923
59.8 x 44.0 cm

PROUNEN

55.3
1° Kestnermappe Proun, (First
Kestner portfolio Proun), print nr.2,
1923
59.8 x 44.0 cm

55.4
1° Kestnermappe Proun, (First
Kestner portfolio Proun), print nr.3,
1923
64.0 x 49.0 cm

55.5
1° Kestnermappe Proun, (First
Kestner portfolio Proun), print nr.4,
1923
64.0 x 49.0 cm

55.6
1° Kestnermappe Proun, (First
Kestner portfolio Proun), print nr.5,
1923
59.8 x 44.0 cm

PROUNEN

55.7
1° Kestnermappe Proun, (First
Kestner portfolio Proun), print nr.6,
Proun Room, 1923
59.8 x 44.0 cm

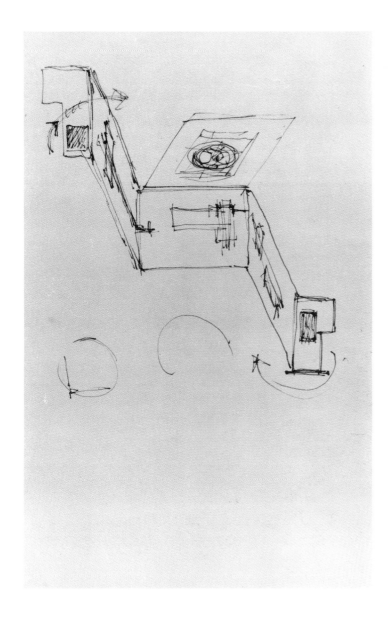

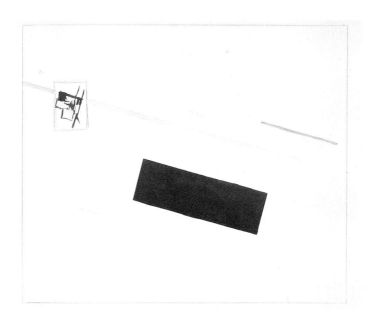

57
Prounenraum (Proun Room), design
side-wall, 1923
34.5 x 47.4 cm

56
Prounenraum (Proun Room), 1923
19.9 x 12.5 cm

58
Proun G.B.A., study, 1923
34.5 x 50.5 cm

PROUNEN

59
Prounenraum (Proun Room), 1923

60
Prounenraum (Proun Room),
reconstruction 1965, 1923
300.0 x 300.0 x 260.0 cm

Figurinen

61
**Figurinenmappe Sieg über die
Sonne** (Figurine portfolio Victory
over the sun), cover, 1920/21
49.7 x 38.0 cm

ЧТЕЦ

62
Ansager, 1920/21
49.4 x 37.9 cm

БУДЕТЛЯНСКИЙ СИЛАЧ

63
Posten, 1920/21
49.4 x 37.9 cm

64
Ängstliche, 1920/21
49.4 x 37.9 cm

ПУТЕШЕСТВЕННИК ПО ВСЕМ ВЕКАМ

65
Globetrotter in der Zeit, 1920/21
49.4 x 37.9 cm

СПОРТСМЕНЫ

66
Sportsmänner, 1920/21
49.4 x 37.9 cm

ЗАБИЯКА

67
Zankstifter, 1920/21
49.4 x 37.9 cm

68
Alter, 1920/21
49.4 x 37.9 cm

69
Totengräber, 1920/21
49.4 x 37.9 cm

новый

70
Neuer, 1920/21
49.4 x 37.9 cm

71
System des Theaters, 1920/21
49.4 x 37.9 cm

Typographic designs

72
**Communicationworkers, remember
the year 1905,** 1919/20
14.5 x 22.8 cm

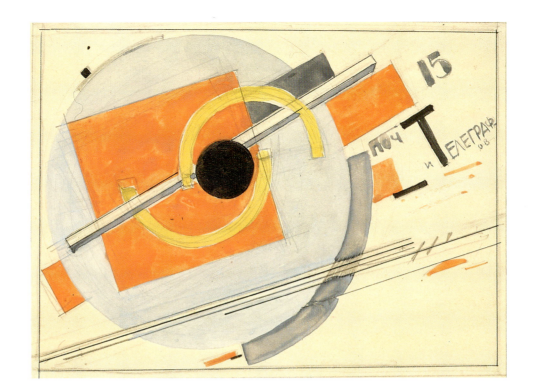

73
**Communicationworkers, remember
the year 1905,** 1919/20
18.2 x 22.9 cm

74
**The factory workbenches await
you,** 1919

75
Untitled, suprematist construction,
ca. 1920
30.0 x 21.0 cm

76
Beat the whites with the red wedge,
reprint 1966, 1919/20
48.5 x 69.2 cm

TYPOGRAPHIC DESIGNS

77
1° Russische Kunstausstellung,
Galerie van Diemen Berlin, cover
design, 1922
27.0 x 19.0 cm

78
1° Russische Kunstausstellung,
Stedelijk Museum Amsterdam,
catalogue, 1923
22.7 x 14.7 cm

79
Vladimir Mayakovsky, **Dlia Golosa**
(For the Voice), cover, 1923
19.0 x 13.5 cm

80
Vladimir Mayakovsky, **Dlia Golosa**
(For the Voice), 1923
19.0 x 13.5 cm

81
Ravvi (Rabbi), cover proof, 1922
20.1 x 28.3 cm

82
Ilia Erenburg, **Shest povestei o
legkikh kontsakh** (Six stories with an
easy ending), 1922
20.2 x 13.8 cm

83
MA, 1922
27.0 x 19.8 cm

84
Wendingen, cover design, 1922
17.2 x 25.8 cm

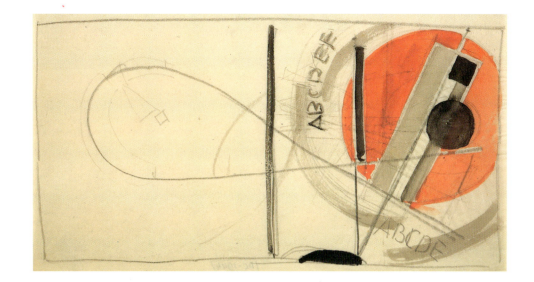

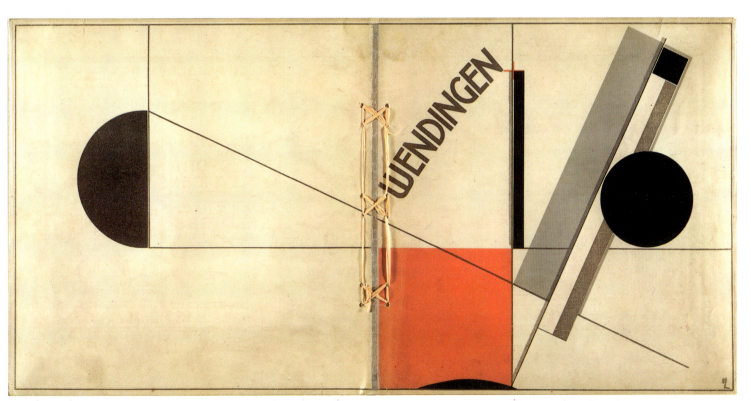

85
Wendingen, cover, 1922
33.0 x 66.5 cm

TYPOGRAPHIC DESIGNS

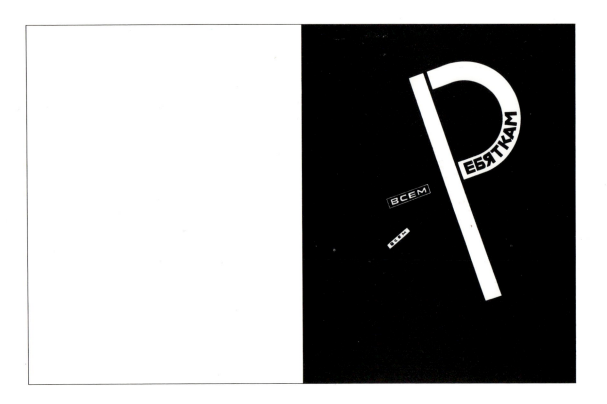

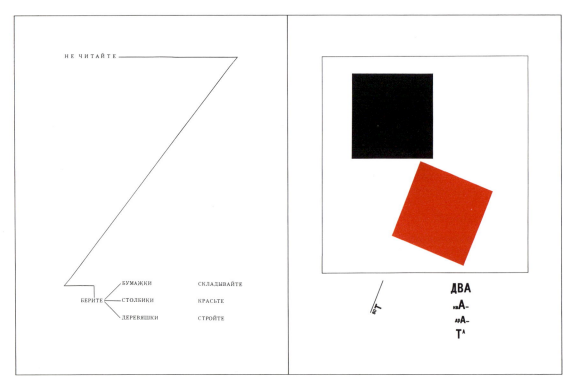

86.1-2
Suprematicheskii skaz pro dva
kvadrata v 6ti postroikakh
(Suprematist story of two squares in
6 constructions), 1922
28.0 x 22.0 cm

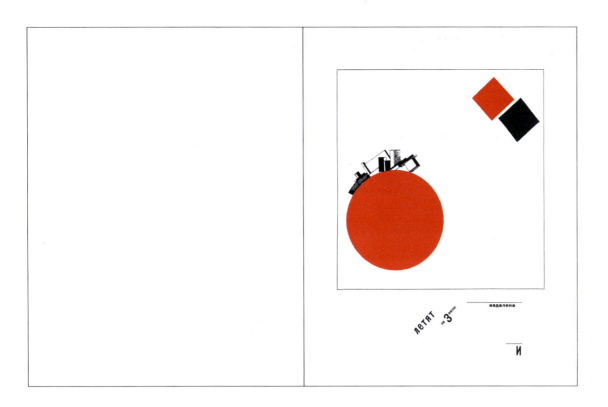

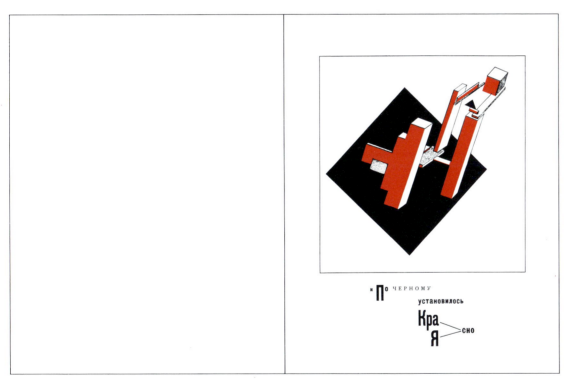

86.3-4
**Suprematicheskii skaz pro dva
kvadrata v 6ti postroikakh**
(Suprematist story of two squares in
6 constructions), 1922
28.0 x 22.0 cm

87
Broom, N 3, June, V.2, cover design,
1922
26.0 x 18.5 cm

88
Broom, No.3, Vol.5, cover design,
1923
27.5 x 20.8 cm

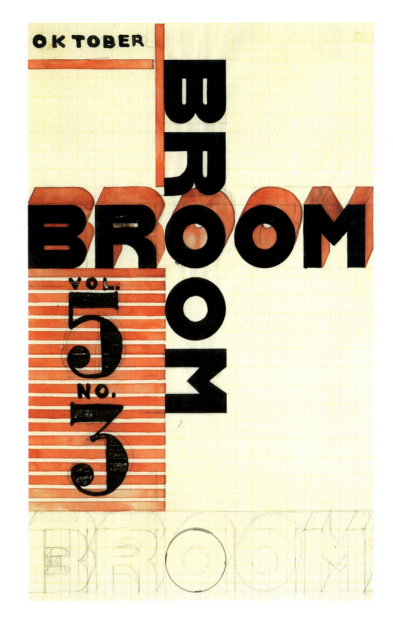

90
Broom, No.3, Oktober, Vol.5, cover design, 1923
36.2 x 22.7 cm

89
Broom, N 3, June, V.2, cover design, 1922
26.2 x 20.5 cm

91
Veshch - Gegenstand - Objet, N 1,
February, cover design, 1922
30.7 x 22.5 cm

92
Veshch - Gegenstand - Objet, cover
proof, 1922
45.1 x 34.4 cm

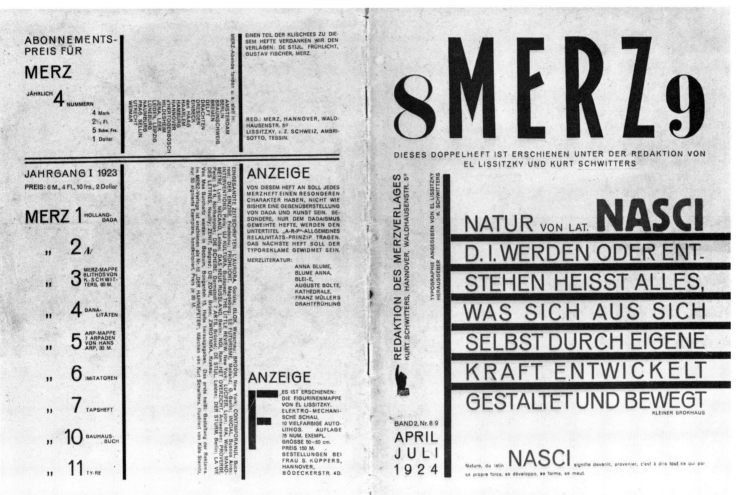

93
Merz, Band 2, Nr.8/9, April Juli,
Nasci, 1924
30.5 x 23.3 cm

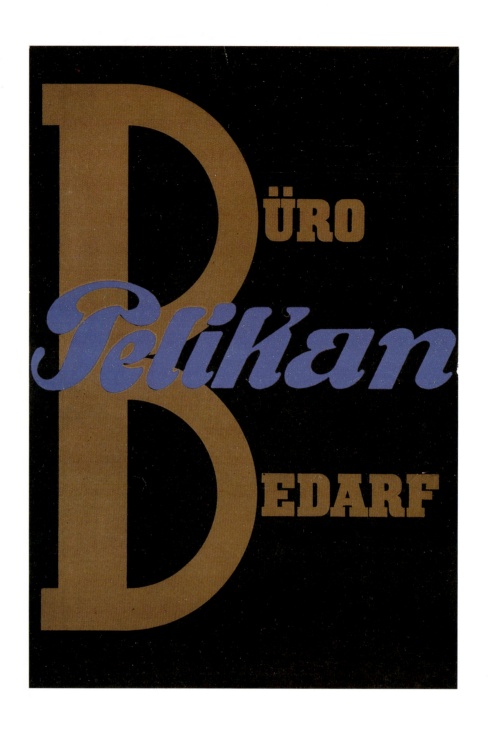

94
Pelikan Bürobedarf, 1924
24.0 x 17.0 cm

95
Pelikan Kohlenpapier,
advertisement, 1925
14.8 x 11.5 cm

96.0
El Lissitzky, Hans Arp, **Die Kunstismen. Les Ismes de l'Art. The Isms of Art, 1924-1914,** cover, 1925
26.3 x 20.6 cm

96.1-2
El Lissitzky, Hans Arp, **Die Kunstismen. Les Ismes de l'Art. The Isms of Art, 1924-1914,** 1925
26.3 x 20.6 cm

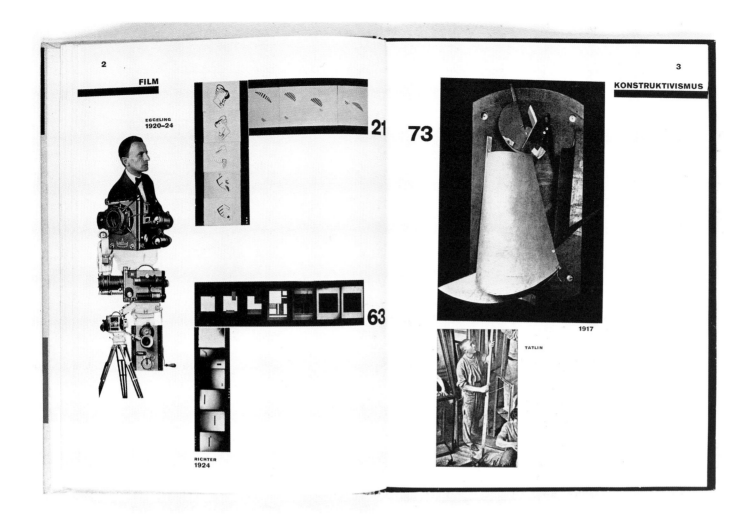

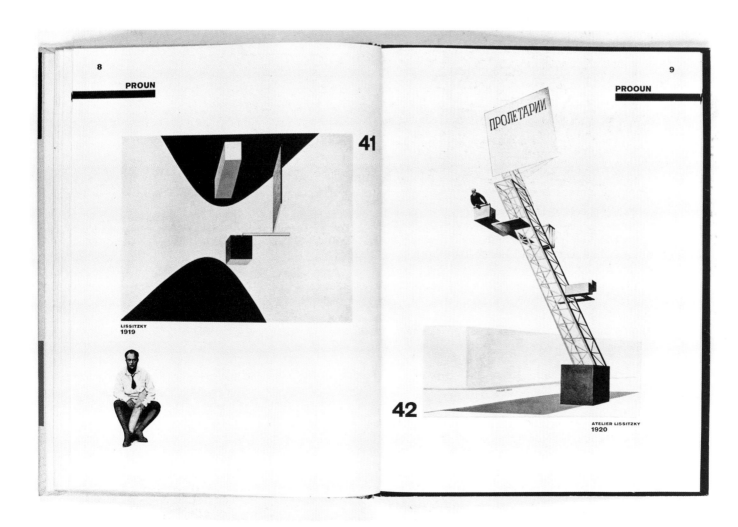

165

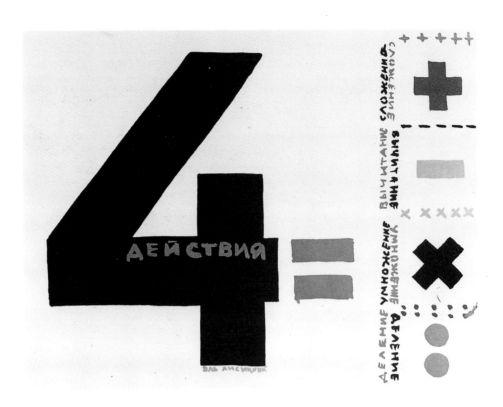

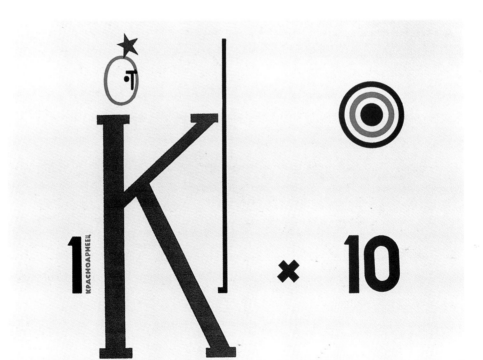

97.1-2
Die vier Grundrechnungsarten (The four arithmetical functions), reprint, 1976
25.0 x 32.5 cm

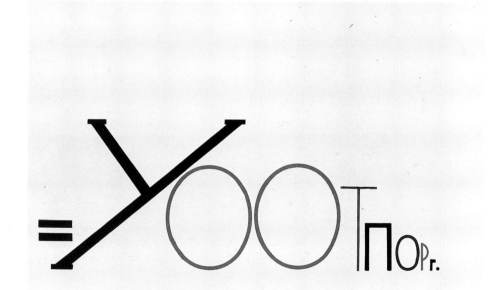

97.3-4
Die vier Grundrechnungsarten (The four arithmetical functions), reprint, 1976
25.0 x 32.5 cm

167

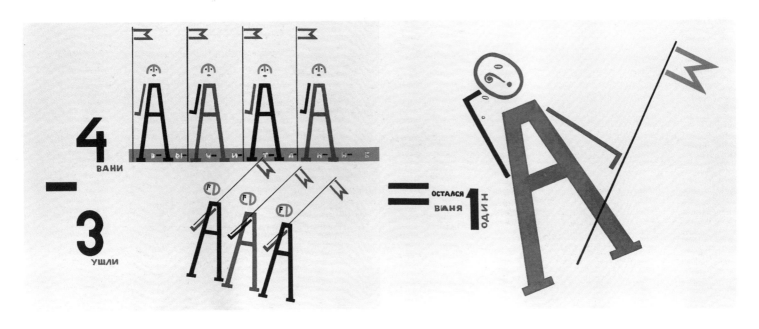

97.5-6
Die vier Grundrechnungsarten (The four arithmetical functions), reprint, 1976
25.0 x 32.5 cm

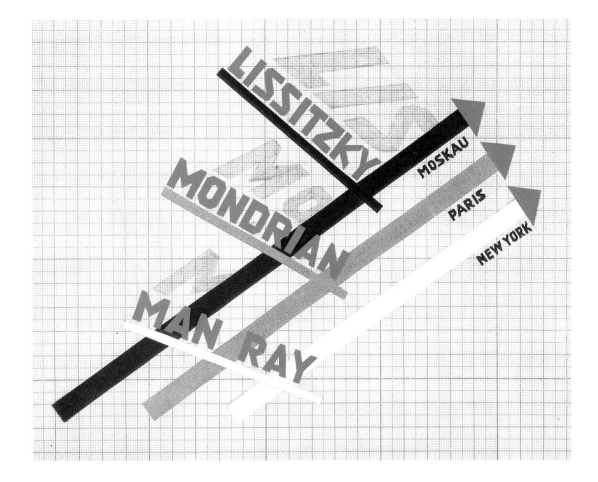

98
Lissitzky - Mondrian - Man Ray,
poster, 1925
19.3 x 24.2 cm

99
Polygraphic Exhibition, invitation
card, 1927
11.2 x 9.7 cm

100
Polygraphic Exhibition, catalogue,
Moscow 1927
14.4 x 10.3 cm

101
**Soviet pavilion at the International
Press-Exhibition Pressa,** catalogue,
Cologne 1928
14.7 x 10.4 cm

102
USSR. Russische Ausstellung,
poster, 1929
128.0 x 90.5 cm

TYPOGRAPHIC DESIGNS

103
El Lissitzky, **Russland** (Russia), 1930
29.0 x 23.0 cm

105
Roger Ginsburger, **Frankreich**
(France), 1930
29.0 x 23.0 cm

104
Richard Neutra, **Amerika** (America),
1930
29.0 x 23.0 cm

106
USSR im Bau, 3 März 1937
42.0 x 29.7 cm

107
USSR im Bau, 9 September 1933
42.0 x 29.7 cm

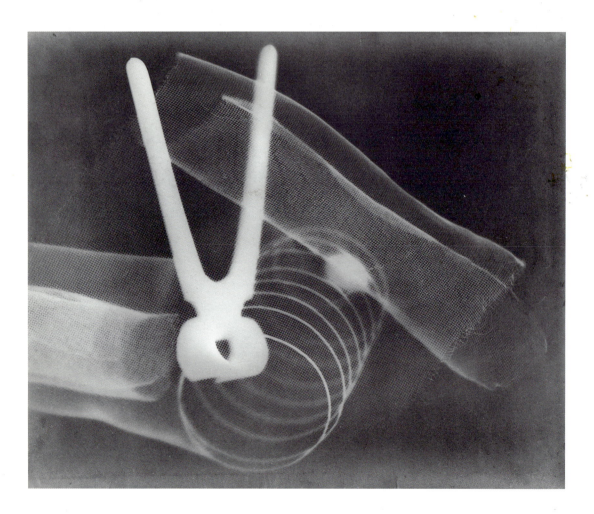

108
Pincers and Wire, negative version,
ca. 1920
23.0 x 29.0 cm

Photography

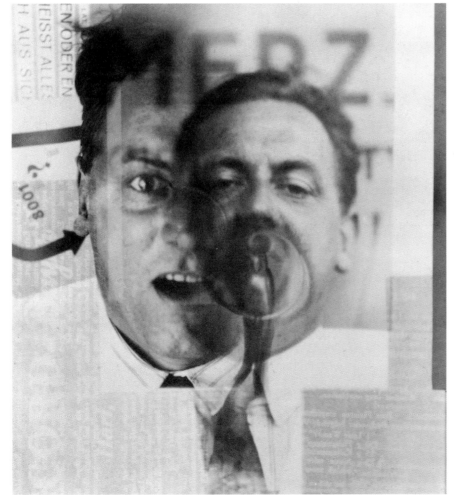

109
Untitled, ca. 1923
16.0 x 11.0 cm

110
Untitled, superimposed portrait,
1924/30
16.1 x 11.8 cm

111
Portrait of Kurt Schwitters, 1924
11.1 x 10.1 cm

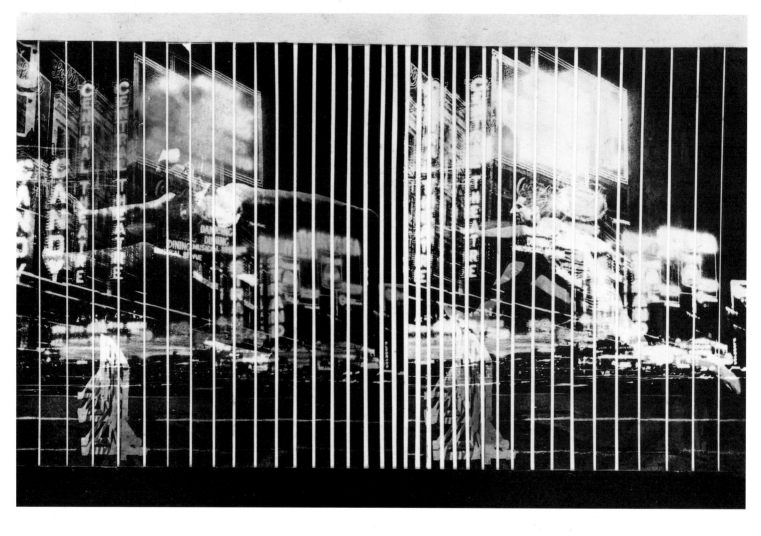

112
The runners, 1930
12.0 x 21.4 cm

113
Footballer, 1930
17.0 x 13.0 cm

114
The runner, 1930

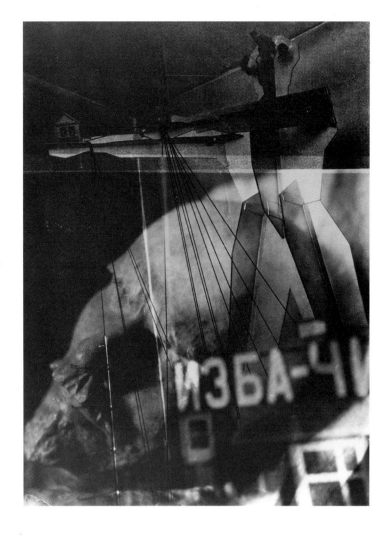

115
Pressa, 1928
11.4 x 8.5 cm

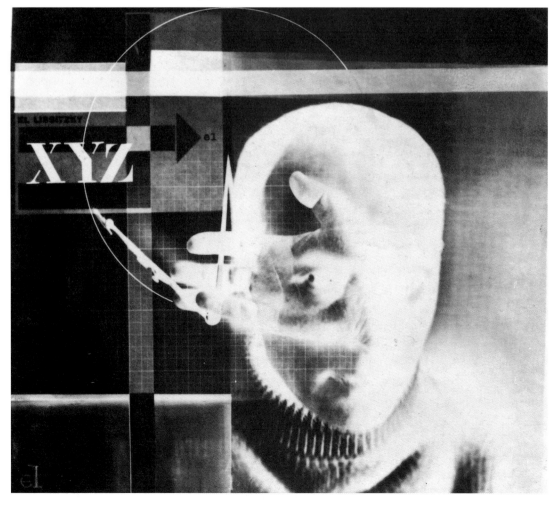

116
The Constructor, self-portrait,
negative version, 1924
12.6 x 14.4 cm

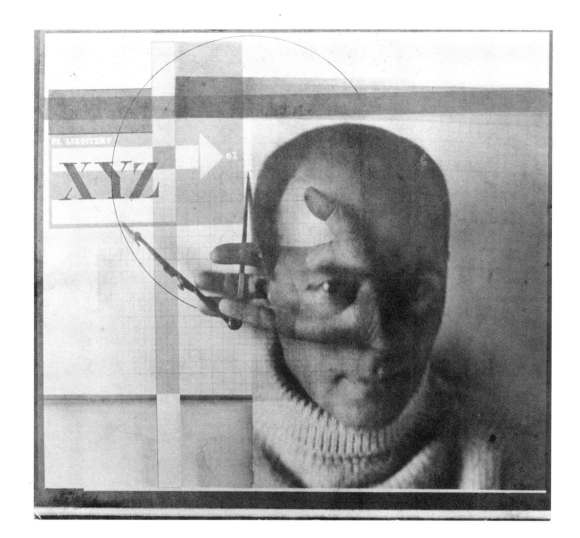

117
The Constructor, self-portrait, 1924
11.3 x 12.5 cm

118
Self-portrait, 1928
8.2 x 9.0 cm

119
Raum für konstruktive Kunst
(Room for constructivist art), design,
1926
16.7 x 22.2 cm

Demonstrationsräume

120
Raum für konstruktive Kunst
(Room for constructivist art),
Dresden 1926
16.7 x 22.2 cm

121
Raum für konstruktive Kunst
(Room for constructivist art),
Dresden 1926
16.7 x 22.2 cm

122
Abstraktes Kabinett (The abstract
cabinet), design, 1927
39.9 x 52.3 cm

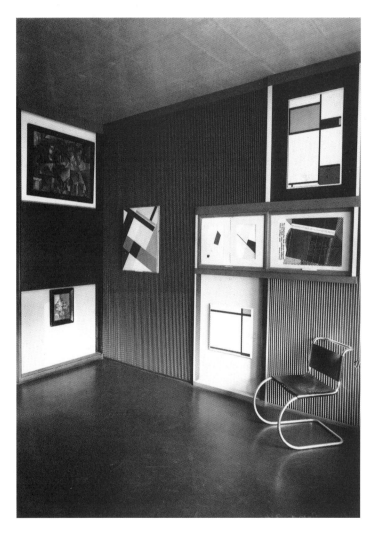

123
Abstraktes Kabinett (The abstract
cabinet), Hanover 1930
17.7 x 23.2 cm

124
Abstraktes Kabinett (The abstract
cabinet), Hanover 1930
17.7 x 23.2 cm

DEMONSTRATIONSRÄUME

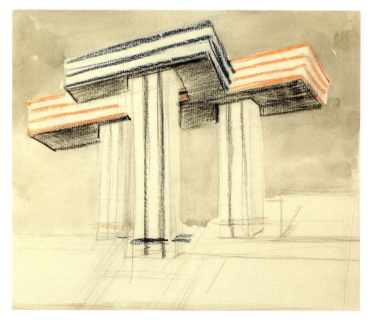

Architecture

125
Wolkenbügel, 1924/25
22.8 x 15.5 cm

126
Wolkenbügel, topographical
drawing, 1924/25
21.4 x 27.0 cm

127
Wolkenbügel, 1924/25
21.4 x 27.0 cm

128
Wolkenbügel, 1924/25
26.9 x 21.4 cm

129
Wolkenbügel, 1924/25

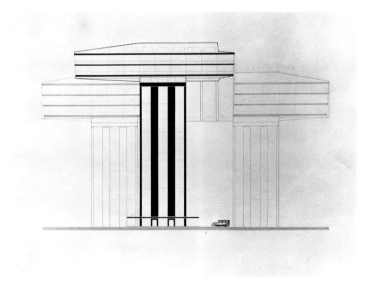

130
Wolkenbügel, design, 1924/25
50.0 x 64.6 cm

131
Wolkenbügel, design, 1924/25

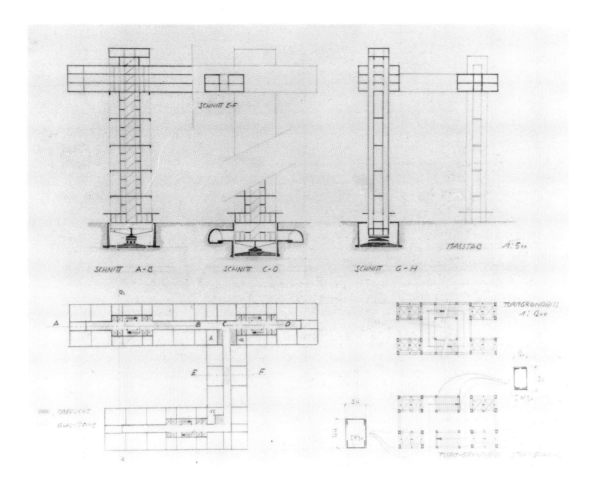

132
Wolkenbügel, working-drawing,
1924/1925
37.2 x 46.0 cm

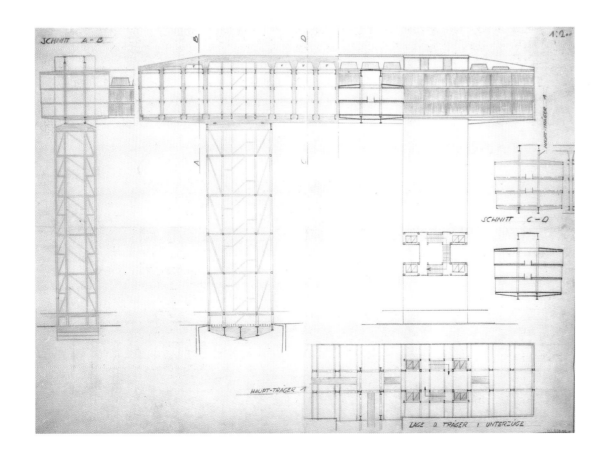

133
Wolkenbügel, working-drawing,
1924/25
49.9 x 69.5 cm

189

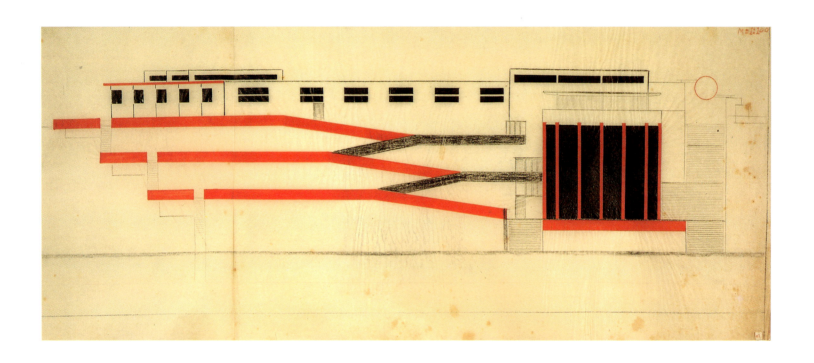

134
Yacht club of the International Red
Stadium on the Lenin Hills, 1925
33.5 x 74.0 cm

135
**Yacht club of the International Red
Stadium on the Lenin Hills,**
axonometry, 1925
38.2 x 45.7 cm

136
Building in Gorki park, design, 1931

137
Clubhouse, model, 1934

192

138
Administration building of a textile factory, design, 1925
28.2 x 31.1 cm

139
House of heavy industry, model,
1930

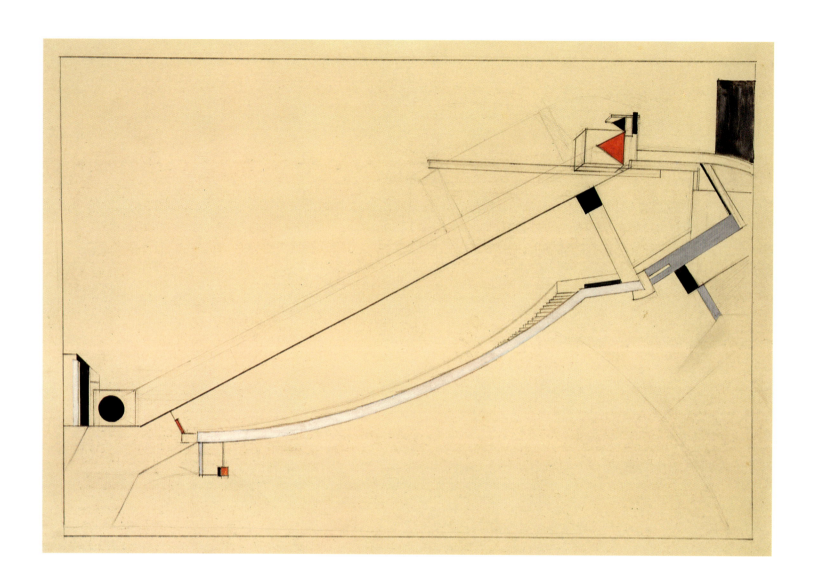

140
Bridge, design, 1925
24.1 x 34.5 cm

141
**International Red Stadium on the
Lenin Hills,** groundplan, 1925
50.7 x 86.2 cm

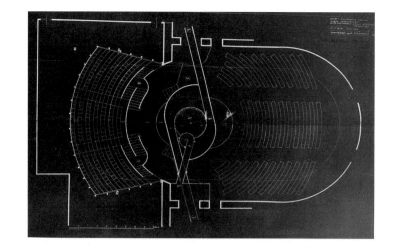

142
The Meyerhold theatre, ground-plan, 1928/29

143
The Meyerhold theatre, model, 1928/29

144
The Meyerhold theatre, model, 1928/29

145
The Meyerhold theatre, model, 1928/29

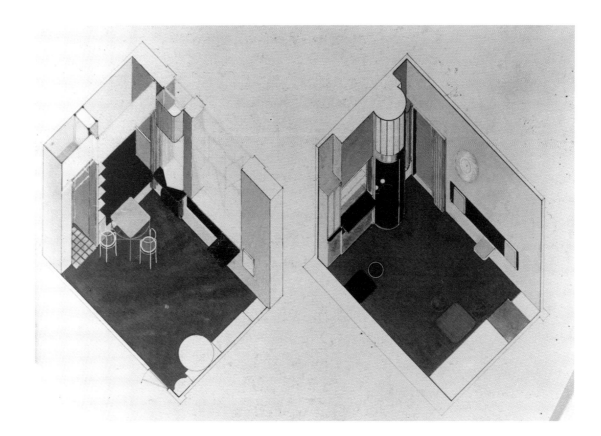

146
Boxoffice, design, 1930

147
House for the architect Ginsburg,
1934

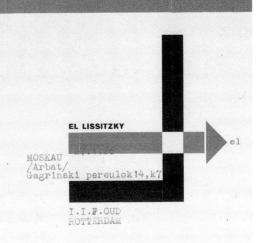

EL LISSITZKY   el

MOSKAU
/Arbat/
Gagrinski pereulok 4,k7

I.I.F.OUD
ROTTERDAM

LIEBER OUD, ich habe erhalten Ihre Rolle mit die beide Zeichnungen.
Ich danke Sie sehr für die Sendung. Die Arbeit ist sehr klar und
durchsichtig. Für uns ist jetzt dies Problem: ein Standart zu schaffen
für das nötige Bauen, das aktuelste. In Holland sind sie in Vorteil,
denn Ihr hat schon dort ein festen Wohnungscharakter und Wohnart. Das
ist alles was bei uns im Werden ist. Und vorläufig sind wir in so einer
Wohnflächenot das wenn mann in Wircklichkeit ein Quadratmeter Fläche
kriegt ist alles gelöst? Mann ist bei uns stark bescheftigt mit all
diesen und es ist ein grosses Interesse zu die Leistungen im Ausland.
So habe ich getrofen in einer Bauausstellung die eben geschlossen ist
auch ein Entwurf von Ihre Rotterdamer Gemeindebauten.
Ich lege auch dabei ein Ausschnit aus einer algemeiner illustrierter
Zeitschrift (ein Aufsatz von mir) wo isch bringe auch Ihre Arbeit. Der
Titel Amerikanismus der europeischen Architektur darf Sie nicht wun-
dern, denn unter Amerikanismus versteht mann bei uns das neue Wollen.

Ich denke das Ihr Buch ist schon endlich im Bauhausverlag erschienen
und werde mich freuen es von Ihnen zu erhalten. Ich habe hier Gelegen-
heiten es in der Presse zu besprechen. Was haben Sie inzwischen schönes
gearbeitet? Haben Sie jetzt wass im Bau? Was gibt in Holland?

Ich leite an der Akademie die Werkstaten für Ihnenausbau. Man muss alle
von Anfang an aufbauen. Mann muss Programme aufstellen, Sitzungen durch-
sitzen, Kunstrichtungkämpfe noch immer kämpfen. Aber ich bin noch immer
optimistisch und behalte meine aktivitet. Also, wenn ich zu Ende des
Semesters durchführe eine Aufgabe die ich der älterer Studentengruppe
gestellt habe, dann werde ich wass Ihnen schicken. Ich arbeite in die
Arbeitspausen auf einer neuen Problem, aber nicht nur problematisch.
Ich fühle das wie ich näher zum Himmel komme desto irdischer werde
ich. Gesundcheitlich gehts mir besser als voriges Winter.
Unser Leben hier ist hart, aber dynamisch und Aussichtsreich. Aus
Deutschland habe ich sehr traurige Nachrichten. Depression. Hoffent-
lich in Holland geht es besser. Ihr hat doch Kolonien.

Schreiben Sie bitte,Oud.
Mit besten Gruss an Ihre Frau und Hans
                    Herzlichst   Ihr El Lissitzky

148
Letter to J.J.P. Oud, 27.1.26
27.5 x 21.3 cm

150
Russian housing shortage and its
solutions, 1930

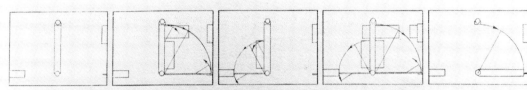

RUSSISCHE WOHNUNGSNOT UND IHRE LÖSUNGEN

27 EL LISSITZKY, MOSKAU. Wandmobil für ein Kommunenhaus, 1929. Möglichkeiten der Raumverteilung · Hingedpartition for a communalhouse, 1929
Possibilities of space distribution · Paroi à gonds pour une maison communale, 1929. Possibilité de distribution de l'espace

149
Model of an apartment, 1930

151
Chair, 1930
72.0 x 48.0 x 56.0 cm

152
Lenin Tribune, design, 1920/24
63.9 x 48.0 cm

153
Flag-post for the Soviet Pavilion at the International Press Exhibition Pressa, design, 1928
70.8 x 52.8 cm

154
Flagpost for the International Press Exhibition Pressa, model, 1928

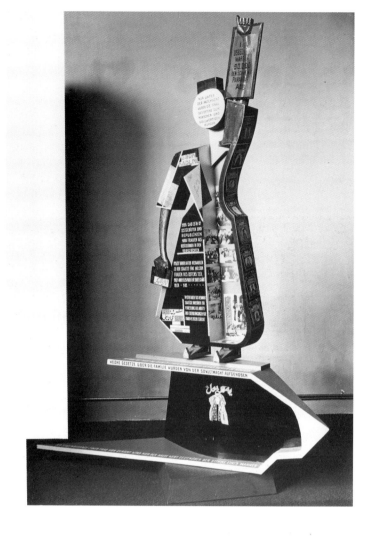

155
Soviet pavilion at the International Press Exhibition Pressa, design,
Cologne 1928
69.0 x 52.0 cm

Exhibition designs

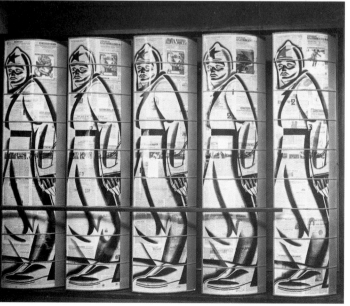

202

157
Soviet pavilion at the International Press Exhibition Pressa, Cologne
1928

158
**Soviet pavilion at the International
Press Exhibition Pressa,** Cologne
1928

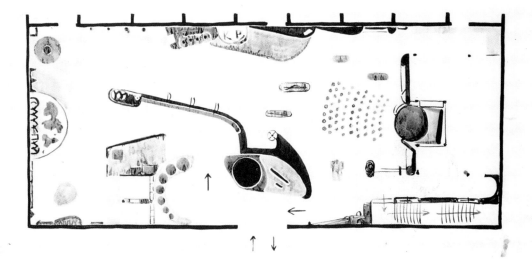

159
Soviet pavilion at the International Hygiene Exhibition, groundplan, 1930
34.2 x 65.5 cm

160
Soviet pavilion at the International Hygiene Exhibition, Dresden 1930

161
Soviet pavilion at the International Hygiene Exhibition, Dresden 1930

162
**Soviet pavilion at the International
Hygiene Exhibition,** Dresden 1930

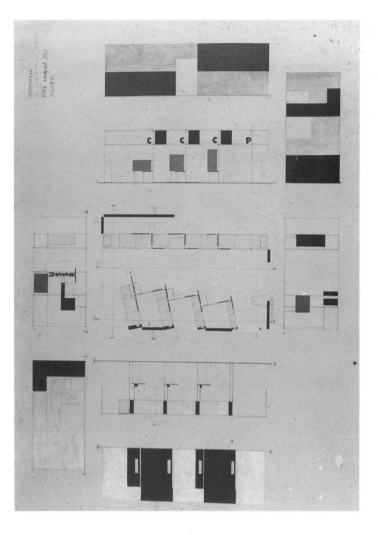

163
International Exhibition Film and Photo, design, Stuttgart 1929

164
International Exhibition Film and Photo, design, Stuttgart 1929

165
International Exhibition Film and Photo, Stuttgart 1929

166
**International Fur Trade Exhibition
(IPA),** model of the Soviet pavilion,
Leipzig 1930

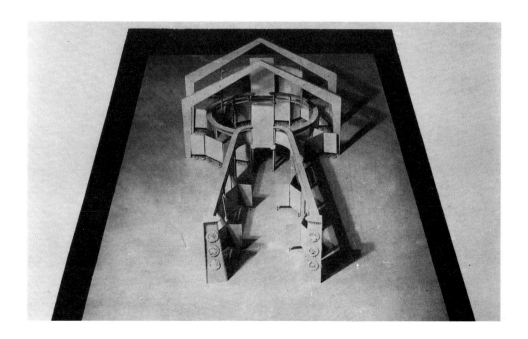

167
International Aviation Exhibition,
model of the Soviet pavilion, Paris
1934

List of reproductions

Since the exhibitions in Eindhoven, Madrid and Paris each have their own character, this book on El Lissitzky does not pretend to be a catalogue of the El Lissitzky retrospective. The choice and arrangement of the reproductions here are separate from those of the works themselves in the different exhibitions.

The list of reproductions is divided into nine categories: Travel sketches, Book illustrations, Prounen, Figurinen, Typographic designs, Photography, Demonstrationsräume, Architecture and Exhibition designs. In this list the first item given for each number is the legend as shown next to the reproduction; where necessary this is followed by the translation. Next the technique used is given, followed by the dimensions (height x width x depth) in centimeters. Lastly, the collection or source of the photograph is stated. Where required, a few explanatory remarks are added.

Lissitzky's original titles have been left untranslated, except when they are of a descriptive character.
The titles of the Prounen are based in the first place on those which Lissitzky gave to his works when drawing up a list for his exhibition in Berlin in 1924.
Book titles have been left in the language of original publication as far as possible.
The original names of periodicals and posters have been retained except where an explanation was required for a better understanding of the artist's work.
In the case of exhibition designs, the original title of the exhibition is given only once.

A question mark indicates that precise details are missing.

Travel sketches

1
The Holy Trinity church in Vitebsk, 1910
Graphite, crayon and gouache on paper
30.0 x 37.7 cm
Municipal Van Abbemuseum, Eindhoven
Underneath in Lissitzky's handwriting: Architek-turafnahme / Die Dreienigkeit-Kirche zu Witebsk (Anfang des XVIII jahr) / (Sogennante "Schwarze" Kirche) / Stud arch Lasar Lissitzky.
(Architecture-view / The Holy Trinity Church in Vitebsk (Begin of the XVIII year) / (So-called "black" church) / Stud arch Lasar Lissitzky)

2
Tower of the fortress in Smolensk, 1910
Crayon and gouache on paper
24.0 x 32.0 cm
Municipal Van Abbemuseum, Eindhoven
Underneath in Lissitzky's handwriting: Zeichnung nach der Natur / Turm aus der Festungsmauer zu Smolensk (1604) / Stud arch Lasar Lissitzky.
(Drawing from nature / Tower of the fortress in Smolensk (1604) / Stud arch Lasar Lissitzky)

3
Venice, 1913
Watercolour on cardboard
26.6 x 34.5 cm
Municipal Van Abbemuseum, Eindhoven
Underneath: Venezia / 13 / Lasar Lissitzky

4
Ravenna, 1913
Graphite, crayon and gouache on paper
31.8 x 23.7 cm
Municipal Van Abbemuseum, Eindhoven
Underneath: Ravenna / MCMXIII / Lasar Lissitzky

5
Italian town, 1913
Graphite, crayon and gouache on paper
24.0 x 32.4 cm
Municipal Van Abbemuseum, Eindhoven

Book illustrations

6.1-5
Khad Gadya (One billy goat), 1917
Portfolio of 11 watercolours
30.0 x 26.0 cm
6.1
One billy goat
6.2
The dog came and devoured the cat
6.3
The stick came and beat the dog
6.4
Then came God and slew the angel of death
6.5
The slaughter came and slaughtered the ox
State Tretiakov Gallery, Moscow
Jewish Passover tale
Variant of the 1919 publication

7.1-5
Khad Gadya (One billy goat), 1919
Coloured lithographs
28.0 x 26.0 cm
7.1
One billy goat
7.2
The dog came and devoured the cat
7.3
The stick came and beat the dog
7.4
Then came God and slew the angel of death
7.5
The cat came and bit the billy goat
Loan Eric Estorick family collection
Published by Kulturliga, Kiev

8
M. Broderson, **Sikhes Khulin, A Prager legende** (An everyday conversation. A legend of Prague), 1917
Lithographs, coloured Indian ink
Scroll 22.1 x 400.13 cm in wooden case
State Tretiakov Gallery, Moscow
Published by Leben, Moscow
Illustrations by El Lissitzky

9.1-3
R. Kipling, **Elfandl** (The little elephant), illustration, 1922
Indian ink, pen, brush
28.7 x 27.5 cm
State Tretiakov Gallery, Moscow
Published by Shveln Farlag, Berlin
Illustrations by El Lissitzky

10.1-3
Vaysrusische folkmayses (Belorussian folk tales), 1919/22
Indian ink, pen, brush
23.5 x 21.5 cm
State Tretiakov Gallery, Moscow
Published by Narkompros, Berlin
Cover and illustrations by El Lissitzky

11
Tatlin, working on the Monument, 1921/22
Collage
29.2 x 22.9 cm
Loan Eric Estorick family collection
Subsequently appeared as illustration in
Ilia Erenburg, *Shest povestei o legkikh kontsakh* (repr.82)

12
Footballer, 1922
Graphite, gouache, Indian ink, varnish, collage on cardboard
33.0 x 24.3 cm
State Tretiakov Gallery, Moscow
Subsequently appeared as illustration in
Ilia Erenburg, *Shest povestei o legkikh kontsakh* (repr.82)

Prounen

13
Proun portfolio, cover design, 1920
Graphite, gouache on paper
49.7 x 38.0 cm
State Tretiakov Gallery, Moscow
Cover design for a portfolio of 11 lithographs
The portfolio in this form was never published

14
Proun 1, ca. 1919/20
Lithograph
25.6 x 27.5 cm (image)
34.2 x 44.6 cm (sheet)
State Tretiakov Gallery, Moscow
Lithograph for the Proun portfolio
In his description of this Proun Lissitzky explicitly indicated that it was essential to turn it around. Accordingly, four views of *Proun 1* are shown here. There is a Proun which shows this happening, *Construction floating in space,* 1920. Underneath it Lissitzky wrote, 'This plan is only a mechanical demonstration of entering the essence of the construction. Only four phases.' The *Proun of 8 positions,* 1924, makes clear how Lissitzky intended to show multiple phases in one composition: it consists of a black sphere inside a rhombus; Lissitzky sets the square on one of its corners.

15
Proun 1A, Bridge, ca. 1919/20
Lithograph
17.0 x 30.0 cm (image)
35.1 x 45.4 cm (sheet)
State Tretiakov Gallery, Moscow
Lithograph for the Proun portfolio

16
Proun 2C, ca. 1919/20
Lithograph
29.9 x 20.0 cm (image)
45.4 x 35.4 cm (sheet)
State Tretiakov Gallery, Moscow
Lithograph for the Proun portfolio
17
Proun 3A, ca. 1919/20
Lithograph
27.6 x 26.4 cm (image)
28.5 x 27.2 cm (sheet)
Municipal Van Abbemuseum, Eindhoven
Lithograph for the Proun portfolio
18
Proun 2D, ca. 1919/20
Lithograph
35.7 x 22.5 cm (image)
45.6 x 34.3 cm (sheet)
State Tretiakov Gallery, Moscow
Lithograph for the Proun portfolio
19
Proun 2B, ca. 1919/20
Lithograph
20.2 x 26.2 cm (image)
35.8 x 45.4 cm (sheet)
State Tretiakov Gallery, Moscow
Lithograph for the Proun portfolio
20
Proun 1D, ca. 1919/20
Lithograph
21.5 x 26.9 cm (image)
35.5 x 40.8 cm (sheet)
Municipal Van Abbemuseum, Eindhoven
Lithograph for the Proun portfolio
21
Proun 1E, Town, ca. 1919/20
Lithograph
22.6 x 27.5 cm (image)
35.5 x 45.6 cm (sheet)
State Tretiakov Gallery, Moscow
Lithograph for the Proun portfolio
22
Proun 1C, ca. 1919/20
Lithograph
23.2 x 23.3 cm (image)
23.9 x 24.0 cm (sheet)
Municipal Van Abbemuseum, Eindhoven
Lithograph for the Proun portfolio
23
Proun 5A, ca. 1919/20
Lithograph
27.5 x 26.9 cm (image)
45.5 x 37.2 cm (sheet)
State Tretiakov Gallery, Moscow
Lithograph for the Proun portfolio
24
Proun 6B, ca. 1919/20
Lithograph
24.8 cm Ø (image)
27.5 x 26.9 cm (sheet)
State Tretiakov Gallery, Moscow
Lithograph for the Proun portfolio
25
Proun P23, Würfel mit Hyperbel, 1919
Oil on canvas
52.0 x 77.0 cm
Loan Eric Estorick family collection
26
Proun 99, 1925
Watersoluble and metallic paint on wood
129.0 x 99.1 cm
Yale University Art Gallery, New Haven,
Connecticut

27
Proun 12E, 1923
Oil on canvas
57.1 x 42.5 cm
Courtesy of the Busch-Reisinger Museum / Harvard
University, Cambridge Massachusetts
28
Untitled, ca. 1920
Tempera on canvas
73.5 x 51.5 cm
Private Collection courtesy of Annely Juda Fine Art,
London
29
Proun 30T, 1920
Oil and mixed media on canvas
50.0 x 62.0 cm
Sprengel Museum Hanover
30
Proun 2C, ca. 1920
Oil, paper and metallic paint on wood
60.0 x 40.0 cm
Philadelphia Museum of Art, A.E. Gallatin Collec-
tion, Philadelphia
31
Proun G.B.A., ca 1923
Oil on canvas
77.0 x 82.0 cm
Haags Gemeentemuseum, The Hague
32
Proun R.V.N.2, 1923
Mixed media on canvas
99.0 x 99.0 cm
Sprengel Museum Hanover
33
Proun G7, 1923
Tempera, varnish and graphite on canvas
77.0 x 62.0 cm
Kunstsammlung Nordrhein-Westfalen, Düsseldorf
34
Proun G7, study, ca. 1922
Collage with watercolor and charcoal on black
cardboard
47.9 x 39.0 cm
Stedelijk Museum Amsterdam
35
Proun G7, study, ca. 1922/23
Gouache and graphite on transparent paper
78.2 x 62.7 cm
Municipal Van Abbemuseum, Eindhoven
36
Proun, ca. 1922
Gouache and ink
50.2 x 40 cm
The Museum of Modern Art, New York
Gift of Curt Valentin
37
Proun, ca. 1923
Graphite, gouache and crayon with collage
45.1 x 41.5 cm
Courtesy of the Busch-Reisinger Museum / Harvard
University, Cambridge Massachusetts / The Fredric
Wertham Collection, gift of his wife Hesketh
38
Proun, ca. 1923
Gouache with red and black ink
35.9 x 27.5 cm
Courtesy of the Busch-Reisinger Museum / Harvard
University, Cambridge Massachusetts / The Fredric
Wertham Collection, gift of his wife Hesketh
39
Proun GK, 1922/23
Gouache, pen and ink
66.0 x 50.2 cm
The Museum of Modern Art, New York

40
Proun, ca. 1919/23
Graphite, gouache, Indian ink on paper
49.0 x 68.0 cm
Municipal Van Abbemuseum, Eindhoven
41
Proun 43, ca. 1922
Watercolour, gouache, Indian ink, aluminium
paint, collage on cardboard
66.8 x 49.0 cm
State Tretiakov Gallery, Moscow
There is a photograph of a wooden panel with the
same composition – but turned 180°. The panel is
lost. The panel is shown on page 162 of the
Lissitzky catalogue from Harvard 1987.
42
Proun, ca. 1921/23
Gouache and crayon on paper
46.5 x 39.0 cm
Municipal Van Abbemuseum, Eindhoven
43
Proun, ca 1922
Graphite, gouache and black ink
24.0 x 22.0 cm
Courtesy of the Busch-Reisinger Museum / Harvard
University, Cambridge, Massachusetts / The Fredric
Wertham Collection, gift of his wife Hesketh
44
Gekläbtes Schwarzes, Proun 84, 1923/24
Indian ink, collage on coloured paper
45.6 x 45.3 cm
State Tretiakov Gallery, Moscow
45
Proun, ca. 1922/23
Gouache and graphite on paper
52.0 x 50.0 cm
Municipal Van Abbemuseum, Eindhoven
46
Proun G7, study, ca. 1919/20
Black ink
13.1 x 8.9 cm
State Tretiakov Gallery, Moscow
47
Proun, study, ca. 1922
Charcoal on paper
40.3 x 39.0 cm
Municipal Van Abbemuseum, Eindhoven
48
Proun LN31, study Karton gross, ca. 1922
Graphite on tracing paper
21.7 x 16.0 cm
State Tretiakov Gallery, Moscow
49
Proun, ca. 1924
Gouache
45.5 x 45.5 cm
Galerie Dr. I. Schlégl, Zürich
50
Proun 88, ca. 1923
Collage
49.9 x 64.7 cm
Staatliche Galerie Moritzburg Halle
51
Kleiner grauer Karton, Proun 30, ca. 1920
Mixed media on cardboard
49.5 x 39.5 cm
Staatliche Galerie Moritzburg Halle
52
Kylmansegg, Proun 1D, 1919
Oil on canvas, mounted on wood
96.0 x 71.5 cm
Kunstmuseum Basel
53
Proun, ca. 1924
Indian ink
24.7 x 21.1 cm
State Tretiakov Gallery, Moscow

54
Konischer, Proun 93, ca. 1923
Graphite and colour pencil, Indian ink, pen,
gouache
49.9 x 49.7 cm
Staatliche Galerie Moritzburg Halle
55.0
1° Kestnermappe Proun (First Kestner portfolio
Proun), cover, 1923
Lithograph, collage on grey paper
60.6 x 44.5 cm
State Tretiakov Gallery, Moscow
55.1-7
1° Kestnermappe Proun, (First Kestner portfolio
Proun), 1923
7 lithographs
59.8 x 44.0 cm (title page and sheet no. 1,2,5 and
6)
64.0 x 49.0 cm (sheet no. 3 and 4)
State Tretiakov Gallery, Moscow /
Sprengel Museum Hanover
Sheets 3 and 4 are missing from the portfolio in
the collection of the Tretiakov Gallery
56
Prounenraum (Proun Room), 1923
Black ink, pen
19.9 x 12.5 cm
State Tretiakov Gallery, Moscow
Notable in this drawing is the round Proun design
– *Proun 43* (?) – that is shown on the ceiling. This
is missing in the later lithograph (repr.55.7) and
the final execution of the Proun Room.
Jean Leering pointed this out to us.
57
Prounenraum (Proun Room), design side-wall,
1923
Indian ink, graphite and colour pencil
34.5 x 47.4 cm
State Tretiakov Gallery, Moscow
58
Proun G.B.A., study, 1923
Watercolour, crayon, Indian ink, graphite
34.5 x 50.5 cm
State Tretiakov Gallery, Moscow
59
Prounenraum (Proun Room), 1923
Cliché
Private archives
The illustration of the *Prounenraum* – four photo-
graphs stuck together – appeared in the magazine
G1 (Gestaltung) Berlin, July 1923, together with an
article by El Lissitzky on his *Prounenraum*. The
article is reprinted in the book by Sophie Lissitzky-
Küppers, 1976, p. 365-367
60
Prounenraum (Proun Room), reconstruction 1965,
1923
Wood
300.0 x 300.0 x 260.0 cm
Municipal Van Abbemuseum, Eindhoven

Figurinen

61
Figurinenmappe Sieg über die Sonne (Figurine
portfolio Victory over the sun), cover, 1920 / 21
Gouache, Indian ink, graphite
49.7 x 38.0 cm
State Tretiakov Gallery, Moscow
62-71
Figurinen, 1920 / 21
Gouache, Indian ink, graphite and black pen, vari-
ous materials
49.4 x 37.9 cm
State Tretiakov Gallery, Moscow

62
Ansager
Announcer
63
Posten
Sentry
64
Ängstliche
The Terrified
65
Globetrotter in der Zeit
Globetrotter in time
66
Sportsmänner
Sportsmen
67
Zankstifter
Troublemaker
68
Alter
The old
69
Totengräber
Gravediggers
70
Neuer
The new
71
System des Theaters
The system of the theatre
Studies for the portfolio: *Figurinenmappe. Die plas-
tische Gestaltung des elektro-mechanischen Schau
Sieg über die Sonne* (Figurine portfolio
The plastic structure of the electro-mechanic per-
formance Victory over the Sun)

Typographic designs

72-73
**Communication workers, remember the year
1905,** 1919 / 20
Gouache, Indian ink, graphite
14.5 x 22.8 cm (repr.72)
18.2 x 22.9 cm (repr.73)
State Tretiakov Gallery, Moscow
Sketch for a poster to remind the postal workers of
the 1905 revolution, 15 years later
74
The factory workbenches await you, 1919
Photo from private archive
Composition of *Proun 1E* as theme for a propaganda billboard, intended to encourage the popu-
lation to go back to the cities.
75
Untitled, suprematist construction, ca. 1920
Gouache and watercolour on paper
30.0 x 21.0 cm
Collection Gg. F. Weisbrod
Cover design for Alexander Kusikov, *Albarrak* (?)
76
Beat the whites with the red wedge, reprint 1966,
1919 / 20
Poster
48.5 x 69.2 cm
Municipal Van Abbemuseum, Eindhoven
Propaganda poster for the Red Army in the battle
against the Whites.
77
1° Russische Kunstausstellung, Galerie van
Diemen Berlin, cover design, 1922
First Russian Art Exhibition
Tracing paper, gouache, Indian ink, graphite
27.0 x 19.0 cm
State Tretiakov Gallery, Moscow
Design for repr.78 (variant)

78
1° Russische Kunstausstelling, Stedelijk Museum
Amsterdam, catalogue, 1923
First Russian Art Exhibition
Letterpress in grey and black
22.7 x 14.7 cm
Municipal Van Abbemuseum, Eindhoven
For the exhibition in Amsterdam, the catalogue
cover of the Berlin exhibition was used and only
the relevant names were changed.
79-80
Vladimir Mayakovsky, **Dlia Golosa** (For the voice),
1923
Letterpress in red and black, on the cover on
orange
19.0 x 13.5 cm
Municipal Van Abbemuseum, Eindhoven
Published by Gosudarstvennoe izdatelstvo RSFSR,
Moscow-Berlin
Layout by El Lissitzky
81
Ravvi (Rabbi), cover proof, 1922
Letterpress in black
20.1 x 28.3 cm
Municipal Van Abbemuseum, Eindhoven
Cover for the book by Olga Forsh, *Ravvi. Pesa v
trekh deistviakh* (Rabbi. Drama in three acts)
Published by Skify, Berlijn
82
Ilia Erenburg, **Shest povestei o legkikh kontsakh**
(Six stories with an easy ending), 1922
Letterpress in black, cover in red and black
20.2 x 13.8 cm
Municipal Van Abbemuseum, Eindhoven
Cover
Published by Helikon, Moscow-Berlin
Cover and illustrations by El Lissitzky
83
MA, cover proof, 1922
Linocut on transparent paper
27.0 x 19.8 cm
Municipal Van Abbemuseum, Eindhoven
Full title periodical: *MA Aktivista folyoirat*
(Today. Activist journal) Vol. 7, No. 8, August
Cover by El Lissitzky
84
Wendingen, cover design, 1922
Gouache, Indian ink, graphite
17.2 x 25.8 cm
State Tretiakov Gallery, Moscow
Design for repr.85
85
Wendingen, cover, 1922
Lithograph / letterpress
33.0 x 66.5 cm
Municipal Van Abbemuseum, Eindhoven
Periodical *Wendingen* IV (1921) no. 11
Cover by El Lissitzky
86.1-4
**Suprematicheskii skaz pro dva kvadrata v 6ti
postroikakh** (Suprematist story of two squares in 6
constructions), 1922
Letterpress in red and black
28.0 x 22.0 cm
Municipal Van Abbemuseum, Eindhoven
20 pages and cover
Published by Skify, Berlijn
Design and layout by El Lissitzky
86.1
To all, all children
86.2
Do not read. Take paper, rods, blocks
86.3
They fly towards earth from afar and
86.4
and on the black is established the red

87
Broom, N3, June, V2, cover design, 1922
Tracing paper, gouache
26.0 x 18.5 cm
State Tretiakov Gallery, Moscow
Periodical, cover by El Lissitzky
88
Broom No. 3, Vol. 5, cover design, 1923
Graphite, gouache on transparent paper
27.5 x 20.8 cm
Municipal Van Abbemuseum, Eindhoven
Periodical, cover by El Lissitzky
89
Broom, N3, June, V2, cover design, 1922
Tracing paper, gouache
26.2 x 20.5 cm
State Tretiakov Gallery, Moscow
Periodical, cover by El Lissitzky
90
Broom, No. 3, October, Vol. 5, cover design, 1923
Graphite, Indian ink and gouache on graph paper
36.2 x 22.7 cm
Municipal Van Abbemuseum, Eindhoven
Periodical, cover by El Lissitzky
91
Veshch – Gegenstand – Objet, N1, February, cover design, 1922
Graphite, Indian ink on paper
30.7 x 22.5 cm
Municipal Van Abbemuseum, Eindhoven
Periodical, layout by El Lissitzky
92
Veshch – Gegenstand – Objet, cover proof, 1922
Letterpress on red paper
45.1 x 34.4 cm
Municipal Van Abbemuseum, Eindhoven
Periodical, layout by El Lissitzky
93
Merz, Band 2, No. 8/9, April Juli, Nasci, 1924
Letterpress in black, cover in red and blue
30.5 x 23.3 cm
Municipal Van Abbemuseum, Eindhoven
Front and back covers periodical
Cover and layout by El Lissitzky
94
Pelikan Bürobedarf, 1924
Pelikan Stationery
Silk screen print
24.0 x 17.0 cm
Private archives
Cover of a box for typewriter ribbon
95
Pelikan Kohlenpapier, advertisement, 1925
Pelikan Carbon paper
Letterpress printing
14.8 x 11.5 cm
Museum für Gestaltung Basel
96.0-2
El Lissitzky, Hans Arp, **Die Kunstismen. Les Isms de l'Art. The Isms of Art, 1924-1914,** 1925
Letterpress in black, cover in red and black
26.3 x 20.6 cm
Municipal Van Abbemuseum, Eindhoven
Published by Eugen Rentsch, Erlenbach – Zürich etc.
Cover and layout by El Lissitzky
97. 1-6
Die vier Grundrechnungsarten (The four arithmetical functions), reprint, 1976
12 Silk screen prints
25.0 x 32.5 cm
Municipal Van Abbemuseum, Eindhoven
Portfolio, based on the original gouaches of 1928

98
Lissitzky – Mondrian – Man Ray, poster, 1925
Graphite, Indian ink and collage on graph paper
19.3 x 24.2 cm
State Tretiakov Gallery, Moscow
Poster design for the exhibition of the same name in Munich
99
Polygraphic Exhibition, invitation card, 1927
Letterpress in silver and red
11.2 x 9.7 cm
Private archives
Original title exhibition: *Vsesoiuznaia poligraficheskaia vystavka*
100
Polygraphic Exhibition, catalogue, Moscow 1927
Photomontage
14.4 x 10.3 cm
Private archives
Catalogue:
Letterpress
17.8 x 12.8 cm
Deutsche Bücherei, Leipzig
101
Catalogue for the Soviet pavilion at the
International Press Exhibition Pressa,
Cologne 1928
Photomotage
14.7 x 10.4 cm
Private archives
Catalogue:
Letterpress in black, offset in brown and red
21.1 x 15.1 cm
Deutsche Bücherei, Leipzig
Original title exhibition : *Internationale Presse-Ausstellung Pressa*
102
USSR, Russische Ausstellung, poster, 1929
USSR, Russian exhibition
Photogravure in red and black
128.0 x 90.5 cm
Museum für Gestaltung Basel
Poster for the exhibition in the Kunstgewerbe-museum Zürich, 24 March-28 April 1929
103-105
Prospectus for the publisher A. Scholl, **Neues Bauen in der Welt,** Vienna 1930
Letterpress in black, cover in red and black
29.0 x 23.0 cm
Contains the announcement of:
103
El Lissitzky, **Russland.** *Die Rekonstruktion der Architektur in der Sowjetunion* (Russia, the reconstruction of the architecture in the Soviet-Union)
104
Richard Neutra, **Amerika.** *Die Stilbildung des Neuen Bauens in den Vereinigten Staaten* (America, the stylistic development of the new architecture in the United States)
105
Roger Ginsburger, **Frankreich.** *Die Entwicklung der neuen Ideen nach Konstruktion und Form* (France. The development of new ideas of construction and form)
106
USSR im Bau, 3 März 1937
USSR in construction
Offset in blue and black
42.0 x 29.7 cm
Municipal Van Abbemuseum, Eindhoven
Periodical, no. 3, March 1937
Layout by El Lissitzky

107
USSR im Bau, 9 September 1933
USSR in construction
Photogravure in blue and red
42.0 x 29.7 cm
Municipal Van Abbemuseum, Eindhoven
Periodical no. 9, September 1933
Layout by El Lissitzky

Photography

108
Pincers and Wire, negative version, ca. 1920
Photogram
23.0 x 29.0 cm
Galerie Berinson, Berlin
109
Untitled, ca. 1923
Photograph
16.0 x 11.0 cm
Thomas Walther collection, New York
110
Untitled, superimposed portrait, 1924/30
Gelatine-silverprint
16.1 x 11.8 cm
The Museum of Modern Art, New York/Gift of Shirley C. Burden and David H. McAlpin by exchange
111
Portrait of Kurt Schwitters, 1924
Photomontage
11.1 x 10.1 cm
Thomas Walther collection, New York
112
The runners, 1930
Photocollage
12.0 x 21.4 cm
Galerie Berinson Berlin
113
Footballer, 1930
Photogram
17.0 x 13.0 cm
Private archives
114
The runner, 1930
Photograph
State Tretiakov Gallery, Moscow
Photograph of the original work
115
Pressa, 1928
Photomontage
11.4 x 8.5 cm
Private archives
116
The Constructor, self-portrait, negative version, 1924
Photogram
12.6 x 14.4 cm
Galerie Berinson, Berlin
Vintage silverprint, from the estate of Käthe Steinitz
117
The Constructor, self-portrait 1924
Photograph
11.3 x 12.5 cm
Municipal Van Abbemuseum, Eindhoven
118
Self-portrait, 1928
Photomontage
8.2 x 9.0 cm
Private archives

Demonstrationsräume

119-121
Raum für konstruktive Kunst (Room for constructivist art), 1926
Photograph
State Tretiakov Gallery, Moscow
The room of 6 by 6 m. was built for the *Internationale Kunstausstellung* in Dresden. It no longer exists.

122
Abstraktes Kabinett (The abstract cabinet), design, 1927
Gouache and collage
39.9 x 52.3 cm
Sprengel Museum Hanover

123-124
Abstraktes Kabinett, (The abstract cabinet), Hanover 1930
Photograph
Sprengel Museum Hanover
The cabinet was originally built for the Provinzialmuseum Hanover. It was removed in 1937 and reconstructed in 1969 (dimensions: 330 x 427 x 549 cm) in the Sprengel Museum Hanover.

Architecture

125
Wolkenbügel, 1924/25
Indian ink, pen, collage on black glazed paper
22.8 x 15.5 cm
State Tretiakov Gallery, Moscow

126
Wolkenbügel, topographical drawing, 1924/25
Watercolour, graphite and colour pencil on paper
21.4 x 27.0 cm
State Tretiakov Gallery, Moscow

127
Wolkenbügel, 1924/25
Graphite and colour pencil, charcoal, watercolour on paper
21.4 x 27.0 cm
State Tretiakov Gallery, Moscow

128
Wolkenbügel, 1924/35
Colour pencil and graphite, charcoal, watercolour on paper
26.9 x 21.4 cm
State Tretiakov Gallery, Moscow

129
Wolkenbügel, 1924/25
Photomontage
Private archives
The *Wolkenbügel,* superimposed on a photograph of Nikitskii-Square in Moscow

130
Wolkenbügel, design, 1924/25
Indian ink, graphite, collage
50.0 x 64.6 cm
State Tretiakov Gallery, Moscow

131
Wolkenbügel, design, 1924/25
Photograph from private archives
Section of the building, showing the entrance to the Underground system beneath the columns

132
Wolkenbügel, working-drawing, 1924/25
Tracing paper, graphite and colour pencil
37.2 x 46.0 cm
State Tretiakov Gallery, Moscow

133
Wolkenbügel, working-drawing, 1924/25
Tracing paper, graphite and colour pencil
49.9 x 69.5 cm
State Tretiakov Gallery, Moscow

134
Yacht club of the International Red Stadium on the Lenin Hills, 1925
Tracing paper, Indian ink, graphite and black pencil
33.5 x 74.0 cm
State Tretiakov Gallery, Moscow

135
Yacht club of the International Red Stadium on the Lenin Hills, axonometry, 1925
Indian ink, gouache, graphite
38.2 x 45.7 cm
State Tretiakov Gallery, Moscow

136
Building in Gorki Park, design 1931
Photograph from private archives
Designed as a workers' rest and recreation centre

137
Clubhouse, model 1934
Photograph
State Tretiakov Gallery, Moscow

138
Administration building of a textile factory, design, 1925
Tracing paper, graphite and colour pencil
28.2 x 31.1 cm
State Tretiakov Gallery, Moscow

139
House of heavy industry, model 1930
Photograph
Private archives
Design for a competition as part of the Five Year Plan for architecture

140
Bridge, design, 1925
Graphite, gouache on cardboard
24.1 x 34.5 cm
State Tretiakov Gallery, Moscow

141
International Red Stadium on the Lenin Hills, groundplan, 1925
Collage, red pencil, white paint on blue paper
50.7 x 86.2 cm
State Tretiakov Gallery, Moscow

142-145
The Meyerhold theatre, 1928,29
Photographs
Private archives
Photographs of the groundplan and Lissitzky working on the model. Lissitzky made a new design for a production of the play *I want a child* by Sergei Tretiakov. Neither the play nor the theatre design were ever realised.

146
Boxoffice, design, 1930
Photograph
Private archives

147
House of the architect Ginsburg, 1934
Photograph
State Tretiakov Gallery, Moscow
Model for a one-room apartment

148
Letter to J.J.P. Oud, 27.1.26
Blue and red typewriter ink on paper
27.5 x 21.3 cm
Municipal Van Abbemuseum, Eindhoven
Lissitzky discusses the housing problem and the subsequent 'Americanisation' of European architecture.

149
Model of an apartment, 1930
Photograph
Private archives
Lissitzky's solution for the housing shortage, shown at the *International Hygiene Exhibition* in Dresden.

150
Russian housing shortage and its solutions, 1930
Photograph
Private archives
In the periodical *Das neue Frankfurt,* Vol IV, no. 11 (november 1930), Lissitzky explains the system behind his model at the *International Hygiene Exhibition* in Dresden

151
Chair, 1930
Wood
72.0 x 48.0 x 56.0 cm
Photograph from private archive
The chair was designed for the *International Fur Trade Exhibition (IPA)* Leipzig

152
Lenin Tribune, design, 1924
Gouache, Indian ink, pen, photomontage on cardboard
63.9 x 48.0 cm
State Tretiakov Gallery, Moscow
Design based on sketches done by Lissitzky and his pupils in 1920

153
Flagpost for the Soviet pavilion at the International Press Exhibition Pressa, design, Cologne 1928
Indian ink, gouache, collage on cardboard
70.8 x 52.8 cm
State Tretiakov Gallery, Moscow
Original title exhibition: *Internationale Presse-Ausstellung Pressa*

154
Flagpost for the International Press Exhibition Pressa, model, Cologne 1928
Photo
Private archives

Exhibition designs

155
Soviet pavilion at the International Press Exhibition Pressa, design, Cologne 1928
Gouache and collage
69.0 x 52.0 cm
Rheinische Bildarchive Cologne/Museum Ludwig Cologne

156-158
Soviet pavilion at the International Press Exhibition Pressa, Cologne 1928
Photographs
Private archives

159
Soviet pavilion at the International Hygiene Exhibition, groundplan, Dresden 1930
Tracing paper, Indian ink, brush
34.2 x 65.5 cm
Original title exhibition: *Internationale Hygiene-Ausstellung*
State Tretiakov Gallery, Moscow

160-162
Soviet pavilion at the International Hygiene Exhibition, Dresden 1930
Photograph
Private archives

163-165
International exhibition Film and Photo, Stuttgart 1929
Photographs
Private archives
Design and realisation of a section of the Soviet pavilion at the *Internationale Werkbundausstellung Film und Foto*

166
International Fur Trade Exhibition (IPA), model of
the Soviet pavilion, Leipzig 1930
Photograph
Private archives
Original title exhibition: *Internationale Pelz-
Fachausstellung (IPA)*
167
International Aviation Exhibition, model of the
Soviet pavilion, Paris 1934
Photograph
State Tretiakov Gallery, Moscow

Bibliography

The first bibliography of literature on El Lissitzky covering the period 1920 to 1957 was published in the monograph by H. Richter (1958). This was later supplemented by the catalogue published in 1965-66 for the Eindhoven/Basel/Hanover exhibition.
The catalogues of the 1987-1988 retrospective exhibitions in Cambridge (Mass.), Hanover and Halle contain the most extensive survey of the literature on El Lissitzky published both in Russian and in East and West European languages. In these catalogues Peter Nisbet included the list of Prounen compiled by El Lissitzky in 1923 and his own catalogue of all the typographic work. In both cases, the entry for each work contains references to all the relevant literature.
The bibliography in the catalogue of the 1990 exhibition at the Tretiakov Gallery supplements these surveys with recent publications in Russian.

Portfolios of prints

Khad Gadya
Kiev, Kulturliga, 1919
Portfolio of 11 prints with imprint
Lithography, 75 copies
Second edition of 1000 copies, Warsaw, 1923

Proun
Vitebsk/Moscow, Unovis, 1921
Portfolio of 11 prints
Lithography

1° Kestnermappe-Proun
Hannover, Verlag Ludwig Ey, 1923
Portfolio of 6 prints with title page
Lithography and collage, 50 copies

Figurinenmappe-Die plastische Gestaltung der elektromechanischen Schau Sieg über die Sonne
Hannover, Leunis & Chapman, 1923
Portfolio of 11 prints, 9 Figurines, title and text page
Lithography, 75 copies
Reprint: Lauenförde, Tecta/Cologne, Walther König, 1988, 150 copies

Books

Suprematiceskij skaz pro dva kvadrata v 6ti postrojkach
Berlin, Skythen-Verlag, 1922, 20 p., ills.
A limited edition of 50 signed copies in hardback was also published
Reprint: Berlin, Paul Gerhardt Verlag, 1969

Van twee kwadraten;
Suprematisch worden van twee kwadraten in 6 konstrukties, Den Haag, De Stijl, 1922, 20 p., ills.
In cooperation with Theo van Doesburg, hardback, signed edition of 50 copies
Also published as issue No. 11/12 of De Stijl, vol. 5, 1922
Reprint: Hilversum, Steendrukkerij De Jong, 1973
Reprint: Maastricht, Gerards & Schreurs, 1986

Die Kunstismen. Les Ismes de l'art. The Isms of art;
Eds. El Lissitzky and Hans Arp
Erlenbach-Zürich, Eugen Rentsch Verlag, 1925, XII, 48 p., ills.
Reprint: New York, Arno Press, 1968 (Arno series of contemporary art: No. 7)
Reprint: Baden, Verlag Lars Müller, 1990

Lissitzky, El
Russland; die Rekonstruktion der Architektur in der Sowjetunion;
Mit 104 Abbn.; Foreword J. Gantner
Vienna, Verlag Anton Schroll, 1930
104 p., ills.
(Neues Bauen in der Welt; Vol. I)
Reprint: *Russland; Architektur für eine Weltrevolution,* 1929;
Foreword W. Hebebrand; Contr. U Conrads
Berlin, Verlag Ullstein, 1965, 208 p., ill.
(Ullstein Bauwelt Fundamente; No. 14)
Translation: *Russia: an architecture for world revolution;*
Transl. and contr. E. Dluhosch
London, Lund Humphries/Cambridge (Mass.), The Massachusetts Institute of Technology, 1970
239 p., ills.

Lissitzky, El
Proun und Wolkenbügel;
Schriften, Briefe, Dokumente;
Eds. S. Lissitzky-Küppers and J. Lissitzky;
Afterword K. Milde
Dresden, VEB Verlag der Kunst, 1977
236 p., ills.
(Fundus-Bücher; No. 46)

Lissitzky, El
Die vier Grundrechnungsarten
Cologne, Galerie Gmurzynska, 1976
12 prints with appendix in portfolio
Silk screen after designs from 1928, edition of 200, signed by Yen Lissitzky

Monographs

Richter, H.
El Lissitzky – Sieg über die Sonne, zur Kunst des Konstruktivismus;
Foreword Chr. Czwiklitzer
Cologne, Verlag Galerie Christoph Czwiklitzer, 1958
60 p., ills., bibliography (1920-1957)

Lissitzky-Küppers, S.
El Lissitzky-Maler. Architekt-Typograf-Fotograf;
Erinnerungen, Briefe, Schriften
Dresden, VEB Verlag der Kunst, 1967
407 p., ills., bibliography
2nd Revised edition. Leipzig, VEB Verlag der Kunst, 1976. 412 p.
Translation: El Lissitzky: Life, Letters, Texts;
transl. H. Aldwinckle and M. Whittall
London, Thames and Hudson/Greenwich (Conn.), New York Graphic Society, 1968
2nd Revised edition. New York, 1980

Tschichold, J.
Werke und Aufsätze von El Lissitzky (1890-1941);
Compiled and introduced by S. Tschichold
Berlin, Gerhardt Verlag, 1970
25 p., ills., bibliography

Birnholz, A.
El Lissitzky;
A dissertation presented to the faculty of the Graduate School of Yale University etc.
New Haven, Yale University
Privately printed
Publication: Ann Arbor (Mich.), University Microfilms International, 1978
2 vols., 515 and 219 p., ills., bibliography

Boomgaard, J.
Theorie en praktijk van de russiese avantgarde;
El Lissitzky's tentoonstellingsontwerpen
Den Helder, Talsma & Hekking Uitgeverij, 1981
58 p., ills.
(Kunsthistorische schriften; No. 6)

Puts, H.
El Lissitzky;
Catalogus van zijn werk in het Stedelijk Van Abbemuseum, Eindhoven;
Dissertation, University of Groningen
Groningen, Puts, 1988
2 vols., 113 and 88 pp., ills.
Privately printed

Catalogues of solo exhibitions

El Lissitzky, Moskau. Schau der Arbeit 1922-23
Berlin, Graphisches Kabinett I.B. Neumann, 1924
4 p.
Contr. A. Behnes, El Lissitzky

El Lissitzky; text A. Dorner
New York, The Pinacotheca Gallery, 1949

El Lissitzky; text A. Dorner
New Haven, Yale University Art Gallery, 1950

El Lissitzky; Eds. J. Leering and W. Schmied; Eindhoven, Stedelijk Van Abbemuseum / Basel, Kunsthalle / Hannover, Kestner-Gesellschaft, 1965
137 p., ills., bibliography
Contr. J. Leering, J. Baljeu, C. Gray, M. Stam
D. Helms, Schuldt, El Lissitzky, O. Zadkine,
H. Berlewy, E. Buchholz,
K.T. Steinitz, E. Winter
H. Richter (bibliography 1918-1965)

An introduction to El Lissitzky
London, Grosvenor Gallery, 1966
6 p. (brochure), ills.

El Lissitzky: text J. Leering
Eindhoven, Stedelijk Van Abbemuseum, 1968
8 p. (brochure), ills.
List of works in the collection of the
Van Abbemuseum, Eindhoven

El Lissitzky
Cologne, Galerie Gmurzynska, 1976
167 p., ills., bibliography
Contr. S. Lissitzky-Küppers, E. Semenova,
D. Karshan,
J. Leering, J.E. Bowlt, El Lissitzky, H. Richter
(bibliography 1918-1965)

El Lissitzky 1890-1941
Oxford, Museum Of Modern Art, 1977
42 p., ills.
texts D. Elliott, El Lissitzky

El Lissitzky – 11 original gouaches for the Chad Gadya and 8 original designs for the Four Mathematical processes.
London, Annely Juda Fine Art, 1979
8 p., ills.

El Lissitzky – Maler, Architekt, Typograf, Fotograf;
Ed. J. Scharfe; Halle, Staatliche Galerie / Leipzig,
Hochschule für Grafik und Buchkunst, 1982
96 p., appendix 16 p.
Contr. H. Olbrich, H.H. Holz, W.I. Rakitin,
S.O. Chan-Magomedov,
E. Frommhold, El Lissitzky, I.W. Rjasanzew,
F. Mierau, H. Ebert

El Lissitzky – 1890-1941;
Catalogue for an exhibition of selected works from North American collections, the Sprengel Museum Hannover and the Staatliche Galerie Moritzburg Halle
Cambridge (Mass.), Harvard University Art Museums / Busch-Reisinger Museum, 1987
211 p., ills., bibliogr.
Texts P. Nisbet, E. Peters Bowron, El Lissitzky
With annotated list of 98 Prouns and annotated survey of typographical works 1905-1942

El Lissitzky – 1890-1941 – Retrospektive
Hannover, Sprengel Museum, 1988
310 p., ills., bibliogr.
Beitr. J. Büchner, N. Nobis, P. Nisbet,
K.- U. Hemken, W. Kambartel,
El Lissitzky, B. Nobis, Chr. Grohn
With annotated list of 98 Prouns and annotated survey of typographical works 1905-1942

El Lissitzky – 1890-1941 – Retrospektive
Halle, Staatliche Galerie Moritzburg, 1988
326 p., ills., bibliogr.
Beitr. P. Romanus, P. Nisbet, K.- U. Hemken,
W. Kanbartel,
El Lissitzky, N. Nobis, Chr. Grohn, N. Nobis,
H. Olbrich,
S.O. Chan-Magomedow, A. Wendelberger
With annotated list of 98 Prouns and annotated survey of typographical works 1905-1942

L.M. Lissitzky 1890-1941
Moscow , Tretiakov Gallery, 1990
132 p., ills., bibliogr.
With articles in Russian by M.A. Nemirovskaya and S.O. Chan-Magomedov
With list of 329 works in the collection of the Tretiakov Gallery, Moscow, and 32 works in the collection of the Van Abbemuseum, Eindhoven, and lists of works by El Lissitzky in the manuscript department, the library and the photographic department of the Tretiakov Gallery. A list of some works by pupils of El Lissitzky is also included. The short bibliography includes recent Russian publications.

Solo exhibitions

1923
Hanover, Kestner-Gesellschaft
1924
Berlin, Graphisches Kabinett I.B. Neumann (cat.)
1925
Dresden
1927
Dessau, Bauhaus
1949
New York, The Pinacotheca Gallery (Rose Fried Gallery) (cat.)
1950
New Haven, Yale University Art Gallery (cat.)
1960
Moscow, Mayakovsky Museum
1965 / 1966
Eindhoven, Stedelijk Van Abbemuseum (cat.), and
Basel, Kunsthalle (cat.), and
Hanover, Kestner-Gesellschaft (cat.)
1966
London, Grosvenor Gallery (cat.)
1967
Novosibirsk / Academy village, House of the Scientists
1968
Eindhoven, Stedelijk Van Abbemuseum (cat.)
1976
Cologne, Galerie Gmurzynska (cat.)
1977
Oxford, Museum of Modern Art (cat.)
1979
London, Annely Juda Fine Art (cat.)
1982 / 1983
Halle, Staatliche Galerie Moritzburg (cat.), and
Leipzig, Hochschule für Grafik und Buchkunst (cat.)
1985
Eindhoven, Stedelijk Van Abbemuseum
1987 / 1988
Cambridge (Mass.), Harvard University Art Museums/Busch-Reisinger Museum (cat.), and
Hanover, Sprengel Museum (cat.), and
Halle, Staatliche Galerie Moritzburg (cat.)
1990
Moscow , Tretiakov Gallery (cat.)
1990 / 1991
Eindhoven, Stedelijk Van Abbemuseum (cat.), and
Madrid, Fundaçion Caja de Pensiones (cat.), and
Paris, Musée d'Art Moderne de la Ville de Paris / ARC (cat.)

Commentary

In M.A. Nemirovskaya's article *L.M. Lissitzky's works in the Tretiakov Gallery*, we read the following statement: "Sofya Khristianovna has repeatedly been approached by representatives of foreign picture-galleries and private collections, who offered to buy work by Lissitzky. She declined, however, even the most advantageous offers, in response to Lissitzky's explicit wish to have his works collected in a gallery in his native country. Only in 1958 was Lissitzkaja-Küppers allowed to go to Moscow to execute the wish of her deceased husband."

This is, as stated in footnote 5, the report of a conversation between the writer of the article and myself before I left the Soviet Union.

I feel obliged to add a few comments to the above-quoted passage.

From 1944 to 1956, my mother and I lived in Novosibirsk, *exiled forever*. We had been banished there from Moscow – my mother was German. *Forever* ended with Stalin's death, but not immediately. In our isolated position, offers from the West to buy my father's works were at that time altogether out of the question. Moreover, one must not forget how paradoxal, until recently, the situation of the avant-garde art of the twenties was in the Soviet Union: on the one hand, this art was considered sheer formalism, having nothing to do with art and *being unnecessary for and incomprehensible to the people*, on the other hand, this art belonged to the people and consequently, in no way could it be exported by a private person to a foreign country. Thus the State could trade this *non-art* in the way it wished, without needing to account for it to anyone. It now appears that, in fact, this regulary happened.

For that reason, I have never spoken about *advantageous offers*, they simply did not occur.

How did El Lissitzky's archives come to be at the Tretiakov Gallery?

When after twelve years of exile there was a possibility of freedom of movement (*freedom* in the Soviet sense of the word), we had to decide what to do with my father's archives. As a matter of fact, to keep everything in one small room in a barrack was not devoid of risk and, on the other hand, we simply had to live - my mother received a pension of 35 roubles (35 kopecs at today's rate).

Only the State could buy the archives and, when my mother went to Moscow in 1958 (she did not move to Moscow, because she was not allowed to return, she only went for a short time) negotiations for this purpose began. It soon turned out that nobody was really eager for this legacy and only after endless bickering did the Tretiakov Gallery and TSGALI acquire El Lissitzky's archives, after having paid half of the beggarly sum agreed upon.

It is further stated that by depositing the archives with the Tretiakov Gallery, my mother executed my father's last will. That is something entirely new for me. I cannot have said such a thing, because there is no evidence whatever for such a wish; neither in my father's papers nor in my mother's reminiscences has there ever been an allusion to such a thing. I think that for him, just as for any other creative artist, it was important that his art should function in life, should be a part of the artistic process. That this art, just because of someone's whim, should not be withheld from society, as had happened with his artistic legacy, which for decades had been locked up in his native land.

Moreover, it should not be forgotten that El Lissitzky executed almost all his important work outside his native land. Therefore it remains unclear exactly where he wished to see his work collected.

This does not give someone the right to put words in the deceased author's mouth and thus create false myths.

Yen Lissitzky

Index

Colophon

This catalogue accompanies the exhibition
'El Lissitzky (1890-1941) architect painter
photographer typographer' organised by
the Municipal Van Abbemuseum in Eindhoven
16/12/1990 – 3/3/1991
the Fundaçion Caja de Pensiones in Madrid
1/4/1991 – 26/5/1991
and the Musée d'Art Moderne de la Ville de Paris/
ARC in Paris
18/6/1991 – 30/9/1991

Exhibition

Organisation: Jan Debbaut, Frank Lubbers,
Mariëlle Soons, Caroline de Bie
in cooperation with Arlette Brouwers, Amsterdam

Catalogue

Final editing: Jan Debbaut, Mariëlle Soons
Editors: Caroline de Bie, Arlette Brouwers,
Jan Debbaut, Dees Linders, Mariëlle Soons
Organisation: Frank Lubbers

Picture research: Mariëlle Soons, Caroline de Bie
Bibliography: Aloys van den Berk

Translations:
Russian-English
Kathie Somerwil-Ayrthon (article by Yen Lissitzky)

Dutch-English
Beth O'Brien, Eindhoven (articles by Henk Puts)
John Rudge (articles by Jean Leering and
M.A. Nemirovskaya, foreword, list of reproductions)

German-English
Joe Manthey, Bonn (article by
S.O. Chan-Magomedov)
R.J.M. van der Wilden-Fall, Rijswijk (article by
K.-U. Hemken, quotations in article by J. Leering,
excerpts from the article by S.O. Chan-Magomedov)

Photographs:
Galerie Berinson, Berlin
Dr. Hüdrun Schröder-Kehler, Dresden
Staatliche Kunstsammlungen, Dresden
Kunstsammlung Nordrhein-Westfalen, Düsseldorf
Staatliche Galerie Moritzburg, Halle
Sprengel Museum, Hanover
Museum Ludwig, Cologne
Stuhlmuseum Burg Beverungen + TECTA,
Lauenförde
Deutsche Bücherei, Leipzig
Kai-Uwe Hemken, Marburg
Gg.F. Weisbrod
Eric E. Estorick, London
Stedelijk Museum, Amsterdam
Stedelijk Van Abbemuseum, Eindhoven (Peter Cox,
Koen van Stokkom)
State Tretiakov Gallery, Moscow
Busch-Reisinger Museum, Harvard University,
Cambridge
Yale University Art Gallery, New Haven,
Connecticut
Thomas Walther, New York
Private collection courtesy of Annely Juda Fine Art,
London
Museum für Gestaltung, Basel
Kunstmuseum, Basel
Galerie Dr. I. Schlégl, Zürich

Design: Arlette Brouwers
and Koos van der Meer, Amsterdam
Lithography: Nemela + Lenzen, Mönchengladbach
Setting and printing: Lecturis bv, Eindhoven
Publisher: Municipal Van Abbemuseum, Eindhoven
Edition: English edition 5300

Distribution in continental Europe:
Nilsson & Lamm b.v.,
P.O. Box 195
1380 AD Weesp
The Netherlands

Distribution in the rest of the world:
Thames and Hudson Ltd.,
30-34 Bloomsbury Street
London WC1B 3QP

Thames and Hudson Inc.
500 Fifth Avenue
New York, New York 10110
USA
I.S.B.N.: 0-500-97393-8

With friendly support of:

Intercolor b.v., Eindhoven

Philips Nederland, Eindhoven

Ministry of Welfare, Health
and Cultural Affairs, Rijswijk